D0297775

THIS
ENGLAND

THIS ENGLAND

PETE DAVIES

LITTLE, BROWN AND COMPANY

A *Little, Brown* Book

First published in Great Britain by Little, Brown 1997

Copyright © Pete Davies 1997

The moral right of the author has been asserted.

A CIP catalogue record for this book
is available from the British Library.

ISBN 0 316 64124 3

Typeset in Bembo by M Rules
Printed and bound in Great Britain by
Clays Ltd, St Ives plc

Little, Brown and Company (UK)
Brettenham House
Lancaster Place
London WC2E 7EN

For Rebecca

Contents

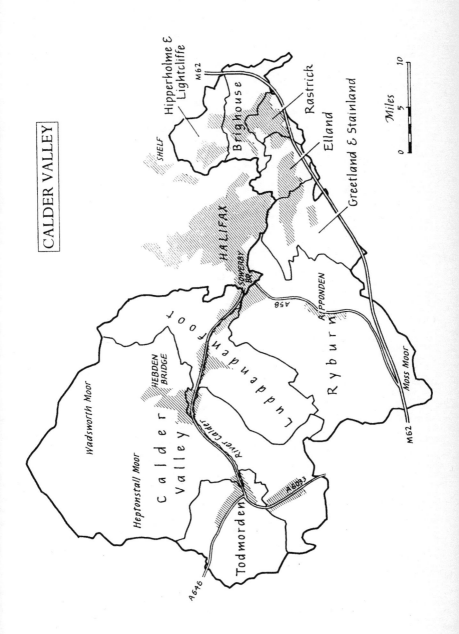

CALDER VALLEY

I

THIS ENGLAND

This England is the eerie, water-sculpted beauty of the grikes and clints in the limestone pavements on the tops of the Dales, and it's the thoughtless gits who leave their crisp packets wedged and fading in between them.

This England is vertigo on Striding Edge, it's the tumbling of Exmoor down steep wooded slopes into the Bristol Channel, it's the endless white sands of the Northumberland coast, and it's the sorry wretches who break into your car while you're having a picnic on the beach. This England is coming back up the dunes to find the broken glass of your passenger-side window in your childrens' clothes, on their books and their toys. This England is coming back from holiday to find you've been burgled, and all they've taken is your six-year-old's moneybox.

This England is St Michael's Mount and Stonehenge, Hadrian's Wall and the Pennine Way, Offa's Dyke and the Settle–Carlisle railway. It's tourists in York and Harrogate, and it's crumpled scratchcards blowing across the empty car parks of lo-cost supermarkets in shut-down pit villages. It's crazy money in the City, and it's prostitution in King's Cross. It's the fatigued desperation lurking in the voices of the people who cold-call you to try and sell you new windows. It's twenty per cent of the population dependent on state benefits, and an average basic pay for your top chief executives of £685,000 a year. Just basic, mind.

This England is the red brick back-streets of Winchester and Salisbury, it's the Royal Crescent in Bath and the Golden Mile in Blackpool. It's Windsor Castle and Alton Towers. It's Lord's and the

Grand National and Wembley; it's village cricket and the Unibond League. It's footballers making twenty grand a week, and fans who can't afford tickets to watch them any more.

This England is Gazza, getting pissed, seeing red. What other country could produce a national icon who thinks farting at foreign journalists is funny? This England is the *Sun* and the *Mirror* and the *Star* pursuing dud celebrities round tacky night-clubs. It's those papers ranting about love rats and sex beasts, and it's huge tits and dirty phone lines in the *Sport* on the rack right next to them.

This England is a nice cup of tea. It's real ale and video games and Crinkley Bottom fruit machines. It's *EastEnders* and *Coronation Street*, Trevor MacDonald and the National Lottery. It's a country where sport and royalty are soap, and we follow the plotlines with the eagerness of addicts because that way we can forget about the news.

This England – it's the Queen on the money, and forged notes in your change. It's sitting in a quiet Yorkshire village writing this and, this very moment as I write – I kid you not – two lads drive down the back lane behind the house, they pull up, one jumps out, he runs into my yard and he steals a dented old metal dustbin. They reverse away with a howling of rubber on the dirt track and I'm sat here thinking, My bleedin' *dustbin*'s just been nicked. What is this?

It's England – a country mired in history and tat and petty crime, where frauds make millions and get away with it while we bang up no-hope kids by the thousand. What are we come to when a barrow-boy loses the best part of a billion, the bank goes under, one of his bosses gets sacked and she turns round and claims a half a million performance bonus? This England – a country where reality went out of the window so long ago that you wonder if we'll ever get a grip on it again.

This England is a country with an antique electoral system whereby, for seventeen years, a minority of the people chose a Conservative Party to rule them that threw away £200 billion of our money – from North Sea oil and privatisation – on buying votes with tax cuts. It's a country where we were told to look out for Number One, that there was no such thing as society – so too many of us did, and then there wasn't.

Thoughtlessness, selfishness — you hardly have to look in the news, or at the last few election results, to know how many people in England can't be bothered to think about the next person any more. It's there every time you get a video from the shop and you open the case, and you find the idle toerags who had the movie before you didn't rewind it. It's there in every supermarket car park in the country, in the feckless way people can't be arsed to push their trolleys out of the road when they're done shopping. It's there in the men — always men — who get up your backside in their fat shiny cars to flash you in the fast lane so they can keep doing a hundred and ten when, for Chrissake, you're overtaking someone yourself. Because we're all in such a hurry, aren't we? We're all hurrying 'cause if we're not broke, we're scared we might be any minute. And in all these things adding up, it's a constant nagging feeling that too many people couldn't give a damn any more — but someone had to set the tone for that, didn't they?

In 1996, as the Tories lurched on through tides of disrepute, their terrible poll ratings suggested that enough people in this England still did care, and that enough people had had enough. But if we were finally to be rid of them, how could you tell the story of the day it happened? Do you bang on, dry as dust, about the policies on offer for the public sector borrowing requirement? Do you zoom round acting gonzo with all the other hacks, gabbling how, if this is Tuesday, the campaign bus must be in Bolton? But neither the campaign bus nor the PSBR are really what this England is about.

Nor is this England about the people with fantastical money, the sham world of *Hello!* and TV mags and lottery wins and share options; nor is it about the people with no money at all, the lost souls marooned in the darkest corners of Liverpool or London, keeping their heads down from the gangs and the gunfire, their kids ripped out of their wits on glue. There are important stories there, and frightening ones, about contract killers and drug dealers and no end of victims — but by definition, they're not stories about the heart of England.

This England, the nub of what the country is about, is in the marginal constituencies: fewer than one hundred places where, because of the absurdities of the electoral system, it is decided who the government will be. This England is in places where the bulk of the people are either moderately prosperous or moderately not; where there are towns, but the towns are not too big, and where the countryside is still beautiful and close. It's in places where, for the most part, ordinary people in recent years have decided that Labour would harm them, but the Tories would see them right. This England, at this island's centre, is a place like the Calder Valley – 210 miles from London, 210 miles from Cardiff, 210 miles from Glasgow – where three-quarters of the people own their houses, where virtually all of them are white, and where the Tory MP who'd been there seventeen years had a majority of 4,800 that, by 1996, was beginning to look pretty friable.

This England, I thought, and the possibility of it changing, resided exactly in a place like the Calder Valley. It was in the agriculture and the landscape, the gritstone and the moors; it was in the industry sprung up along the river and the canal in the defining moments of our history, when we went out into the world and sold it all that we could make. It was in the dense mix of urban and rural, and in the character of the people formed there against a harsh terrain – bloody-minded, proud, pernickety, independent. It was in the traditions of Nonconformism and Chartism and Cooperation, of hard labour and rights won. It was in the mill chimneys and the dry-stone walls; it was in the centuries of history since a Roman road first crossed this way over the Pennines, and it was in all the private moments of decision when the descendants of that history would go once again to the ballot box.

It was in the fact that, no matter how much we English may dislike politics and the people who practise it, we do at least remain a democracy. It was in genial old Sir Donald Thompson, the Tory MP for Calder Valley, contentedly convinced that the place was paradise – and it was in Christine McCafferty, the Labour candidate who meant to take this paradise from him. She was a well-built woman of fifty with straight, short blonde hair, an attentive, piercing blue gaze and an unashamedly loud laugh; a talkative, friendly, basically ordinary person who wanted this England to change, after seventeen years. And she knew that if it was going to change, it was exactly in a place like the Calder Valley that the change would be made.

2

I Intend To Win

The road out of Huddersfield to Halifax climbs gently through the grand houses of Edgerton, houses built on the money West Yorkshire once made in textiles and engineering. At Ainley Top it passes through a gracefully arched tunnel beneath the M62, and the Calder Valley opens wide far below. You zoom down the sweeping curves of the hulking bleak hillside – and the biggest building in view is the Gannex mill, where Harold Wilson's dodgy mate made raincoats. Wilson – another guy who came over all modern, and aimed for Downing Street bearing promises about the kind of country we could live in.

Late in the afternoon on July 1st 1996, I was whipping down that hill, looking at that mill, when the tape in the car radio finished and I was pitched into Five Live. It was the day after the Germans won Euro '96; they were running a highlights show, and like half the population I knew each highlight by heart. Gazza chipped Hendry and thumped the dropping ball home, England tore Holland to pieces, the crowd sang 'Three Lions', Wembley was jubilant and visceral, Nadal stepped up to the penalty spot and Seaman saved, we were in the semi-final and Gareth Southgate stepped up . . .

Was there ever a time when we retained a degree of proportion about football? Certainly, these days, it's completely out of hand. Euro '96 came with no end of think pieces attached on what the game had to tell us about England; but the extremity of the euphoria, the intensity of the involvement, reminded me most of what we always used sniffily to say about Argentina or assorted other Latin hothouses. We used to shake our heads and pity them and say, well, they've got nasty sleazy governments, shabby economies, loads of poor people – so of course they go crazy over football, it's all they've got. And now here we were, all England singing along to a pair of second-rate comedians with the cross of St George slapped on our faces, excused all contemplation of reality for the sake of three weeks of football.

Reality: football does not house the homeless or make jobs for the unemployed, it does not provide decent education or health care, it does not fight crime or make our food safe. Politicians are supposed to do those things – but after seventeen years of the Tories, with the government mired in a fractious and cynical torpor, politicians as a class were sunk so low in our esteem that we thought they didn't get out of bed without taking a bribe for it, or climb back into it afterwards without the company of a whore or a lover. And who'll pay attention to that when there's football on?

In the week after Euro '96, with the general election due inside a year, the Labour Party launched a document entitled *The Road to the Manifesto*. It purported to say that politicians could indeed still do what we wanted them to do; it claimed, specifically, that Labour would cut infant class sizes and NHS waiting lists, get young people off benefit and into work, get tough on young offenders, and be economically virtuous all the while. These were cautious pledges and expedient ones, but they were nonetheless the opening shots of an historic campaign; a campaign in which, after nearly two decades, it seemed likely that middle England would bite the bullet and go for Blair. If it did, we'd get a result more significant than any football game could ever arrive at; we would, literally, be making a millennial decision. So, late in the afternoon on July 1st, having quit football and turned to politics for this vital season, I drove down the hill towards Halifax, past an ominous and hulking emblem of the last time Labour had a chance – and that evening I saw a woman moved to tears for reasons altogether less trivial than some bloke fluffing a penalty.

T he Asian Women's Swimming Project. They'd love that at the *Mail*, wouldn't they? Brown People Splash Out On Taxpayer Shock.

Hire of the pool in the year to April '96 had, in fact, cost the Calderdale Well Woman Centre £469, out of an annual grant from the local authority of £35,280 – and in a tricky social context, it was a modest and sensible exercise in preventative health care. Britain's Asian communities have a higher rate of heart disease and related illnesses than the population as a whole; getting them to take more exercise is a valid goal. In Halifax, however, many Asians are Muslims from backwoods Kashmir; as one of the Centre's staff put it, 'These women, if their husband's out and their nephew comes to the door, they don't open it. It's that bad.' So providing at least a few of them with some women-only time in the pool was one of the small but worthwhile deeds these people got up to.

The Centre shares a council building with three other welfare agencies in the middle of Halifax; its literature promises, among other things, free pregnancy tests, free condoms, a crèche, a nurse, interpreters, or just a cup of tea and someone to talk to. Staffed mainly by volunteers, in the past ten years it had helped thousands of women with any number of medical or personal problems – and for the past seven years, it had been Chris McCafferty's place of work.

Now, as the Labour Party's candidate for Calder Valley, she'd served out her notice; attending the AGM that July evening was her last formal duty. She sat with twenty other women in a big airy room, lately redecorated, amid shelves of health-care books and filing cabinets with 'No Smoking' signs, and they went through their minutes and their apologies, their matters arising and their accounts. The treasurer said she didn't always know what the accountants were on about, what a fixed asset was, or a deprecia- tion – but she did know they had money in the bank, and she apologised for that. It was, she stressed, all marked down to be used; she said, 'We do know we're a charity, and this money will be spent. We just don't want to fritter it, is all.'

It was the kind of meeting you could find on any evening in any town up and down the country: a small group of mostly unpaid people trying invisibly to do a bit of good on an annual budget that'd barely buy you a decent footballer for a fortnight. But you don't get paying crowds at the AGMs of welfare agencies and as a result they were, said the chair, 'a vulture organisation'. She announced the oddments they'd scavenged for a raffle: an old answering machine, a tin of Quality Street, some beechwood easels, a trip to Leeds–Bradford airport with a complimentary meal, two tickets to Flamingo Land. I wondered what the women who'd visited from the Kabardino-Balkariya province of the Russian Caucasus would have made of this cheerful, game, underfunded side of England; they might, perhaps, have found that evening's *Courier* headline more familiar: Guns And Drugs Found In Halifax. Then it came time for the chair to thank McCafferty for her work down the past seven years.

She went to sit on a cheap sofa at the end of the room. They gave her a bunch of flowers, and people had little personal presents for her too, and there were quiet embraces. McCafferty said, 'Well, I promised myself I wouldn't cry. It's been a very, very important part of my life, it's been really, really . . . I'm getting upset. This isn't like me.'

Someone beside her said gently, 'It's allowed. It's allowed.' They all knew, of course, that McCafferty's mother had died the week before, and that she'd had little or no time to grieve. Being a parliamentary candidate doesn't leave you a lot of space for yourself; she'd put it away, she said, and would grieve at a later date. At least it wasn't a surprise; eighty-seven years old, her mother had been ill for a long while. She'd become blind and deaf and very dependent, and she hadn't liked that at all; McCafferty told me later, 'It's difficult to want somebody to stay with you, when you know they're ready to go. But I've not really had time to consider what my feelings are.'

Briefly, they welled up now . . . then she dried her eyes and said her piece. She said, 'If you're in a so-called normal environment, if you're down or distressed, you don't want to go to work. But here, if you're down, you do want to come, because you know there's people who'll support you, and I'll find it very difficult to do without that. But I've already said to people that should my life change dramatically, and should I be elevated, and should I get very stressed out, I'll come here. Because there's not many places just for women in Calderdale, or in West Yorkshire. Or in Britain altogether, come to that. But I hope I'm around enough to see how you grow and change, and I hope you'll be here for me. And,' she smiled, 'can I have a drink now please?'

★

Christine Livesley was born on October 14th 1945 in Hightown, in inner-city Manchester. She was a surprise baby, one who came late, and she was very much cherished; ten years earlier, her sister Pauline had been born poorly during the Depression, and had lived only a few months. Their mother, who worked occasionally as a waitress, and for Ferranti during the war in their laboratories, was severely disabled with rheumatoid arthritis; Chris remembers being very happy, an only child made to feel very special, but she also remembers having to take responsibility for her mother from an early age. It's no surprise that, when she left school at eighteen, her first job was working with disabled people.

If it was a happy childhood, it wasn't a wealthy one. Her father was a warehouseman; they were council tenants who moved about as slums got knocked down and new housing was built. She remembers when she was young the toilets being outside, one cold-water tap in the kitchen, and people going to the public baths in Elizabeth Street to wash. The area was mainly Jewish; the way she'd heard it told, people fleeing across Europe from the pogroms of 1904 had arrived at Manchester Victoria and walked up the hill until they dropped. Where they dropped, up sprang Hightown.

The Livesleys weren't Jewish, but what their daughter calls Christian Socialist; she was born into the Labour Party. She remembers going to Whalley Range Grammar, and how genteel it was; she recalls the day she went to a friend's house for tea. She asked if the man in the garden was her friend's father and her friend told her, No, he was the gardener. Then their tea was given them by a domestic – and that was incredible to her, that her friend had two people working for her parents in her house.

After Whalley Range, she went to Footscray High in Melbourne; her father had dreamed of emigrating since he'd left the Royal Air Force at the end of the War, and in the late 1950s they finally tried it. But it wasn't a success, and you could date the start of McCafferty's adulthood to when they got back off the boat train from Tilbury Docks in a freezing January and saw with a weary shock how England, after Australia, just looked filthy – miserable, cold, stark, and filthy.

Still, if you'd have told her then that she'd end up standing for parliament, she'd have laughed in your face. From twenty years old she was active – going to meetings, canvassing – but she had no great ambition. She worked, at first with the disabled, then with young people; she got married in '68 to a computer engineer (whose surname she retains) and had their son David in '72. Twenty-four now, he'd just finished an M.Sc. in renewable energy at Loughborough – and for the first sixteen years of his life, before she started work at the Well Woman Centre, she'd been, she said, 'A full-time mum. Just an old-fashioned girl.'

Not completely old-fashioned, of course. She'd divorced, ami-cably, and remarried – she was, she conceded, a child of the Sixties – but she'd not been new-fashioned enough that she ever thought she'd stand for parliament. So how had it come about? She laughed and said, 'Not a clue. Not a clue.'

The McCaffertys moved to Hebden Bridge in the mid-1970s; the marriage broke up, she met her second husband David Tarlo there, and in 1980 they bought a ruin for £9,000. Hebden Bridge back then was still broke and remote, before the car commuters and the Pennine tourism came, and a fair few children of the Sixties were moving in on property so cheap you could buy it for cash. The local term for the incomers is 'off cumdens'; I asked Tarlo if, as one of them, he'd been a hippy back then, and he smiled and denied it. He said, 'I worked in the theatre, I roadied with bands, I had long hair – but I wasn't a hippy, I worked. I gave hippies lifts.'

Before the War (before the arrival of white sliced bread) the place they bought had been Hebden Bridge's bakery. It had no roof, and no back wall; it had an old flour-sack hoist that they donated to a Salford museum. The gas ovens were still in, under a collapsed glass ceiling; the original shopfront's still there now, shedding dusty light on the basement where Tarlo keeps his joiner's tools. A devel-oper would have turned it into two dwellings, one atop the other; the Calder Valley at Hebden Bridge is so tight and steep that there's barely a house on flat land, and what they call 'under-over dwellings' abound. It was another reason property went so cheap. Shared floor/ceiling boundaries were called 'flying freeholds' – and who was going to lend on places where, if Party A didn't look after the ceiling, Party B's floor collapsed?

They turned the old bakery into a family house by themselves;

McCafferty did the labouring, because Tarlo was the one with the skills. Sixteen years on, it's still not finished – it's a Forth Bridge job, this one – but it's worth a bit more than nine grand. Meanwhile, they were active in the local Labour Party and, in 1991, Tarlo stood for election as a local councillor in their ward, the Calder Valley ward. This straddles the A646 as it runs towards Todmorden and the moors, and it's fairly solid Labour – whereas Luddendenfoot ward, next along to the east, is more inclined to vote Liberal or Tory. Partly as a consequence of that, while Tarlo knew he'd be standing for a reasonably safe seat a year ahead of time, down the road in Luddendenfoot they still had no Labour candidate eight weeks before the poll – so McCafferty was asked to stand.

At first she was reluctant. She'd worked on every local and general election since the Sixties, she knew the stress it involved, and the idea of both of them running at the same time was daunting. What swung it was, firstly, that she was always saying there weren't enough women in politics, so it was time she put her money where her mouth was; and secondly, a general view that she couldn't possibly win in Luddendenfoot, so that in the end it didn't make any difference.

They campaigned, it came to the count – and she doesn't like counts. There's a knack to reading the boxes, seeing the slips tumble out and registering how many crosses are on your bit of the ballot, and it's a knack she'd never acquired; without it you can get deeply paranoid if you stand there trying to gauge how you've done. So she stood outside, talking to a policeman, fretting all the while – not about her own result, but because Tarlo's hadn't come through from up the road. It was a solid seat, they should surely have heard by now that he was in – while in the building behind her she was close, but not close enough, until they found another bundle; the votes in it were mostly hers and, to her surprise and elation, she'd scraped a win by twenty votes. Unprepared, she hurried to the toilet and scribbled a quick speech on the back of an envelope; then she ran to the car. Driving to Tarlo's count she was thinking, Why haven't we heard? He can't have lost. God, if he's lost and I've won, it'll be awful, awful. I'll have to leave home.

When she got there, people laughed – what was she worrying about? Of course he'd won. It had just taken a little longer than usual, because one of the counters only had one arm.

★

The morning after the Well Woman's AGM, McCafferty took a seventy-seven-year-old woman to see a solicitor. The case came to her notice over the question of the woman's entitlement to a concessionary TV licence, but it turned out there was more to it than that. The woman owned a house, which disbarred her from receiving benefit, but she didn't live in it; her son, who'd previously shared it with her, had moved in his partner, then somehow wangled a council flat and moved his mother out to that. Now he was paying her a rent of £20 a week, this generous fellow, and his mother was in penury.

McCafferty told her she should sell her house; if she still couldn't get benefits, at least she'd have the money in the bank and the interest on it. The old lady fretted that she'd be being a bad mother, the son went ballistic – but the injustice of the case was transparent, and McCafferty wanted to see this woman properly advised.

Trying to resolve people's thorny little griefs is what local politicians of every stripe are regularly engaged in – some, of course, rather more so than others – and generally they get little or no credit for it. Credited or not, however, it was work McCafferty enjoyed. When she was elected, she said, 'I hoped I might be able to help people with their problems, and I think on a lot of levels it's perfectly possible to do that. But on the grand scale, where you're dealing with the big ideas, wanting to change the world – or change Calderdale, anyway – it's much more difficult.'

Like most new councillors, she spent the first year overwhelmed by the amount of information coming through the letterbox. Politicians get whole trees' worth of paper every day; Tarlo and McCafferty fill a bin-liner virtually every time the postman calls. So you have to learn to assimilate that information, to discern what's important – then you have to learn the structures of the council, and how to work through the bureaucracy just to find things out, never mind get things done. 'You can,' she said, 'get very disappointed; you can feel you're not getting very far. But we had a hung council my first four years so every item, every line had to be argued, and it was good training. I've found that I enjoy it; I may have arrived there by default, but I do enjoy it, and I think I'm good at it.'

Good enough that in 1995 she was returned with a substantially increased majority; good enough that she now wanted to be an MP. Her name had been put forward, and she thought about it a long while – then she was awake one night and she said to her husband, 'I can do this.'

So he told her, 'Of course you can.'

She was selected as the Calder Valley's candidate in February '95; the selection process took four months. The constituency's eleven branches had to winnow thirty-three names down to a short-list of six; you were, in effect, interviewed for the job eleven times over before you even made the last round. In that last round, there was a morning hustings in Halifax, another session in Hebden Bridge in the afternoon – it was, she said, a very long day.

It was an all-woman short list. She was up against a Co-op candidate, a councillor from Leeds and a solicitor from London; she was up against Sheena Whittingham, the wife of the candidate in the '92 election, and she was up against Ann Martin. Martin, secretary to the area's MEP, would subsequently oust a Tory from a council seat in Brighouse in May '96 and become McCafferty's agent.

McCafferty won the first ballot, but not quite by enough; she came home easily in the second. The constituency may be progressive enough to have an all-woman list, but in other regards it's a parochial place, and wasn't ever going to choose some lawyer up from London; there was no question that they'd only support a local candidate. Among those, McCafferty said simply, 'I always thought I'd win.'

So why do it? Ego? Belief?

'Ego? You'll have to ask other people. But it's just wanting this country to be a better place. I want to do my bit to improve my home, I want something better for my son, and my grandchildren when they're born, and I know what that is. I want Britain to be a place where wealth isn't measured by profit and loss. I want Britain to be a place where we care about vulnerable people and we don't just talk about it, we actually do it. I don't like the way things have gone and being an MP, for me, means having access to people who can change things. It means becoming part of the establishment, and helping to change the rules to benefit people.'

Was this not, I wondered, a shade rosy-tinted?

'Probably. But my bottle's always been half-full. You get further by being optimistic. Although I suspect that the country's finances are in a far worse state than we're being led to believe, and that it'll be very, very difficult to turn things round. We'll certainly need more than five years.'

So would she win? Could she knock off a Tory majority of 4,800?

She said, 'I intend to win. A friend said to me right at the start of the process, Never stand for what you can't win. And I'm standing.'

And if you lose?

'I'll be very, very disappointed. Not just for myself but for all the people that have worked on my behalf, people that are working even now. And looking at the bigger picture . . . I can't bear to think. It gives me a pain even now to think what that loss would mean. Because if we don't win here, then we aren't winning in a whole wide range of places, and that would be far more than just a personal disappointment, it would be *awful*. I mean, I could barely speak for twenty-four hours after the last election, and I wasn't the candidate then. So I can't imagine. I feel this time that it's crucial to win, it's *absolutely crucial*. If we don't do it, it's curtains for the Labour Party, and it's curtains for a lot of people in this country.'

After she won selection two Tory councillors, disgruntled at the endless disorders of their party, the quagmire of corruption and incompetence and Euro-craziness, called to tell her she had the votes in their houses. One of them said, 'Just don't expect a poster, OK?'

She'd been told by her seat organiser to be prepared for the possibility of an election on October 10th, in the first week of November, or the first week of December. Local Labour MPs said the state of the Tories in Westminster was so bad that, when parliament reconvened in the autumn, they'd not be able to hold it together any longer; there was also a theory that Major would cut and run to avoid another triumphal Blair performance at the party conference. Herself, McCafferty favoured October 10th. When I asked why, she smiled and said, 'Because I don't want to wait any longer.'

It was, said Tarlo, 'Like waiting for an appointment with the dentist. There's a protracted fear.'

So were they battening down the hatches in the old bakery? Well, not quite. After the Well Woman's AGM that summer evening, as we talked late into the night, we were briefly interrupted by a waifishly pretty young girl toting a rosy-cheeked blond boy on her hip. The girl, it transpired, had just turned sixteen, and her son was lately past his first birthday; she'd fallen pregnant with him at fourteen, her parents had wanted her to have an abortion, she'd refused, and she'd ended up with her baby in a charity home that wasn't really appropriate. Efforts had been made to find them a foster home; but, said McCafferty, 'There were plenty willing to have the little boy, because he's beautiful, and there were plenty willing to have his mother, because she's beautiful too – but nobody would have them both. And she'll get a flat, she's a wonderful mum – but it's just a case of seeing how she does, so she's here with us for a few months first. And,' she smiled, 'it's really very nice.'

Effectively conceding that they'd not landed a punch on Tony Blair in two years, the Tories responded to *The Road to the Manifesto* with their New Labour, New Danger business, and were ruinously mocked for it. 'The *Sun* says: Never mind New Labour, New Danger. The real problem is . . . *Same old Tories. Same old claptrap.*'

A day or two later, Blair used the phrase 'same old Tories' at a press conference. When the Labour leader's soundbites are being provided by the *Sun*, you know the moon will be rising in the morning and that anything – even a Labour victory – really is possible. But the Blairification of the people's party was stirring assorted Labour MPs to much low grumbling. He ruled by dictatorial decree, he was surrounded by spin doctors and policy wonks barely out of short trousers, he was a pink Tory – maybe not even that pink. On the morning of July 1st, the lead headline in the *Independent* said, 'Labour Leader To Crush Dissent'.

McCafferty laughed. 'I've been banned from talking about that.'

But really, I said, 'Labour Leader To Crush Dissent?' Who did he think he was, Stalin?

'It's interesting.' She chuckled. 'But he's a very bright young man. Should go far.'

What did she think, though, about all the changes, all the policy reversals? Did she miss Clause IV?

'No – that was absolutely right. To me it was antiquated, out-dated – because nobody ever asked me about Clause IV on the doorstep, not in thirty years. And there's got to be something wrong about a party statement that nobody wants to ask about. So it was a dead duck years ago.'

And the other changes? The apparent disappearance of the word socialism? You could say they had to do anything within reason to get Labour elected – but at what point does it stop being within reason?

'Right, listen. What I've discovered in the past five years is that your average voter isn't really political at all. In fact, they don't *like* politics. Now this might well be Englishness – it might not apply in Scotland, it certainly doesn't apply in Europe – but in England, people aren't political. They know what they want, and they almost hate it when getting it has to involve party politics. So I'm totally supportive of the move to the centre, because I've come to realise that for ordinary people, it's as much as they can take – and a party that doesn't grow and change to reflect what people want, it dies. It's happening to the Tories now, it happened to us in the Eighties. We were stuck with all that old dross, and a lot of it *was* dross, and nobody had the guts to take it on and shift it. There's been some stunning moments, I'll grant you – but he's on the right lines, and there's a lot to be admired in Tony Blair.'

He'd just said he'd push the button . . .

She laughed out loud. 'Has he said that? I haven't heard that.'

I said I'd look back through the papers, I'd find the reference, and again she laughed. She said, 'Must have been the *Daily Mail*.'

Blair's confirmation at a press conference that he'd push the button was referred to in an editorial in the *Independent on Sunday*, which went on to ask whether there was anything he'd not say to achieve election. I told McCafferty this later, so she thought about it and said carefully, 'Well. Let's just say there are some things I'd not say to get elected myself.'

While we talked, Tarlo served us food to keep us going: broccoli quiche and some exquisite, hot chilli'd little vegetable samosas – and

I was, by now, developing my Buffet Theory of English politics. Vote Labour, I reckon, and you'll get a better class of canapé.

A few months earlier, John Prescott had come to give a gee-up speech to party workers in the adjoining key target seats of Halifax, Keighley, and Calder Valley. The meeting was held in Dean Clough, a gigantic old mill in the centre of Halifax now converted into an art gallery, workshops, small business space – and once there'd have been Labour firebrands outside this place protesting, saying you'll never turn our mill into some glitzy emporium of enterprise and fancy art. Now, however, the Labour Party was inside it, and looking right at home.

There was wine and orange juice and mineral water; there were delicious chilli'd olives and crisp, fresh crudités with an assortment of tasty dips. Prescott gave his speech against a backdrop of white walls hung with large abstract canvases. Along the way, he said he wasn't ashamed of the word 'socialism', and he had a few digs at 'private affulence' – the slip making it sound like the rich had wind – but the scene said more than the speech did. There wasn't a cloth cap in sight; this was Labour '96, smart, confident and comfortable in one of the glossy new institutions of late-century, post-industrial England, eating (for heaven's sake) felafel balls. And what's the Labour Party coming to, eh? Every summer in the Calder Valley, they even play *croquet* . . .

On a Saturday morning, six days after the Well Woman AGM, I found Tarlo at his front door with the hoover in one hand and a baby bird in the other. Not content with housing a teenage mother and her child, the old bakery was now rescuing the local wildlife as well. Tarlo wasn't sure if it was a finch, maybe a wren, but he'd found it in the road the day before and he'd managed to keep it alive. A wiry, ironical fellow with a greying mop of curly hair, he grinned and said, 'It needs feeding every hour. So I've got to macerate some worms now.' The chair of Calderdale Leisure Services, responsible for an operation worth some £8,000,000 a year, currently much exercised with his wife about whether car-parking charges should be introduced in the valley – he was for it, she was against – here he was on his weekend, wondering if he should take a baby bird to a croquet party.

He'd made the mallets and the balls himself five years back, and once he'd done it they had to use them, didn't they? So, every summer, some fifty Labour folk gathered at Stoodley Glen, west up the valley towards Todmorden, to play a knockout competition, and you couldn't imagine a more perfect English scene. Wedged between the steep, wooded, lushly green sides of the valley, down a single-track lane across a lock-bridge, our hosts lived in a row of 1910 millworkers' cottages by the banks of the Rochdale Canal. Holidaying narrowboats puttered past and on the far side of the canal, just visible through the trees, a village cricket match was in progress. The sun shone down warm from a cloud-flecked blue sky on a thoroughly eatable buffet – sensational desserts – and people sipped wine in lively conversation to the slow, staccato soundtrack of mallet thwacking ball.

We got there in Tarlo's D-reg Volvo; they had a small G-reg Rover as well. ('It's not too flash, and it's British. So that's the election car.') The bird travelled in a cardboard box on the back seat, with a saucer of chopped egg and pineapple, an eggcup of milk and a tiny pipette to feed it from. By the gate on to the lawn, snapshots had been taped to a board and entries were invited for a caption competition. 'As a power symbol, Nick felt the push mower left a lot to be desired.' Count Basie tinkled from an open window. McCafferty sat on a bench and told how a Tory councillor had looked at her copy of *The Road To The Manifesto* – just at the cover – and he'd said ruefully, 'I've got to hand it to the guy. He's really pulled you lot together.' Then he'd paused and sighed, 'I wish someone would do it for us.'

Tarlo wandered up with the bird in the box. 'Surreal, eh?'

An expert pronounced the bird to be a coal-tit – so it would, they decided, be a Labour voter. I drifted off to the nosh, and tried the Buffet Theory on another guest tucking in. 'Oh aye,' he said, 'you get better eats with us all right. And I'll tell you another thing – the Tories make you pay for theirs too.'

3

THREE LUNCHTIMES

Between Warley Moor and Midgley Moor – their bleak tops rising nearly 1,400 feet above sea level – Luddenden Brook flows down to join the Calder. Early in the nineteenth century, when the mills sprang up along the fast-flowing soft water-courses off the Pennines – producing cotton in Todmorden, fustians and velveteen in Hebden Bridge, wool and worsteds in the lower valley – Murgatroyd Mill was built here, above the village of Luddenden. Now it stands derelict, a rubble-littered wreck of boarded windows with a tall, grubby chimney looming against the steep valleysides, the dry-stone walls and pretty cottages.

Below the mill, Luddenden is a desirable place; in 1973, it was made Calderdale's first village Conservation Area. It was also part of the nineteen square miles of McCafferty's Luddendenfoot ward, but it wasn't natural Labour territory; her fellow councillors there were Liberals. Rural quaintness, on the other hand, concealed the place's share of poverty; commuter gentrification did nothing for the single mothers and pensioners in the drab brick-and-stucco of the Kershaw estate.

Across the road from the estate's boxy flats and houses, behind a ragged hedge clogged with brambles and Himalayan balsam, Greave House Fields looked down over the tributary valley – and changes in the Calderdale Urban Development Plan now threatened to open this site for development. A building speculator could get fifteen or more three- and four-bed 'executive' homes in there – but sixty-seven houses had already been built in Luddenden since 1988, it was beginning to merge with Luddenden

Foot at the valley's end, and people in Luddenden weren't too pleased about it.

At noon on August 13th, McCafferty met five objectors in the Coach and Horses in Luddenden Foot. She arrived a few minutes late; both her and Tarlo's cars had been broken into and ransacked. With the paranoia of the candidate upon her she asked, 'Was it just kids mucking about? Or was it political?' Kids mucking about, after all, don't leave two perfectly good car radios behind them.

At the bar, men in ties and shirtsleeves sank pints; a few children played on the fruit machine. In a quiet corner, under horse tack and hunting prints and hanging brass ash-pans, McCafferty asked whom the objectors wanted to speak for them and a woman told her, 'Jim's the one who does the talking.'

'Fine. I'll do the listening then.'

The woman was smartly dressed, around sixty; the men were younger, in their forties, three of them casual in T-shirts and trainers. Jim was open-collared, with faintly rosy cheeks, and a manner about him of suppressed agitation. He delivered an account of the objectors' position, laced with a sense of frustration and powerlessness in the face of planners, bureaucracy, building speculators and John Gummer. The inspector who'd approved the planning recommendations that threatened Greave House Fields, it transpired, came from some office in Bristol – and there was a strong feeling at this meeting, on both sides of the table, that decisions affecting these people were taken in a country far away, which knew little of them.

McCafferty had been active, and was able to offer an informal meeting at which the residents could put their objections; she coached them gently towards a notion of how they should make their case. They'd need to be ready on short notice; they'd need to think in bullet points. Could they get slides, or at least some photographs? 'And don't be more than half an hour, or they'll nod off.'

Asked if she'd speak for them herself, she said she would; she didn't believe development at Greave House was appropriate, and had ideas as to where more urgently needed low-cost housing might better be sited. She wanted the shell of Murgatroyd Mill converted into flats, and felt the owner's agents were sympathetic to that; they could keep the mill ponds and make them safe, they could have a little shop and a few benches and a playground. Developing the mill, she hoped, was the planning trade they could make that'd save Greave House Fields – but it would have been easier to provide low-cost homes if the council weren't barred from using its Housing Revenue Account to build such housing itself. While the market was skewed towards the private builder, and the housing stock grew steadily more depleted, Calderdale had £7,000,000 sitting there, ring-fenced and doing nothing. It was, she sighed, 'Dogma gone mad.'

The discussion became more general. Jim said, 'This is about emptying town centres of population. Property prices fall, developers move in and snap it up for shops or offices or whatever, and out here the villages get clogged up and merged, and then everyone's a commuter.' He started in about John Gummer again . . .

McCafferty grinned. 'You know what my answer is. Get rid of Mr Gummer.'

When she was gone, I asked what they made of their councillor, and this process they were in. Jim sighed, 'It's taken us months just to learn how it works. But all the councillors have been good, not just her. They don't like central government telling them what to do in their own back yard.'

'It's the first time I've met her,' said one of the others, 'but she seems very receptive. Another councillor's been good at sounding sympathetic, whereas this one's saying she'll actually stand up for us.'

So when it came to the election, might they vote for her? The last speaker said, 'I think there's a ground-swell; I think she has a very good chance. Having met her, certainly, that could influence the way I vote.'

Jim said, 'I vote Tory – but they seem to be losing track of what we want at the minute. They need to come down here with us and get their shoes mucky. But I think it's high time they brought in proportional representation; there's too much fractional politics.'

I raised my eyebrows – there's not a lot of Tories believe in PR.

'I know,' he said. 'It's a bugger, that.'

'You've got to understand,' laughed one of the others, 'this bloke – if the Tory candidate was a donkey in that field he'd vote for it.'

The following morning, McCafferty went on Radio Leeds to launch a petition against handgun ownership; by midday she was back in Luddenden, at the Church of England's vicarage on Carr Field Drive. On the north side of Greave House Fields from the Kershaw estate, this was a different world, a cul-de-sac of big new houses with conservatories and double garages; but if the people of Kershaw were out of sight, in the vicarage they weren't out of mind.

The vicar was a smiling, pleasant man named Michael Morphy; with two members of his church, he was trying to save the Parish Pop-In Shop on the Kershaw estate. The estate had four retail units, all owned by the council; three had been knocked together into a little supermarket by a Mr Singh. The council had spent the last two years trying to rent out the fourth unit, without any joy, and in the meantime the church shop had used the space to sell cast-off clothes and junk, raising money for local people. They'd helped the youth centre and the playgroup, they'd given money to the school so poor kids could go on field trips, they'd even paid for one family's wedding outfits.

There were, they said, people in terrible trouble on that estate. But financially speaking, Calderdale was in terrible trouble too, casting round wherever it could to sell assets and raise revenue; and while the church wasn't paying even a peppercorn rent, Mr Singh fancied buying all four units. No one was suggesting he'd then jack up his prices and hold the residents to ransom, but a lot of these people had no cars, they had nowhere else to go – so if the church shop went, they'd lose an asset and gain a monopoly supplier.

McCafferty was unhappy about it, and was able to report that she'd secured a verbal agreement that, if she insisted, the property would not be sold. 'But – and it's a very big but – there's still the issue of money. If it's not sold we'll have to advertise it, and you'll have to put in a tender, and you'll have to pay a rent. Then, if the Property Committee wants to choose you instead of a higher bidder, we're not allowed to decide that ourselves; it has to go to the Secretary of State.'

They went around it – and somewhere along the way, news came up that a proposal for a car park in Luddenden had also gone to the Secretary of State. Morphy beamed, this was fine news; Luddenden being tight and steep, every time he had a wedding or a funeral the place got gridlocked.

I didn't beam; I gaped. I said, you want a car park in a village, you have to ask Whitehall? You want to let a church shop on a cheap rate in a housing estate, you have to ask Whitehall? Or you want to sort out a development plan in West Yorkshire, and the inspector comes from Bristol? What was this?

McCafferty said, 'Local democracy's been squeezed to the point where it barely exists. When I got elected we still had four members on the local health authority; we've none now. And you don't have to go much further back to find councillors, people you elected, on the water boards or the other utilities. But in one field after another, the decision-making power's been stripped away – which is ironic, really. Don't you remember Margaret Thatcher talking about the Nanny State?'

The last two lunchtimes there hadn't been any lunch; not the Labour Party as I'd been coming to know it, that. So the next day we made up for it with roast pork at the Shoulder of Mutton in Mytholmroyd (particularly fine crackling) where Tarlo and McCafferty were meeting two waste-management officers from the West Yorkshire Waste Disposal Authority.

Since they were elected, they'd tried to avoid ending up on the same committees or boards. 'We're both very opinionated,' McCafferty smiled, 'and we both have verbal diarrhoea. It wouldn't be fair on the other members, never mind on us.' They had, however, landed up together on waste management – and now the two officers were going to show them the state of play at a closed landfill on Scout Road. In the Fifties and Sixties, a lot of asbestos had been dumped there: maybe twenty tons, or forty, no one knew for sure. In Luddenden, Michael Morphy remembered when he first came to the valley how he'd dealt with a lot of families bereaved because of odd tumours, and it might have been anything – where there's textiles, there's chemicals – but certainly for McCafferty, asbestos struck a chord. Her father had died of lung cancer; his employer had made a small settlement out of court.

Scout Road closed at the end of the Seventies; the site was fenced off behind tall metal gates, chained with a padlock as big as a man's hand, and the concrete track up the hillside was blocked by two large boulders. But there was a junior school on the road

beneath it, and in the Eighties building societies had stopped lend-
ing on properties nearby. Now, to ease that blight and to eliminate
the health risk, the site was being decontaminated.

It was a painstaking job which would take several years; much of
the hillside over which the asbestos had spread from the tip was precipitously steep, and it was heavily overgrown. The way they'd
opted to do it was to send in a dozen men, wearing protective suits
and respirators, who bagged the poisoned topsoil by hand, then
winched the bags to a dumper truck on a cable and pulley. The bags
were sealed in a skip and taken away for burial at a licensed site;
they'd shifted 18,000 bags so far. The next bad hot-spot, until they
got round to it, was covered with layers of geotextiles and plastic
webbing, with a blanket of shredded wood over that.

One of the officers said, 'It may seem slow and archaic, but do
you know a better way? Sure, you give me a million quid, I could
get a machine in – but then we'd gouge and scar the hillside, and
we'd take out dozens of trees, and we'd end up with fibres blowing
down over that school there. No thanks. Because it's asbestos, your
mind just runs amok.'

One of these two men said he'd prefer not to be identified; as a
public servant, he didn't want his private views attributed. So I'll
call them Bill and Ben; they were a cheerful pair after all, one greying and roly-poly, the other taller and sandy-haired, and they were
good company. But they had their gripes and one of the biggest (as
with Luddenden's car park, or the tender for the Pop-In Shop) was
that everything they tried to do was forever hanging fire on financial approval from Whitehall.

Bill said, 'It does seem to us, up here in the wild outreaches of
the country north of Watford that nobody gives a bugger about,
that they sit round the table in April, and by the time they've
approved anything you're halfway into winter, and you can't do the
work. On both a personal and an engineering level, I feel there's
too many faceless chinless wonders down there telling us how to do
our job when they don't know a damn thing about it. And what's
annoying isn't just that it's messing up the environment – it's that it's
messing up my family's quality of life. And they can bugger me
about – but not my family.'

We walked through the quiet, poisoned woods under a grey,
humid sky. 'You'll get the feeling,' said Ben, 'that me and Bill are

very sad – I won't say bitter – but very sad, certainly, about the way local government's going. Everything's being tipped into the private sector; the bottom line seems to be just to smash and break things up. It's all this *dismantling* . . .'

This was a man who'd always voted Tory. Next time, however, he'd most likely be abstaining.

There was no doubt where Bill's vote lay. He said, 'My parents were Labour, I was brought up Labour, and I've always voted Labour. It's true I've done better than my parents did, and that's what every parent would hope for – and you might think now I'm managerial, I might try the other lot. But there's no way I could bring myself to vote Tory. It's not just what's happening to local government, or to my job here – it's the welfare state, and the health service. The first two houses I lived in were taken down in the slum clearances, we were council tenants; so the sort of background I'm from, I see my elderly relatives who never had money, and who were never able to accumulate money, being totally dependent on the welfare state, and now they're taking it apart. You get all this talk of people looking after themselves – but there's too many who can't, and it's not through any fault of their own. They've paid their dues, they've expected that help, they're not getting it, it's the Tories who've taken it away, and the arrogance with which they do it . . .'

The trees shifted under the muggy sky; we were coming back to the heavy gates of the landfill, looking out over the high narrow valley with its thin line of industry along the river. Bill shook his head and said, 'Example. Portillo's been an MP ten years so he gives that party to celebrate, and it was however much a head to go there. Well, pardon my French, but who gives a fuck how long he's been an MP?'

4

THE RIGHT HONOURABLE MEMBER

It was the last day of August, and in clement weather a festive crowd gathered for the Mytholmroyd Gala. Stalls and bouncy castles lined the main arena on the Hebden Bridge Saints' football pitch; at the back of the ground, a bunch of lads in scuffed trainers and baggy jeans bunked in over the fence. Having saved on the entry money, they tried their skill at chucking footballs into the Rotary Club's toilet bowls for fifty pence a go.

The Labour Party stall was wedged between St Michael's Church and the RSPCA; it boasted lollipops, leaflets and organic courgettes. Chris McCafferty gathered signatures for her anti-handgun petition on a clipboard. 'Everyone's signing,' she said, all smiles, plainly relaxed. She and Tarlo had been hiking on the Lleyn Peninsula; the election, she now believed, would be held in November. Tarlo showed holiday snaps, his wife striding out in her walking boots; he grinned, 'Your active MP.'

I wandered by the Scouts' tombola and the Nursery Action Group, past Amnesty International, the MS Society, and the Calderdale Badger Monitors. It's a strange thing how, as a nation, we're so peculiarly dedicated to good deeds and causes in multifarious profusion, how we'll round up cuddly toys and bake cakes until our dying day for children and furry animals and hungry people far away – and then we vote Tory. Do we think caring should be a private matter, and the public domain all emotionless business?

The parade arrived, led by the City of Bradford Pipe Band. Behind the pipers, the Gala Queen with her attendants and her cushion-bearer jolted precariously on a flatbed truck through the narrow gateway from the road, smiling hectically and clinging for dear life to a fetching assortment of plastic garden furniture. Then came majorettes twirling their rods to a Queen song, the music provided by a gigantic boombox wheeled along in a pushchair. A New-Life-In-Jesus crew followed, then the Hebden Bridge Junior Band, the Judo Club, an assortment of children fantastically costumed as carnival insects, more majorettes and cheerleaders, Joseph and his coat of many colours on a truck with two wobbly fake palm trees, and an eager tailing bevy of ice-cream vans. In the watching crowd, I asked the retiring Gala Queen what she'd done for the past year in her demanding role; she was tall, very striking and a little shy. She said, 'You're supposed to get invitations. But I were away at university, so I couldn't go to any of 'em.'

Her mate said glumly, 'You only got one invitation anyway.'

Speeches were made, and the national anthem played. At the back of the little stage the Conservative MP for Calder Valley, Sir Donald Thompson, sat stout and silver-haired in a blue blazer, a white carnation in his lapel. Afterwards I found him exchanging pleasantries with David Tarlo and a Council Countryside Officer on the save-the-badgers stall. I told Thompson I was writing about the Calder Valley and he said heartily, 'You're writing about paradise then.'

At Labour's stall, McCafferty bobbed and weaved through the strolling crowd with her clipboard. 'Would you sign a petition against handguns?'

A tall, fit-looking old man said sternly, 'Of course I will, love. And if you don't get in this time, I'm giving up bloody voting.'

'If you don't get in this time,' said another man, 'there'll be no point bloody voting.'

McCafferty waved her clipboard about. By the end of the afternoon, only four people had refused to sign it. Two, she said, were of questionable lucidity, the third owned three shotguns, and the fourth was Sir Donald. Having thus voted resoundingly against handgun ownership, the public of Mytholmroyd went to watch the Wild West show. This featured a clutch of embarrassed-looking fellows trying to act macho in black duster coats, bandannas and spurs, mumbling cowboy lines in broad Yorkshire accents – 'You took mah woman' – and then shooting each other.

★

At the Royd Regeneration stall, signatures were sought on another matter. Mytholmroyd, stranded along the valley road between Halifax and Hebden Bridge, had in the past five years lost three banks and a building society; that in turn impinged upon local businesses and shops, and was particularly felt by the town's older people. So Royd Regeneration had a petition to get some banking facilities back; at least a cashpoint machine.

The agency was six weeks old. It was McCafferty's baby, housed (ironically) in premises vacated by Barclays and set up on funds begged, borrowed and whistled for from private and public sources alike. I'd attended the opening, with a brass band playing on a drizzly evening in the war memorial gardens; short speeches were given, mostly inaudible under the rumble of traffic just feet away on the main road. No one had remembered to bring a ribbon or scissors, so the local snappers photographed the Mayor of Halifax putting the key in the lock instead. The Mayor sighed that her chain of office weighed as much as two bags of sugar.

She went in, chain-laden, and an acne-spattered youth of fourteen or fifteen with a crew-cut, ratty trainers, jeans off his hips and four surly girls in tow slouched up to ask what it was all about. I said it was about trying to get new businesses started; he said, 'I could start a business, me,' and headed in to scarf great mounds off the buffet. His appetite was healthier than the local economy, for sure.

Six weeks later, the agency's development officer Shaun Green was running his petition to the banks. He said, 'Sir Donald came in. He told me, this petition, I was to send it to him when it was done, and he'd sign it and add a letter. I said, Great. And I was thinking, You might be out of office by then, pal.'

Sir Donald Thompson was a Conservative of the old school, a genial and contented man of about five foot six with expensive spectacles, a belly like a barrel and a wheeze like dodgy air-brakes. He lived in Hipperholme, up the hill from Brighouse; on a small road by a little garage and a bridal shop, the house was substantial but not detached, and suggested moderate rather than extravagant wealth.

He was born in Harrogate in 1931; his family moved to Hanson Lane in Halifax in the Thirties, and his father rented a butcher's shop. They lived over the shop; there was no bathroom, and the toilet was outside. In the evening, while his parents worked, the apprentice would give Donald and his younger brother their bath by the fire. One night during the War, after his bath, the bomb that fell nearby killed the apprentice on his way out, and several other people.

The Thompsons moved to the suburb of Northowram, and Donald went to Hipperholme Grammar; his father bought a farm in Mixenden and when Donald finished National Service in 1951, he went to work on it for ten years. It was mostly pigs and poultry, supplying three shops the family owned by then – but he got farmer's lung, an extreme form of asthma, so he went into running the butcher's business with his brother instead. They supplied schools, prisons, hospitals; then, sparked by a need for moulded liners to go in their vans, he moved into fibreglass manufacture with a company called Armadillo Plastics in Brighouse. If he'd not gone into politics, it would have been an ordinary, unspectacular small businessman's career; but during the Sixties, he said, 'I became a bit worried about Harold Wilson. It sounds ridiculous now, but I thought we were going to finish up like East Germany. So I walked round to the local Tories in Hipperholme and said, I want to help.'

In 1967, he won a seat at County Hall in Wakefield on the old West Riding County Council; his slogan was, 'Don't Emigrate – Vote Conservative'. Then he decided he wanted to become an MP. He went to London, and was interviewed by a man called Sharples who told him to go away; they could do better than him. Thompson recalled the memory with a breathy chuckle; he'd now been an MP for seventeen years, a good foot soldier who'd never voted against the government in his life and had a knighthood to show for it.

He stood for Batley and Morley in 1970, and chewed off half Labour's 14,000 majority there. In the elections in 1974, he stood for the Calder Valley seat – it was called Sowerby then – and he lost by 115 the first time, 646 the next. He said he lost by more the second time because he'd gone negative and, in retrospect, he thought it turned people off. In the February election, when Labour won, some of their supporters unfurled a banner with a hammer and sickle over Todmorden Town Hall; in October the Tories used that in a last-minute leaflet and, said Sir Donald, 'It didn't do. So I lost.' Later, in light of that remark, I asked him what he thought about the poster of Blair with the demon eyes. He said he wouldn't have done it.

When Thatcher went to Downing Street in 1979, Donald Thompson won Sowerby by 1,180 votes. The seat's boundaries were then redrawn, giving the Sowerby Bridge ward to Halifax, and the more well-heeled Hipperholme and Lightcliffe ward to the new seat of Calder Valley. This made a marginal much safer for the Tories; between that and the Falklands, in 1983 his majority was 7,999. He said people would ask him why he bothered canvassing at all – and Labour did all they could to help. Nationally, there was Michael Foot and the 'suicide note' manifesto; locally, they had some woman up from London who, said Sir Donald, 'Got it entirely wrong. Dressed like a politico, went on about the *Belgrano*. Well, they'd cheered about the *Belgrano* in the pubs round here.'

I asked why he'd wanted to become an MP and he said, 'I thought I could do better. I was genuinely disturbed about the Labour Party, all the strikes, it got worse and worse – so I thought I could do better, and I still think I can. Look – everybody in Westminster either has been a minister and still thinks they ought to be, or would like to be a minister and can't understand why they aren't. That's on the Conservative side and the Labour side and in the press gallery too. They'll never say so – but all my colleagues think they could do better. It's like anyone. You write books because you think you can sell them, don't you?'

Looking back, he was more proud of privatisation than anything else. He said, 'If we'd have known we'd be there for seventeen years, we'd have done it all sooner.' On the debit side, he felt they'd not been successful with local government. 'We didn't know where we were going, and we haven't got a framework or a formula yet. But,' he shrugged, 'I don't think the Opposition have either, God bless 'em.'

In success or in failure, he loved his job. He was, he said, 'The luckiest man in England. To be an MP is the best job an

Englishman can have. I don't know what a Scotsman thinks, or a Welshman or an Irishman – but I know I can, and have, for the last seventeen years, been able to influence what we were doing. And then, I've a wonderful constituency.'

I said the book would be called *This England*, and he quoted 'Jerusalem'. He said, 'You used to be able to stand on Beacon Hill over Halifax and your schoolteacher would say, I'll give you a shilling if you can count all the mill chimneys.' The fact that much of the work those mills represented had gone didn't appear to give him pause; he seriously believed the Tories had been good for manufacturing industry.

He struck me as a kind of roly-poly Candide; in Sir Donald's world, on the whole, all was for the best. His definition of the 'strong culture' locally was priceless: 'We have the cricket. I'll go to Walsden or Todmorden, I'll have a tea – if I haven't ordered one I don't get one, mind – then we've amateur dramatics and operatics, Rotaries, Round Tables, Soroptimists, nine golf courses, hundreds of soccer teams, strong rugby league, rugby union, a bit of hockey, bit of tennis, all that. A strong culture.'

Amid this orgy of hale civic endeavour there were, he conceded, problems. 'There's a lot of underprivilege. It isn't in great lumps, but there are areas that could do with more resources. There's some fairly low wages. There's some *misunderstood* low wages, mind, because outworkers *like* to work out – and when I've spoken to them they take it as an impertinence if you say they're only getting £2 an hour. They say that doesn't matter 'cause I've got all me kids, me mother's next door, I can earn £70, £80, £100 a week, and it's nothing to do with you.'

I was in Sir Donald's living room for an hour and a half, and there were moments when I struggled to keep my jaw from heading floorwards. He was a pleasant and convivial fellow, genuinely well-meaning, but he appeared to live in a world bearing no relation to the one I see every day. The notion of these outworking peons (doubtless tugging on a forelock, if they've not gone bald with stress) gamely declaring, 'Eh oop, ah'm '*appy* with two pound an hour, me – this was only one of several radiant moments.

He was, for example, unfailingly polite about Chris McCafferty (just as she was plainly fond of him). The manner of her selection, however – the all-woman short list – he described as, 'A hen pen.

A load of girls picked by the old cocks.' The delivery of this gem
was blithely, I'd say almost giddily innocent.

He said one way to tackle deprivation was to get more resources
to women. I said that sounded like moderate Conservatism . . .

'The only possible reason for privatising Britain, for turning it
round as we have done, is to make sure people get a better quality
of life. Everybody. Not just the guy whose tax went down from
ninety per cent to forty, but the ordinary man and woman. Look,
I met a girl the other day, sixteen, just started life as a hairdresser.
Now she should have as full and interesting a life as you or I do, and
it's part of my job to see that she does. Which is why I make such
a fuss about our culture. Life's got to have wide margins.'

Not a right-winger, then.

'I'm right wing as far as privatisation goes. I'm not sure I believe
in ID cards; soon as they give you one, somebody'll be wanting to
confiscate it. That worries me. And I'm *very* worried about remov-
ing the right to silence; that's what all the Chartists up these valleys
fought for.'

So, on social matters, definitely a moderate.

'I don't know. I think the guys up here think I'm a bit left, a bit
soft.'

I asked him what he thought about the likes of Teresa Gorman
and he said, 'She's not middle England. She's embarrassing. Bill Cash
is a bit less so, at least he's got an intellectual base – but at the end of
the day, people don't like tap-room politics, and they don't expect me
to deal in the small change of it. I mean, Hitler had tap-room politics, y'know – kill them bloody gypsies, chuck the old folks in the
incinerator, all that – that's not what my constituents want.'

Relieved to hear it, I reeled away from this peculiar formulation
to the election date; it would, he said, be on May 1st, and the sceptics would be a problem. 'Europe hampers us, and it would hamper
the Labour Party if they let it. But they've more sense. They want
to get in, and they aren't talking about it. So Europe isn't an issue
across the country, but it might become one. I mean, pae-dee-o-
philia, quite rightly, pae-dee-o-philes, is the issue this minute. Or
law and order – we might go very strongly on law and order, or we
may come out, if there's a Dunblane half-way through . . .'

He was up there with James Joyce for your stream of conscious-ness. If the Tories suffered from the Gormans of this world, he said, 'They suffer on the other side from the smoked salmon socialists, the North London dinner-table socialists. Guys who've no idea what it is to get up in the morning and catch the bus and go to work and sew gussets into jeans, or wait on tables, or cut up beef, and can't understand how important it is for people to be tret well at work, and to have margins in their life outside, and not have their Saturday afternoons spoilt by yobbos. I mean, they swear, I was always amazed at how much chaps working for us'd swear – but that doesn't mean they were rough and crude. They work. And they don't want their weekends spoilt, and bloody . . . well, there's me swearing. But these North London dinner-table . . .'

Blair was one of these?

'I count him as one, yes. He's a Scotsman, isn't he? I don't know. But he's of that ethic and of that ilk. Now he's doing a very good job of trying to get the Labour Party elected, and he will be let down by his friends, as we have been. But I think we'll win in May. I think I shall win. The tide will turn. My job is to convince my constituents that 1996 is a different world to 1980, that it's more prosperous. That the health service works, and it does – it does *here*. That the schools are good. And I've got to convince them that if they think it's time for a change, it won't be a change for the better.'

What if they say they don't believe you?

'They will. So I'll ask them, where's the evidence? Un-employment in Calder Valley is five per cent . . .'

And if they bring up their wages, the insecurity of their jobs, the gulf between rich and poor . . .

'They'll say that. The answer, of course, is that as the gap's widened, the bottom's gone up too. The prosperity of people at the bottom is greater now, in disposable income, in goods they've got, in every measurable thing, than it was in 1980. We are now regard-ing as poor people who we would have regarded as not very well off then – because they are better off.'

I left, baffled. He was a decent man, but what had he been doing these past seventeen years? Where had he been? In the Houses of Parliament, of course – where, it would appear, there's a risk that the longer you stay there, the less you know.

★

Opposite the Crazy Teapot Tea Rooms and a glitzy boutique, all palmy bits and sub-Biba, the Bridge Mill is now workshops, a pottery, a New Age gift shop called Magpie's; it houses a pizzeria, and a licensed café called Innovation selling Breton crêpes and designer greeting cards. The mill chimney stands by the riverside, a pleasing relic for your holiday snaps; on the bridge itself, a man playing a clarinet had half a dozen little watercolours for sale on the pavement. I was in Hebden Bridge, two days after talking with Sir Donald, and in the market Chris McCafferty was on the anti-gun case with her clipboard.

Eileen Jones, Kinnock's biographer, turned up fulminating about Gordon Brown's dream of a 10p tax band. 'Don't we all know we've got to *raise* taxes if we want to sort things out?' It was that Mandelson's fault – but she felt guilty saying rude things about the prince of darkness, she said, because he'd given her book a good review.

Kevin Barron, MP for Rother Valley and a member of the shadow health team, had come to support McCafferty's petition, his presence in turn drawing the *Halifax Courier* and the *Hebden Bridge Times* – the point of the exercise. They went into the market to be photographed; at a rather wonderful cheese stall, a woman behind me said, 'What the hell's that about? Bloody rates going up, I'll bet.'

When they were done, Barron put the argument against even *talking* about higher taxes with great clarity. In 1987, when Labour voted against the 2p cut in the rate to 25p, he'd been Kinnock's PPS. And it didn't matter what people said – when they were in the privacy of the voting booth with three boxes in front of them, and one of them meant more money out of their pocket, they didn't put their cross in that box, plain and simple. So Barron and Kinnock went about the country in that campaign, and in private somewhere they looked at each other and said, 'We've dropped a bollock here.'

I asked if he was more confident this time and he said, 'Twenty points ahead, it's a good start. But if no party's ever come back from that far behind, look – no party's ever won from opposition with a six-point swing either.'

I went home, and that evening in my local a smartly dressed man told me he didn't like the Tories. But he earned over £20,000 a year, and last time they told him Labour would hit him on that.

'Never mind the average household,' he said, 'never mind two kids and half a dog, or what happens if you drink three pints of beer. My income, I can count that. So I voted Tory.'

And is that, in the end, all this England comes down to? Tolerance, adaptability, baking cakes for the poor and the sick and the hungry – are all those things just guilty do-goodery to cover up the fact that when we get in the voting booth, all we think about is our wallets?

'It's fear, fear, fear, every time. If the electorate didn't have that fear over tax, we'd win with a majority of 120. But there's a generation of people whose image of the last Labour government is so deeply ingrained in their whole being that, yes, they see the party's changed, they see it'd be good for Britain – but in the polling booth they'll look and think, Oh God. No way. So you're asking people to make a leap of faith, to make a courageous act, to not have that fear. In our private polling we're ahead on strong leadership, on being a united party, on the One Nation thing – but what the Tories have going for them is fear, and their entire election strategy will be based on it.'

The Labour Party's offices on Kirkgate in Bradford were a dingy tip. You went in through a murky doorway labelled 'General Buildings', and rode an antique elevator to the third floor. On an ill-lit corridor, Ian Carvell's office had a grimy window, tatty cast-off furniture, and an overflowing wastebin on a worn old carpet scattered with flecks of paint. Stacks of leaflets and newsletters teetered on dented filing cabinets; random strips of sticky tape hung from faded woodchip wallpaper.

Carvell was as worn as his office; he was twenty-seven but looked appreciably older, a heavy smoker with a frayed nervous energy, wrecked teeth, and dark bags beneath his eyes. He was the Labour Party's Area Organiser for Bradford and Calderdale: as he put it, 'the NEC's person on earth' in this patch of West Yorkshire, responsible for the political management of seven constituencies. Among these, Halifax, Keighley and Calder Valley were key targets into which he had to funnel the party's strategy and resources. He'd got the post in spring '95, two weeks after winning a council seat in Tunbridge Wells; between the two jobs, he'd put

48,000 miles on a B-reg Granada in fifteen months. He looked, frankly, shattered.

His father was a teacher; he was born in Malawi ('when Dr Banda was still only eighty') and he'd lived his first four years there. The family moved through Derby, Essex, Nigeria and Plymouth before settling in Kent in 1980; when he was fifteen, he'd worn a badge supporting the miners, and in the lower sixth he'd read *Socialist Worker*. I asked if his views had moderated since then; he said they had. But then, he grinned, 'I'm not allowed to have views now I work for the party anyway. I'm here to sell soap powder, not discuss policy.'

The campaign was entirely about marketing; there were 89 key seats, and they had to be won. Alice Mahon's majority of 400 had to be shored up in Halifax; of 61 targets with Tory majorities, Keighley and Calder Valley were 39th and 47th on the hit list respectively. Reeling these in was all about hard work; about an 80 per cent contact rate, getting all your voters on computer, getting newssheets and manifestos through letterboxes. Carvell said, 'There's no such thing as a leaflet too many.' In the local elections last May, he'd been leafleting at seven in the morning; that afternoon he'd told me, 'You might have noticed I'm pretty paranoid. But that's a trait of all organisers; you throw yourself into it, you roll your sleeves up. You need to.'

Labour won control of Calderdale Council that day; the general election would be different. Of the timing he said, 'I've always thought it'll be May. Their best chance is to get our lead down to 10 per cent, and they're spending £2,000,000 a month doing it. They'll do it for ten months if they have to, and we can't counter that. And if they can instil New Labour, New Danger into people's minds, and pull us back by 2 per cent a month, once they're inside 10 per cent they can beat us. They whittled that away last time, and they can do it again.'

I asked if he wanted to be an MP, putting in time as he was in the party machine. He said, 'There's half an eye on it. I've seen MPs and candidates that are a lot less capable than I am – but there's other things in life. After the election I'll have done five long, solid, hard bloody years, and I might want to look at other things. There's a long queue of people more ambitious than me, a long queue of people who think they'll be MPs in the government after the next one. You can see them, completely ambitious, the researchers, the people working for the party, the people straight out of student politics . . .'

McCafferty, I said, certainly wasn't one of those.

'She's a character, she's not a machine politician – and it works to her advantage. Frank Dobson said it'd be very nice to have a woman like her in the House, 'cause she's so different to a lot of the new breed of Labour woman MPs. I can imagine who he meant by that,' he smiled, 'and I'm not saying. But y'know, they're thin, they've got the designer dresses. Chris is big, she'll laugh out loud – and occasionally she doesn't know totally how the party works in its darker moments, but that doesn't matter. She doesn't need to, that's what me and her agent are for. She's the public face of the party – and she's one hell of a campaigner.'

There was an implication there, I suggested, that if she got to Westminster she'd be in for a shock.

He said, 'Everyone will be in for a shock. Sitting Labour MPs will be in for a shock. They don't know how hard it's going to be, especially if we've got a tiny majority, or there's a hung parliament – because after seventeen years of the Tories, the shit's going to hit the fan. Every single constituency party's going to be throwing everything at their MP, wanting Blair to deliver, and deliver fast. And people are going to be so disappointed; it's going to take a lot of political guts to hold the line.'

So, I asked, was Blair doing the right thing?

'Yes. You can't change the way the country thinks from opposition. When Thatcher got in, the country wasn't thinking about privatisation, that whole right-wing agenda – but gradually, with them being in so long, the country's moved that way in its ethos. Now you cannot pull that back unless you win the election, and Blair's single-mindedly determined he'll do that. I've seen him in the Commons and he's ruthless, and he's got ruthless people around him. I could tell you stories about the day John Smith died, the weeks after that . . . well, I will in my memoirs. But he's not mucking around. And he's probably more in tune with the country than he is with the party – but that's what a prime minister needs to be.'

To get in, however, he had to beat that fear; he had to overcome

the nation's embedded small 'c' conservatism. And then, as Andrew
Marr had written in that morning's *Independent*, 'The difference
between Labour machiavellis and Tory ones is that Labour sprites
are very good at getting themselves written about, and Tory sprites
are good at getting re-elected.' Labour, Marr observed, was 'utterly
hopeless at knee-in-the-groin politics of the Conservative variety'.

Carvell agreed; the Tories, he said, 'Are the best election
machine the world has ever seen. They've got no problems with
lying, no problems with playing dirty – and we've not responded as
hard as we could have. There's an ethos in the Labour Party that we
shouldn't have to be like that to win – but unfortunately, we do.'

Sometimes, I said, he talked as if it were hopeless.

'No. But it is going to be very, very hard. It depends on places
like Calder Valley – and we know our lead is there to be disappeared.'

How would he feel if Labour lost?

'I'd go more in favour of PR than ever, just to guarantee they
never get in again. But,' he said grimly, 'I'd be gutted. I don't know
who I'd start blaming. But I wouldn't be ridiculously surprised.
They're just too good, and the gap we've got to make up is astro-
nomical. From '87 to '92, we hardly moved our percentage vote of
the population at all – because there are more Tories in England, in
their gut feeling, than there are people who vote Labour. There just
are.'

5

OLD LABOUR, NEW LABOUR

There were, said Ian Carvell, two people who mattered more than anyone else to the business of getting McCafferty elected: her agent Ann Martin, and her campaign co-ordinator Tim Swift. Nor could you have found two people who more perfectly represented the old and new wings of the Labour Party.

Martin turned fifty in September. She was a miner's daughter from the pit village of Willington, and played in her school brass band at the Durham Miners' Gala. In her family, she said, 'There was nothing else but Labour.' She began her working life as a telephonist with the Post Office and, apart from her family, what she was proud to call her 'socialist beginnings' came with her role as a shop steward in that job. Joining the party through the union, she'd been active in it all her life – whereas Tim Swift had left the Liberal Democrats to join New Labour just eighteen months ago.

Martin worked in Bradford City Hall as personal assistant to the area's Labour MEP Barry Seal; she was a forthright woman with straw-coloured hair, a reddening face, and a mellifluous north-eastern accent gone gravelly with smoking. Swift, by contrast, was a jacket-and-tie southerner, an 'off cumden' from Leicester with a precise, faintly effete manner; he was a white-collar computer whiz, and he was Age Concern's Chief Officer in Calderdale.

Conveniently, this job barred him from any public role; because, had he been McCafferty's agent, a fair few members of the Calder Valley Labour Party wouldn't have lifted a finger to help. Never mind how gifted he was; he wasn't 'one of us'. When I quoted a Polly Toynbee comment on the fierce tribalism of grass-roots politics, he laughed and said, 'Quite accurate. I've not seen a great deal of overt hostility, and I hope I've tried to avoid that. But I'm sure there are undercurrents.'

'We have,' said Martin, 'a slight problem.' Swift and his wife Megan started working with McCafferty very early after her selection; Martin, on the other hand, only became her agent in the summer of '96, when the previous occupant of that role didn't work out. So they still had to define her place in the team *vis-à-vis* the Swifts. They'd had, she said carefully, several 'discussions' to work out how they could come together — and it was clear these discussions hadn't always been temperate.

She said, 'Tim's a genius at what he does, but the party's not happy with his close relationship to Chris. He's come to us, he's got the ability, we've absolutely got to use it — but he doesn't see the role of an agent as I do. I see an agent having complete control of what goes on — because at the end of the day, if anything goes wrong, I'm the one who goes to prison.'

Carvell knew about these hints of inner tension; he thought the election would be in May and that was Plan A. But it was now September and if it should come in November, while he had a Plan B for Halifax and Keighley, for Calder Valley he didn't. Right now, if the election came early, Plan B for Calder Valley was just 'to get everybody running like fuck'. If it came in November, he said, in Calder Valley they'd lose.

Bradford City Hall stands between a modern office block housing the Abbey National, and a multi-storey car park. It's a wonderful building, ornate and towered, strutting with the municipal pride of a more confident time; it is, today, an architectural galleon marooned in a sea of pavement. Down the dim corridors of this grand and gaudy pile, Martin's office was decorated with posters promoting the work of the European Socialist Group; she'd worked for the MEP since 1980.

Eighteen months ago, she'd stood for selection herself, and the process had involved a spot of tribal infighting. As chair of the constituency party, Martin had been (or was seen to be) instrumental in their decision to have the all-woman list. This meant the previous candidate, David Chaytor, was out of the game; his wife, Sheena

Whittingham, therefore stood in his place. Now Whittingham was from the top of the valley, McCafferty from the middle, Martin from the bottom – and, said Martin, 'It was a very amicable contest, apart from one person who made it very difficult. Chris and I got on well throughout and I was delighted when she won, honestly. We're friendly, we've known each other a long time – and it seemed we gelled together against Sheena. It was just the antics the top of the valley got up to, they were really vicious, slagging me off in the press, naming me – because they blamed me for the all-woman list. There was a lot of bad feeling.'

Still, she thought the right woman had won. She said, 'She works extremely hard, she's refreshingly free of ego, and she's very personable. Since she became the candidate, the acrimony over the list has disappeared; the place has come together because of her. If I'd been the candidate,' she shrugged, 'the top end of the valley wouldn't have bothered.'

The agent's job is to organise the election, to be legally responsible for everything that happens, and to organise the candidate – to make sure she's happy, briefed and on time. Come the campaign, said Martin, she'd be with McCafferty every moment. I asked if she'd have any life of her own in those weeks, and she laughed at the very idea. She said, 'Oh no. You just work for ever. I don't sleep a lot anyway so it doesn't bother me, but it'll be seven in the morning to one the next night every day. But look, when we come to it, I'll love it. It's my life. The Labour Party is my life.'

If they lost, she said, 'I'll be absolutely devastated. The country will never be the same. They've wrecked it beyond recognition already; we've become a selfish society, and if they get another term it'll be worse.' She sighed, a long pause, then she said, 'I've not words for it. The Labour Party will split, I fear that. It's this time or never.'

The idea of the party splitting, should Labour lose, was not at all far-fetched to her; of Scargill's break to form a party of his own, she said only that he'd got his timing wrong. Of her own views she said, 'I'm certainly not New Labour, and I'm quite concerned at the moment as to where we're going. It's all right getting middle England, but what's going to happen to traditional Labour voters?

There's a percentage out there who might think, What are they going to do for me? What are they going to do about social benefits, things like that?'

So did she think Blair was doing the right thing? There was a long, long pause, then she said, 'He's doing everything he thinks is possible to win, with the guidance of Mr Mandelson' – and here she peeled the guru's name off her tongue as if it tasted of ash. She continued, 'I don't know personally whether he's gone too far; I feel he has. The party has to modernise – but if you're leaving your traditional electorate behind, they've got nowhere else to go. And if they don't vote for us, what we've gained at one end, we've lost at the other.'

If Martin and Swift came to Labour from diametrically different positions, on this point they were entirely united. Asked that same morning if Blair was doing the right thing, Swift said, 'Most of the time I think he is. I'm always hesitant about second-guessing someone who's doing a job the pressures of which one can barely imagine – but I'm becoming concerned. I've no doubt that in 1992, when people got in the polling booth and pictured Neil Kinnock in Downing Street, they decided they had to vote Tory. I don't think that'll happen this time, because of the changes Blair's made. But the difficulty is balancing that with the need to recognise that most of the people who actually go out and do the work are long-standing Labour Party members who do believe in . . . well, in socialism. Or at least, who have some pretty deep beliefs that have been rather trodden on. And while they'll accept so much, we still want and need those people to be active. But John Smith House has just done a batch of telephone canvassing for us, six or seven thousand calls – and I've been concerned, going through them, that there's the odd traditional Labour person in there saying they're not sure it's worth bothering to vote for this lot. They may just be saying it, they might still bother – but it's more than one or two now, it's one in every couple of hundred. And you start to think, we can't afford to shake those people off.'

At a candidates' briefing at the party conference two weeks later, Mandelson – with whom McCafferty was much impressed – said the message to get through to the voters about the Tories was simply, 'Enough is enough.' Inside the Labour Party, however, from old socialists to new converts, people wanted Mandelson and Blair to hear that message themselves.

Thirty-nine years old, Swift was a trim, slight, greying and bespectacled man who'd moved from Leicester to Hebden Bridge in 1990. He'd come to work for the Association of Liberal Democrat Councillors; the following year he became a councillor himself, in McCafferty's Luddendenfoot ward – and after polite, flat Leicester, the council culture he found in Calderdale was a shock.

He said, 'It was a bit rough. There were some quite strange, unpleasant personal relationships between councillors, inside parties as well as between them. The general level of animosity was really quite difficult; in the early Nineties every group had one or two very strong individuals who were convinced they should have their own way, and when they didn't get it, watch out. They were capable of being very, very cruel.'

In the coming election, the Liberal Democrat candidate for Calder Valley was a councillor for Greetland and Stainland named Stephen Pearson; and while everyone was fond of genial old Sir Donald, very little that anybody had to say about Pearson was printable. Pearson, however, was not the only reason Swift left the Lib Dems. He'd come to think simply that *the* most important thing was that the Conservatives shouldn't win the next election – and that the Liberals were a hindrance to that.

Besides, the whole landscape had shifted. He still saw himself as a liberal with a small 'l' on the touchstone liberal issues – racism and equal opportunities, civil rights, freedom of information – but those were positions you could happily hold in the Labour Party. So he moved; Blair, he said, wasn't directly relevant, but ditching Clause IV was. In the past, he'd used Clause IV as his excuse for not joining Labour; he could say, I don't believe in the common ownership of the means of production. He suspected 97 per cent of Labour Party members never believed in it either – but it was gone now, and he'd joined because he wanted to see a Labour government, and he wanted to help bring that about.

In May '91, he'd stood against McCafferty, not expecting as an 'off cumden' to win; he didn't, but he got on the council a little later in a by-election. There was a year or so when relations

between himself and McCafferty weren't too good; the campaign
had involved unpleasantness on both sides. The Liberals had gone
personally after the then Labour leader, David Helliwell; they said
all the money went to Halifax and not the valley, they said Labour
councillors didn't pay their poll tax, they slagged Helliwell for
bringing the Northern Ballet to town. It was, said Swift, 'Pretty
tacky.'

Over time, however, Swift and McCafferty found they had a lot
in common, not least a strong interest in social services. I asked if
she'd invited him to come over to Labour, and he could only recall
her saying it once – but he'd been finding life among the Lib Dems
intolerable anyway. He said, 'What at first was a perfectly justifiable
set of local campaign techniques, about mobilising the community
and being involved in an active way, has become just a mechanism
that they use quite divorced from reality. Liberals in the ward I
represented would, with a perfectly straight face, put out leaflets
saying they keep in touch all year round, when in fact you've not
heard from them in nine months. But they do it with so much
volume for the last two months that they con people into believing
it – and I find that totally immoral.'

Sick of the party in general and Pearson in particular, he quit the
council to work for Age Concern. He joined Labour some months
later, and started working with McCafferty at about the same time.
Now he'd been engaged for months in what, nationwide, the
Labour Party was calling the biggest exercise in voter identification
ever seen in British politics – so while Martin looked after the candidate, Swift ran the computer that told them where the votes
were.

It involved doing what people have always done: collecting
canvas information. But what the party had done nationally, and
what some people locally found difficult to grasp, was to say that the
traditional way people canvassed – to ask, How will you vote? –
wasn't actually too helpful. People lie, and canvassers are over-
optimistic – so they were trying instead to understand where people
really come from. You don't ask who they'll vote for; you ask who
they identify with. You ask, if they're in the pub and there's an argument, do they say, I'm Labour? Do they say, I'm Tory? Or do they
say, I'm Tory, but I'm never voting for those buggers again?

Traditional canvassing put that last person down as Labour in the same way you'd put Ann Martin down as Labour, and that was meaningless. So they were trying to get people to differentiate, and it was a sound idea. Swift said, 'I don't know if a lot of local parties can deliver on it, because it's very difficult to go to a member of forty years' standing who's doorstep-canvassed all that time and say, "Sorry, not right. Please do it again". But the fact is, from being a Liberal, I do know that Labour canvassing was lousy.'

Long from end to end, curled round three sides of Halifax, socially and geographically diverse, the electoral map of the constituency was a nightmare. Up the top, Todmorden was the most solid Labour ward; next along, Calder Valley and Luddendenfoot were more mixed, split between Labour and Lib Dems, with a fair slice of Tories who might sway to the Liberals – and a crucial part of the voter identification process was finding out the Liberals' second preferences. Labour squeezed the Liberal vote very successfully in '92; unfortunately, they squeezed most of them to go and vote Tory. So it was important to know which Liberals wanted a change of government, and to leave well alone those Tories who sometimes voted Liberal. 'We're very happy for the second lot to vote Liberal,' Swift smiled, 'so long as we can get the first lot to come to us.'

Next along, south of Luddendenfoot, Ryburn ward had a pocket of council estates by Sowerby Bridge; the job here was to get their votes out, without too much exciting the good folk of Ripponden and Rishworth towards the moors next door, these last being solidly Conservative. 'Let's hope,' he said, 'the carrier pigeons don't get through up there with the date of the election, eh?'

As to the five wards at the lower, eastern end of the valley – Greetland and Stainland, Elland, Rastrick, Brighouse, Hipperholme and Lightcliffe – these were smaller, more compact and urban, and for Swift they represented a problem. The top of the valley had been hard-fought between Liberals and Labour for years; as a result you had active, competent local parties there. But in the lower valley there'd been a more traditional Labour-Tory thing, a feeling that you won your seats in the good years, you lost them in your bad. So something like 60 per cent of the party's membership lived in the top three wards – when in a general election the other wards were vital, and they didn't have the resources or the people to work them properly. 'But the trouble is,' he shrugged, 'the party's always tended to be run from the upper valley – and lower valley people don't like upper valley people coming in and saying, you're not doing it right. And,' he smiled, 'they certainly don't want *me* coming and saying it.'

All in all, he sighed, it was a hell of a constituency. People lived all over the place; towns, villages and hamlets were slung down any which way, merging one into the other along every roadside. In Leicestershire, you'd not bother with every farm, every odd house; you'd do where the bulk of the population were, and you'd hit 90 per cent. Here, the first time he did Luddendenfoot that way, he missed 1,000 houses. There were no clear boundaries; you'd get a core of forty or fifty homes, a terrace of six or seven up behind them, then if you knew about it you went up a track and there were three more hid away round the back. 'And that,' he said, 'is another reason why knowing where your supporters are matters so much – because there's nothing worse than trudging up a four-hundred-yard farm track to remind a Tory to go out and vote.'

He believed Labour could win. Nationally, support would be higher than in '92 – while locally, both Calderdale seats had under-performed that year anyway. The council had been unpopular; they'd got messily involved with the football club, the Northern Ballet – and the ballet summed it up. Here was a council facing poll-tax capping, and they were spending all that money on some nancy southern art form.

All the same, the 20-point poll lead was fantasy. Swift said, 'What worries me is that for a couple of years most Labour members have given the impression it's in the bag, and it very definitely isn't. I think the most likely outcome is that the national swing will place Calder Valley right on the boundary. We'll just win it, or we'll just lose.'

He said McCafferty might make the difference. 'It's a good sell-ing point that she's not gone into this just wanting to be an MP. She's not your cardboard cut-out candidate who's hawked her way round the constituencies; she's someone with a real interest in the valley, who happened to be in the right place at the right time to become the PPC. So if she doesn't win here, she'll not go and stand in Bradford or Bury; she'll stand here or nowhere. In a time when people are cynical about politicians and their motives, that's very sellable.'

But what if she lost? What if Labour were to lose? He gave a deep, deep sigh and said he'd be utterly demoralised, not just about politics but in his job as well. Working for Age Concern, he knew only too well how many people out there were juggling like mad to cope, living with financial anxiety all the time. It depressed him; he saw an underlying fear in people that things just weren't going to get any better, that more and more would be taken away from them. He said, 'I think that's the worst legacy of the last seventeen years. Our parents thought the world would be better for us, but do you feel that for your children? They seem to have destroyed so many people's expectations, and it's the worst thing, that nobody believes we can do better any more. I just think that's awful.'

6

CONFERENCE

———————

Over breakfast in Blackpool on the Sunday morning before conference, McCafferty and Tarlo spoke with an old couple about the weather and the shows. The pensioners asked if they were up for the politics, and Tarlo said they were. The woman looked at McCafferty and said, 'Never mind, dear. You can always do some shopping.'

The hotel's front room had red plush banquettes, a tiny pool table, a fruit machine, a football video game, and a TV on the wall. There were two weird collages of dried flowers – one adorned with white wooden pigs wearing bows and shawls, the other with a *Good Housekeeping* cover dated November 1931. Around the seats lay four empty pop cans, an assortment of crumpled fag packets, and an ashtray losing its battle to contain a mountain of butts. In the street outside three Scottish girls, all navel and thigh and black leather, attracted the admiration of a bevied pack of lads while their car failed to start. Raucous cheers and oiled advice echoed through a window edged with bilious yellow-green striplights.

Blackpool lately has attracted a dash of favourable press, sometimes of the so-awful-it's-great variety, but usually awed at its continuing ability to draw gigantic legions of fun-seekers. So let's get this straight: Blackpool is a tawdry, dispiriting dump strewn with litter, fast food, pissed kids and chewing-gum. Amid a prevailing odour of chip-fat, it's a monument to the English taste for getting catatonically drunk and having crap one-night stands. Throw in 1,300 Labour delegates, 4,500 media, armies of police, and an accreditation centre sunk under the keening weight of world attention into a baffled state of lethargic chaos, and I could see hysteria setting in in short order.

Certainly, wherever Blair went, the edge of excitement did verge on hysterical. Arriving on Sunday evening, I went with Tarlo and McCafferty to an eve-of-conference reception for the Party's North and Yorkshire Region in the Pembroke Hotel; two minutes after we got there the leader arrived, and it was as if you'd plugged every person in the room into the mains. He swept into the room with John Prescott in tow, and Alexis Powell – a bright, feisty twenty-seven-year-old delegate from Calder Valley – was so startled with the sharp potency of his presence as he passed that she backed flailing into McCafferty, and knocked the latter's red wine down her blouse. Mortified, Alex fled; McCafferty retired to the ladies' room thinking, 'You clot. You spent all that money on a new blouse when you *knew* something would be spilt on it.'

With a wry grin Tarlo idly inquired, 'How much money exactly?' Mind you, she might have been blouseless altogether; in the confusion of their arrival the night before, when our tatterdemalion hotel got their reservations wrong and they'd ended up sleeping in the owner's daughters' beds, they'd lost their car keys. 'And,' she sighed, 'I'd packed all my power dresses in the boot so carefully.'

They found the keys, rescued their clothes and went to see Blair. In person, buzzed up on the adulation and desire of his supporters, he's a tall, lean man who packs a dizzying charisma. Close up and live, the smile that looks cheesy and insincere in press pictures is fiercely dynamic, an energy field of gleaming incisors. Back in the B&B, there were leaflets for Sea World yelling that we should go and see the eight-foot-long sand shark – but when you've seen Tony Blair, who needs sharks?

The room was big, packed and humming; the wine was a most acceptable Vin de Pays de Vaucluse, and the chicken-liver canapés were a knockout. I tore myself from the waiters to jostle through to the front, where Prescott was at the mike. 'You can see I do what I'm told,' he joked. 'He said, You go first.' He introduced Blair, who spoke fluently for six or seven minutes without notes about how the conference would lift them, and they'd go home from it to fire up their constituencies. His manner was easy, his humour natural – he was comfortably unfazed by Sadie from Whitby, maybe three years old in a pretty floral dress, who kept running round his feet until he laughed that he couldn't compete – and I'd see him do a turn like this three nights running, each speech smoothly tailored off the cuff to the audience in each room. When you consider that every night he had to do this in half a dozen different rooms, the energy, the facility, the sheer drive of the man was astonishing. You think – as you're meant to, without hesitation – that you're in the presence of the next Prime Minister.

On this occasion, he spoke before a display stand mounted by Northumbrian Water, the sponsors of this particular bash. 'Very generous of them,' he said, with a puckish grin, 'considering our policies.' But of course it wasn't just me, or the thrill-dizzy delegates, who figured this man was on his way to Number Ten; big companies and trade associations had packed the conference hall with their PR stalls and the hotels with their parties, all cosying up to where the power was flowing. Without exception, everyone I spoke to said they'd never known a conference like it – that there were so many people and organisations crowding its halls and corridors, its bars and meeting rooms, that the Winter Gardens this year simply wasn't big enough.

Up at the mike, Blair pointed himself out in Northumbrian's montage of pictures and copy; the picture, he said, had been taken at the opening of a sewage plant. 'And I can tell you,' he said, puckishness hitting overdrive, 'that giving a speech at the opening of a sewage plant is the hardest speech you'll ever give.'

We moved to another do three hotels along, and Robin Cook told me that at conference you barely had time to clean your teeth. 'But,' he smiled, gnomic, cocksure and foxy, 'the pressure's OK when you're winning.'

A wild-eyed, somewhat teetery woman with vivid lipstick, cropped ginger hair, a lopsided jaw and a pint of bitter – looking confused, as well you might if you're not at the reception you'd been looking for – said fiercely to Tarlo, apropos of nothing, 'Where are all these new members of the party then? You never see them.'

'Never mind,' Tarlo told her, emollient, 'so long as we've seen the colour of their money.'

Some time after eleven, we walked back to our sorry hotel – £17 a night for a room the size of a shower cubicle; no suites at the

Imperial for your humble PPC – and McCafferty and Tarlo spoke of how this was the big world here. 'Some of these people,' said Tarlo, 'they're not interested in who you are. They want to see Chris elected, sure, but they don't give a monkey's otherwise. Them, they're elected already.'

McCafferty shrugged. 'They're human. Some help, some don't.'

When I'd said to Tarlo in a room full of suits that the place was plainly seething with ego, he'd answered gently, 'The grass is there to be scythed. And we're the grass.'

The 95th Annual Conference of the Labour Party in the Empress Ballroom of Blackpool's Winter Gardens began on the morning of September 30th, and was tediously difficult to get into. A long queue snaked round the corner from the entrance under grey, windy skies; with every pace that you crept forward, another leaflet was thrust in your hand. The Punjab, unemployment, human rights in Leicester, abortion, housing, drugs, fishermen, Cyprus, the Shabab Indian Restaurant, Miss Patricia's Music Hall Tavern, you name it – if you couldn't worry about it, you could eat and drink in it.

A bloke in a beret stood by the railings with a placard announcing, 'Blair Is A Tory.' An old woman behind me tut-tutted and said, 'Dear, dear. Have you seen his membership card?' Further along, a man with a guitar stood on the steps of a sealed doorway with a sign round his neck, demanding that the sale of cigarettes be banned from childrens' sweet-shops.

Inside the entrance there were airport X-ray scanners, walk-through metal detectors, and Group 4 bods with Star Trek-type clicking things to check you had no Semtex on your palms. (Crazy – do the IRA not wear gloves?) Once you'd funnelled through this, you were pitched into a seething scrum of commerce and good causes. Oxfam, the Post Office, British Gas, the NSPCC, DHL, Luton Airport, Sky, the UK Brewers – these last at a stand made up like a pub, the pub sign showing a picture of our Tone looking intently, perhaps even demonically, at a pint of ale. Monitor screens scrolled through infinite lists of fringe meetings; badged and labelled, delegates, party staff, the media, corporate and international observers all swilled about in a murmuring throng. Tarlo wandered over to a stand set up by whoever quarries gravel and chalk and stuff, and fell into earnest conversation about aggregates.

McCafferty had gone back to Halifax; at short notice, the meeting for the Greave House Fields objectors had come up that morning, and she had to go from that to the opening of a business park in Mytholmroyd. Left alone, I drifted into the hall to find shadow health minister Chris Smith announcing that a Labour government would ban tobacco advertising. Good for him.

'If you are ill or injured,' said Smith, 'if your health is damaged or under threat, there will be a National Health Service with the resources and the will to help . . .

'We will restore it.

'That's our promise.

'I repeat that: We will restore it. You will have a National Health Service again.

'Ask me why you should vote Labour. That reason will do alone. You will have a National Health Service again.'

Cue applause. Me, I went to the press centre to get a copy of the speech and to check I was hearing right. Sure enough, large chunks of Smith's speech, and of every speech I heard subsequently, seemed to have been written by an idiot.

An idiot who couldn't handle paragraphs longer than a sentence.

Who didn't like sentences with verbs in.

Who liked his sentences . . .

Really short.

Well – I'm sure Smith's no idiot. I also heard Brown, Cook and Blair, and I'm sure they're not idiots either; Cook, indeed, was universally deemed to have a brain not the size of one planet but of several. So I just wonder if it isn't enormously frustrating for intelligent people to have to reduce difficult and complex subjects into morse code.

So they can sound good on TV.

But that's politics now.

Reducing the world to the verbal equivalent of canapés.

For lunch, I went to a thoroughly enjoyable and completely pointless fringe meeting about football. Basically, we all agreed that there was too much money in it, that it was all rotten and corrupt and we had to do something about it but we hadn't the first idea what and, Lord help us, in the meantime we just couldn't stop watching it.

I went because I wanted to see Tony Banks, and he was great. After Rogan Taylor gave a witty and erudite little speech on the creation by the Hungarians of 'socialist football' – bet you didn't know it was the Budapest branch of the KGB who first cooked up the concept of someone playing 'in the hole' – Banks said, 'We used to discuss nothing else in the Shed. Where are you coming from dialectically, my son?'

He also said, 'The Labour Party at the moment is trying to pretend it hasn't got a past, and it's embarrassing. It's like Chelsea saying they started when Ken Bates showed up.'

Labour MEP Glyn Ford said this meeting was the only place at which the class struggle would be mentioned all week.

A Scotsman asked, 'I wonder when the Labour Party's going to legislate against referees in Scotland forever giving penalties to Rangers. I wonder, could you put that in the referendum?'

Taylor said, 'If fans want to be heard, they have to hit the sponsors. The politicians are just squabbling at the edges. The big decisions now are taken by the corporations – so you've got to pour Coca-Cola down the drain in front of the ITN crew.'

Banks laughed. 'It's all right trashing a Snickers bar, Rogan. What are you going to do if you're a Spurs fan? Smash up a Hewlett-Packard?'

Sky were there, to ask how the politicians meant to get 'the sports vote'. I felt like saying, By getting on Sky, dimwit – but I was polite, because they wanted to interview me. They're promiscuous, that Sky lot, they'll interview anybody. The Sky bloke asked, 'If Labour used to be the party of the terraces, what are they now? The party of the executive box?'

I wandered back to the hall to hear Gordon Brown deliver another collection of extremely short sentences and – amid the Tidy Britain Group and the anti-hunting people, amid Shelter and War on Want – I decided that the conference was just an enormous version of the Mytholmroyd Gala, but with better speakers, and multinationals instead of local churches. Then you had the surreal business of stepping out from it, and quickly finding yourself amidst some knot of drunken twerps in kiss-me-quick hats who wouldn't know a ballot paper if it butted them in the schnozzle.

In procedural terms, tradition was maintained; arcane rituals were duly observed, constituency resolutions went through the syntactical Moulinex and re-emerged as cumbersome composites to be moved or remitted, while delegates waved their papers at the chair in the mostly futile hope of three minutes' spouting time. But antique images of Labour were otherwise rapidly dispelled; there were no bug-eyed Dave Sparts in slogan-bedecked T-shirts here, no furious lesbian skinheads, no humourless *Morning Star* merchants dreaming of the militant millennium. Indeed, drinking a muddy impersonation of a cappuccino by a kiosk in the hall, I watched the good folk of New Labour eyeing the hopelessly tacky Blackpool postcards of naked totty with oiled and sandy tits, and some were even buying them.

Eighty per cent of these delegates had never been to a party conference before – and I'd venture that 80 per cent of them, male and female alike, wore suits. They were, by and large, so sensibly humdrum that at a Young Labour party, Alex Powell ended up having a go at Mandelson on the grounds that it was all too normal by half, that they might as well be the Young Conservatives. And my only quibble with that would be, who said the Young Conservatives were normal?

If sensible, however, it wasn't wholly void of passion. On the platform, a rather striking young woman demanded, 'How dare Michael Heseltine, seventy-four million rich, oppose this minimum wage policy, when he spends more on one lunch than a million families have for food in one week?'

Suitably stirred, I wandered out to find McCafferty returned from her day trip. The Greave House meeting had gone well – then her car broke down, she just made it on a bus to the opening of the business park, and now that she was back someone wanted a radio interview. She passed; she said, 'There's no point doing interviews when you feel like death on a stick.'

Knackered or not, you've got to do your rounds. The evening's first party was given by the Government of Gibraltar in the Imperial, the hub hotel where the shadow cabinet stayed. It was four storeys of giant brick box, with a white rim of fortressy crenellation round the top, and it was completely sealed off; scanners and metal detectors were set up in a portakabin in the parking lot, and the queue snaked down from there to the illuminations along the shore. Absurdly, a policeman allowed me and my media pass to go in by a short-cut entrance, while the parliamentary candidate had to linger in line. There's priorities for you.

We did the Gibraltar party, then swapped hotels to attend the MSF bash, the Manufacturing, Science and Finance union; they had a section for the voluntary sector, and McCafferty had joined when she worked at the Well Woman Centre. So far, they'd given her £650 towards telephone canvassing, plus a further £1,000 just recently, and she was hoping there'd be more. There is, of course, a legal limit on what any candidate's campaign can spend – but in reality, neither main party adheres to it. You get round it by spending a good bunch before the election's actually called – so Labour in the Calder Valley might spend £18,000 or £20,000, Sir Donald's lot more – considerably more – and the Lib Dems somewhat less (though Stephen Pearson had private money, which might put him in better stead than others in his party). But wherever it comes from, you have to go and say thank you.

There was a fine, airy onion quiche, scrummy chicken breasts in a BBQ sauce, and there was that buzz again: 'Blair's coming, Blair's coming, he'll be here in two minutes.' I stood up from the table where we were eating to watch him arrive and Tarlo said, 'You're going to get wafted away by his graciousness then?'

Not everyone loves him. As I squeezed down the corridor towards the main room I passed two MPs, and in the dim, packed hallway I didn't clock the names on their badges – but one was saying to the other, 'They say only 20 per cent of the new intake will be Blairites. Bollocks. They might not all be true believers, but they'll be with him.' The tone was aggressive and mortified.

In the main room, fans turned under chandeliers; there was a small dance floor surrounded by tables, but most people were standing, and the place was thrumming with talk and body heat. Prescott came in, nudging through the pack in the doorway, with Blair and Cherie Booth behind him – a small, sharp-looking woman in a two-piece apparently made of aquamarine fuzzy carpet. MSF's General Secretary Roger Lyons said, 'Good

evening, sisters, brothers, gatecrashers. You've all experienced
the feeling of electricity in the air, and we're pleased to greet
Tony and Cherie tonight – and under Tony's leadership we're
going to *win*.'

He also said something about MSF now having 97 members
adopted as candidates; Blair quipped that with that many, they'd
practically *be* the government. He took off his jacket to speak,
handing it behind him to his wife; it was 9.30 p.m., he was giving
his keynote speech the next afternoon, but here he was. He said,
'It's a fairly daunting thing when you pick up *Newsweek* and you're
on the front cover. Without the red eyes, even. But it's an extraordinary thing – a year from now we can be the government. It's a
historic thing. And it really can be done.'

When he was gone McCafferty said simply, 'This guy has the
potential to be the greatest leader we've ever had. You contrast
him with Major,' and then she sighed and shook her head. 'The
potential for letdown is mega-heartbreaking.'

We went to a humid, seething affair hosted by the Cable
Communications Association; we left about eleven. A policewoman
on the door said she'd be there until eight the next morning, a
twelve-hour shift; Tarlo asked her, 'Do they give you leggings?' She
patted her jacket pocket, and said they did.

'And do they bring you a cup of tea?'

'Sometimes.'

'Well, I hope it doesn't rain for you.'

'So do I,' she laughed, 'the rain here's horizontal.'

The same policewoman told me the following night that she
couldn't believe the arrogance of some of these people, especially
the media people, the way so few of them had a word for you when
you were stood there all night, the way they swanned past as if it
were simply too much trouble to show a pass – but arrogance was
not a fault you'd have found in Chris McCafferty or David Tarlo.
They walked back arm-in-arm, and when he lit a cigarette she had
a right good go at him. When he looked mock-pained she said, 'I
just don't want to lose my soulmate, that's all.'

'Oh,' he smiled, 'did I get promoted then?'

★

The next morning, Neil Hamilton was branded 'A Liar And A Cheat' by the *Guardian* (sitting on the fence a bit there) – and I was left wondering if it'd be, y'know, a bit sleazy to get a free massage from the Health Education Authority in the exhibition hall. Tarlo and I also decided to award Best Carrier Bag '96 to the National House Builders' Council; they were dispensing handy little plastic houses full of paper clips too. I mean, paper clips. C'mon, guys – where are the used notes?

I was beginning to think in speech chunks. New Labour. New carrier bags. New Britain. New battered prawns on little sticks. I'd been there forty-eight hours, and I was going utterly barking.

The whips' office gave lunch for the PPCs in Annie's Bar. They got induction guides on what awaited them at Westminster, they got barbecued ribs and fish bits, and the meeting was sponsored, appropriately, by the Police Federation. 'The Tory conference next week,' said one of the whips, 'will be the first conference where the police are keeping the criminals *in*.'

Donald Dewar said that doing PR for the whips' office was something of a contradiction in terms, rather like a publication called *Practical Anarchy* that he used to read so eagerly when preparing for life in the Labour Party. But, he said, the whips were there to help – which in his dry, quiet Scots accent sounded distinctly sinister. McCafferty said one deputy whip had told her firmly that they didn't keep dirt files on their MPs like the Tories did, and she professed herself reassured. She laughed and said, 'You do think of *House of Cards*, don't you?' But they told her, if you weren't there to vote, they'd be down on you like a ton of bricks.

Of course, they had to win before she could do any voting. I left early to be sure of a seat to hear Blair and, on my way back through the hall, watching them mill about in all their taut aspiration, was to see with sadness how few figures of note this party had produced in recent years. There was Tony Benn, stooped and shuffle-footed, like some kindly old uncle; there was Glenda Jackson, sucking in her lips like she'd swallowed a lemon; there was fish-eyed Paul Boateng. But is that it? Who else do you know? Does the name Doug Hoyle mean anything to you? Tom Pendry? Nah. For the most part, passing among the chattering members and the teeming media, the folk with the 'Ex Officio' badges were little more than a procession of

nondescripts and apparatchiks. Only when Neil Kinnock zoomed
by did you get any real sense of lift or energy, a tingly gust of
enthusiasm – and he never made it to Number 10. So could Blair?

It was a good job I left early. At 1.15, ninety minutes before he
came on – and I assure you we're talking gig here, we're talking
theatre – the whole wide corridor to the three entrances into the
hall and the balcony was packed shoulder to shoulder. The
entrances were sealed, with party staff and security bods scooting in
and out. Sky's Adam Boulton barged through with a singular lack
of good grace, but the scrum was mostly good-humoured. A cock-
ney voice behind me said, 'I think this could be one of the happiest
days of my life.'

Mobile phones pressed to ears; pagers bleeped. One fellow said
mildly, as we wriggled like sheep in a truck, 'Shows how disciplined
we are, doesn't it?' His mate beside him started quietly singing,
'Moving on up, moving on out . . .'

A cry went up, there was a surge forward, a pause, then people
at the front loudly shushed us, demanding silence. We fell silent and
there came . . . silence. People laughed, nervously eager. Then an
announcement was made about having your passes clearly visible,
the doors were flung open, the press of bodies steamed up the
stairs, and anyone who'd tried to check a pass would have been dead
meat underfoot. Once in, we fought – politely, but I'm telling you,
we *fought* – for a seat with a view unobscured by pillars or cameras,
until I found myself parked in a breathless sweat by a Sloane Ranger
lobbyist with her mouth jammed in overdrive. 'This place in the
evening it's wall-to-wall security tape,' she spooled, 'and even the
tape's printed New Labour. I'm telling you, in ten years of conferences I've never seen anything like it, I mean just now, that fellow,
he was just *scrambling* over the seat backs, my goodness, and the
crush back there, the *crush*, there were fire officers on the phone,
I've never seen anything like it . . .'

Obviously, I said, she'd never been to a football match. The look
of incomprehension she gave me suggested she'd more likely have
been to Mars – at which point I saw David Davies passing by,
Chief Mouth at the Football Association. I thought, hey – didn't I
get into this to get *away* from football? But given what was coming,
if I'd really wanted to get away from football I'd have needed to go
to Mars myself.

The platform had been changed; the 7-seat politburo desk had been moved to the side so the leader could stand at the lectern in splendiferous solitude. With its two thin black mikes and its pair of autocue screens, the lectern looked like something from which a Klingon boss might berate an assembly of his intergalactic foes. The chandeliers were turned off so just the dais where the lectern stood was lit, empty in the shadowed austerity of the stage. Only a kind of vent in the back flat was lit otherwise. Around the base of the lectern, knots of photographers and TV people roamed before the delegates, festooned with cables and flashbulbs. The hall was noisy with talk, tense with desire. Prescott, Cook, Brown, Beckett and three others trooped to the desk, and showed us a review of the past year in the form of a pop video. It was glib, shallow, bright, fast and hugely optimistic – a year in politics, disco-style. Then the applause died down and the chair announced, 'Conference. Tony Blair.'

He appeared as if by magic through the lit vent, the modernising genie suddenly popped up centre stage to stand before us; he raised his hands, and got a standing ovation just for being there. After all the long empty years, the explosive, keening welcome was nothing less than the hailing of a saviour.

'This year,' he told them, 'we meet as the Opposition.

'Next year, the British people willing, an end to eighteen years of Tories, and we will meet as the new Labour government of Britain.

'A chance to serve, that is all we ask.

'John Smith's final words from his final speech the night before he died.'

It was a quiet start, but you could feel the tension crackling in him, you could hear the catch of emotion in his voice. As he spoke, the flashing of the photographers' bulbs at his feet cast giant, eerie, strobing shadows of himself upon the backdrop. Solemnly he appealed for peace in the Middle East, for peace in Northern Ireland, for the freedom of Aung San Suu Kyi in Burma. Then he ad-libbed: he looked at the snappers beneath him and said, 'You must be careful with those flashlights, you know. You're making my eyes go red.'

The applause and laughter was a great wave of relief and release. Come on Tony, *take us with you* . . .

'About this nickname business.

'First it was Stalin. Then it was Kim Il Sung. Now it's the devil with the demon eyes.

'Can't we just go back to Bambi?

'Or maybe Kim Il Sung's official title? "The Great Wise Leader, President for Life, Dearly Beloved and Sagacious Leader."

'Why not? That's what John Prescott calls me.

'Sometimes.'

He segued flawlessly from the knockabout to the serious again, praising up Prescott, tearing into the Tories. He was flying now, absolutely flying, voice rising, passionate, knowing where each next thunderclap of applause was coming from, holding for it, and then ripping on as it died. Cook and Brown had been academics by contrast – engaging, earnest, instructive – but this was immaculate stuff on another plane altogether, evangelical and rousing and very, very deliberate indeed, because all of it was leading to an in-your-face lesson. Anyone out there still harbouring romantic notions? You listen to Tony now.

'I can vividly recall the exact moment that I knew the last election was lost.

'I was canvassing in the Midlands on an ordinary, suburban estate. I met a man polishing his Ford Sierra. He was a self-employed electrician. His Dad always voted Labour, he said. He used to vote Labour too. But he'd bought his own house now. He'd set up his own business. He was doing quite nicely. "So I've become a Tory," he said . . .

'That man polishing his car was clear. His instincts were to get on in life. And he thought our instincts were to stop him.'

This is not, of course, what a Labour conference wants to hear, even one as buttoned-up and single-minded as this one was. They want to hear the Tories and all their moneyed mates flayed for the evil bastards they are, and they want to hear how Labour's going to be infinitely kind to the poor, the old, the sick, children, and any passing furry animals. They don't want to hear about guys with Sierras and small businesses, they don't want all that superhighway stuff – and for a long central passage of the speech now, the fizz went out of it. I started wondering if we could have an interval, if someone could come round with a tray on their waist and sell me a Cornetto. I began to imagine Blair tearing off into his enterprise future, his Age of Achievement, and one day he'd look around him in New Britain plc and there'd be nobody behind him, nothing but his own dustcloud.

But for now they were following, for now they were listening, because for now they were all agreed. If this was what the man had to say to get Major out of Downing Street, fine, go on and say it. So he got through with all that – then a couple of furlongs out he began using the whip, building for the winning post. He produced his vow-list, his ten mostly vague but very resonant promises. He produced his big ideals, 'The marriage of ambition with justice, the constant striving of the human spirit to do better.' He told them what being British was about: 'Common sense. Standing up for the underdog. Fiercely independent.' He refused to accept the destruction of so many people's hopes and expectations, claiming, 'Britain can do better. Britain can be better than this.' And he was flying again now, easily a hot enough orator that he had them all back up and flying with him, and I could see trembling lips and quivering eyes all around. When he cried out, 'I say to the British people, have the courage to change,' I could feel belief all about me that if Tony asked them like that, then this time they would.

There's a bloke who goes bowling in Todmorden. He's in his seventies, he fought in the War, and he'd always voted Tory – but he said he couldn't vote for them again now. The trouble was, he didn't know if he could ever vote Labour instead, it was such a big, big step . . .

'Well,' McCafferty asked him, 'it took courage to fight in the War, didn't it?'

I was thinking of that man, and I was feeling all the desperate, yearning pride and desire in that huge packed hall, when Blair on the podium hit Kennedy mode. 'I don't care where you're coming from; it's where your country's going that matters.'

Then he did the Skinner & Baddiel number out of Euro '96, 'Labour's coming home. Seventeen years of hurt. Never stopped us dreaming. Labour's coming home.' I was gobsmacked; I didn't know whether to laugh or cry. As a piece of theatre – as a piece of marketing – it was brilliant, and I don't doubt that on telly it looked packed with vim and verve. But if the political discourse of this country is now so debased that the way to win power is to peak your speech on a football song, *and you get acclaimed for it* – then God help us.

Ah well, it worked for the crowd. He hit the last sentence and reeled back from the podium as if unleashed, looking shattered and high, exhilarated and wrung out all at once. People rose, gasping as the applause and the cheering boomed and thundered and roared – gasping because, for a while now towards the end of the speech, high on the flats behind him there'd been this odd pattern of light, these abstract little flecks of red and blue. Now, as Blair collapsed backwards under the tumult of approbation, the full picture in the pattern of light was revealed above him – and it was the Union Jack.

It was a *coup de théâtre*, stunning in its shameless simplicity. So the applause redoubled, Cherie came on for hugs and kisses, the shadow team marched across to stand behind them, Cherie and Tone stepped down among the crowd, and the D-ream tune started pumping from the PA at ear-splitting volume. *Things can only get better, can only get better, now that I've found you . . .*

So there we have it. Official. Party conferences are now game shows, party creeds are now football songs, and the next government of Great Britain will be a rave.

The audience was not so much persuaded as shell-shocked. They squeezed from the hall in a gabbling pack, stunned, wide-eyed, walking on Blair. The young woman who'd had a go at Heseltine for being seventy-four million rich said, 'Great. Amazing. New Life For Britain.' She was grinning hugely; she could have been coming out of an Oasis gig. Everywhere around me, the corridors bubbled with faith and hope and adrenalin. TV crews ran interviews from every niche and alcove. I found McCafferty, who professed herself inspired, drained, wrung out with emotion. Everyone sat around her, she said, had been crying, or close to it.

We were supping Tango by the kiosk with the titty postcards. A Halifax delegate said grimly, 'We can kiss goodbye to November after that. All I can say is, it's been the longest twelve months of my life. And we've only had six months of it.'

I'm told the parties you really want to get to are the ones thrown by the Arab embassies, that their tucker's so tasty it must have come in by magic carpet. Unable to locate any Arabs, however, I had to make do with Safeway.

While a lot of companies were networking with what they took to be the next British government, it wasn't the case that they'd all just turned up opportunistically this year. Yes, there were more of them now, but even when Labour was an unelectable rabble of bearded Trots and woolly dreamers and scary wimmin in boiler suits, a lot of them still came. Someone like Safeway, after all, wants planning permissions, and where better to buttonhole local councillors than the party conference?

McCafferty and Tarlo went to a sit-down dinner with the Duty Free Association. 'Have fun,' said Tarlo, 'loitering in the garden of delights.' I hoisted my flute of Safeway's bubbly and went to talk with MSF's General Secretary Roger Lyons. Blair's speech, I said, seemed to have gone down a storm.

Lyons said, 'You never know where the next hand grenade's coming from. Look at '91, we were exuberant then, *exuberant*. John Major? How could we lose? And everyone forgets how exuberant we were, with what happened to us after. But look – there are powerful vested interests in this country, and they don't give up easily. They're cosying up to Tony now and he's talking about it, he thinks it looks good – but I've said to him, they'll not be there on Day Two.'

In the Imperial Hotel alone, outfits hosting lunch meetings that day included the UK Offshore Operators, BBC Public Affairs, the Prison Officers' Association and Yorkshire Electricity. In the evening, there were receptions and dinners given by, among others, the Industry Forum, the British Cement Association, GWR Group plc, two supermarkets, Tarlo's chalk and gravel diggers, ITN, BBC Public Affairs (again), and the Advertising Association. Seeing how I started my professional life writing commercials for tampons and masking tape, this last seemed the natural place to be.

The Churchill Suite was a sauna, packed to the gills and broilingly humid. As we supped Rioja, Andrew Brown, our host's Director-General, a tall, flushed bloke in a grey pinstripe, had repeatedly to mop at his sweat-slicked brow. So, I inquired – handing him a Craven A – what did they make of this ban on baccy ads?

There were, he said, three reasons to oppose it. Firstly, freedom of speech; cigarettes were a legal product. Secondly, if the tobacco firms suddenly had their ad budgets sitting idle, they'd switch that large sum into below-the-line promotion – in other words, cigarettes would become cheaper. Then thirdly, he played the old line about tobacco being a declining market in which ads didn't get people smoking, but merely got smokers to plump for one brand against another.

There's logic in this, and he had stats to back it: for example, that the three most declining markets in Europe were Germany, Holland and the UK, in all of which ads were still allowed. But I still don't buy it. Freedom of speech is a high-sounding red herring; being harmful is more important than being legal, and governments have a right – it's what we elect them for – to take action to limit harm. As for cigarettes becoming cheaper, you simply hike up the tax on them to counter that – a Good Thing, no? Then finally, the notion that cigarette advertising is only brand-competitive has always struck me as specious, self-serving nonsense. The overall effect, I said, is to create an environment in which cigarettes are widely pictured in an attractive light.

'That,' said Brown, 'if you don't mind my saying so, is a pretty crappy argument.' He added, 'If you really want to stop kids smoking, you stop selling cigarettes in sweet-shops and newsagents. Have you seen the guy with the guitar outside the conference? He's right. But you tell a politician to take on 80,000 Asian small shop-owners. It's much easier to take the moral and emotional high ground with a policy that doesn't work.'

Besides, the Advertising Association wasn't in Blackpool just to talk about tobacco. They were there because the Labour Party still contained a lot of people who didn't understand advertising, who were just generally against it, 'And people who don't come and talk to people who have different views from themselves are very silly.' So they were there in the hope of preventing undue regulation because, 'We want the freedom to do business.' Moreover, they were there because they were apolitical, and next week they'd be in Bournemouth to talk to the Tories – and a fair few Tories, he said, were, 'Thick as pigshit. It's sometimes better to have enemies who understand you than friends who don't.' But anyway, he said, 'We don't expect to change the world with a reception.'

Maybe not. But between throwing receptions, and whatever more private briefing goes on, they were there not to change the world but to change minds, and it works. A little later I saw Kate Hoey across the room and, being an admirer of her dogged and unpleasantly derided pursuit of corruption in football, I went to introduce myself. I was, I said, pleased that Labour was going to ban tobacco ads . . .

'Well,' said Hoey, 'it's policy. But it's very easy to take the emotional high ground. And I really don't believe kids start smoking 'cause they see Damon Hill whizzing round with Rothmans on the back of his car.'

Then why do they put it there? So a few corporate drug-dealers in suits can get tickets to the race? I don't think so. But as politicians tend to be, Hoey's a forceful person, and I couldn't face arguing. Disheartened inside, I changed the subject. As to whether Labour bans tobacco ads, watch this space.

I'd been in the Imperial three hours, and was beginning to lose it; I could never be a politician. I can't remember names, I'm useless at small talk, I've no desire to go about the place smiling 'til my face aches, and rooms packed with strangers fill me with all the confidence of a mole. I moved on to the Washington Suite for a reception for the Rt Hon. Tony Blair MP, hosted by the Labour Party's North and Yorkshire Region, the North-West Region and the Sedgefield Constituency Labour Party – all this sponsored by Manchester Airport – thinking by now that the best course of action was to get seriously drunk. So drunk that I ended up paying five quid for raffle tickets, opening myself thereby to the ghastly possibility that I could win a Sunderland shirt.

Alex Powell was there, high on Blair. She said, 'I've got neighbours who totally fancy him. One's a Lib Dem, but she just thinks he's gorgeous. There was a Teletext poll – who'd you most like to be with on a desert island? And Tony Blair came ahead of Mel Gibson. Really.' Then she sighed – she's a single mum, with two kids – 'And that's what my life's like. Watching Teletext polls on who you fancy.'

This to the tune of a guitar duo doing 'Imagine'. Around us the room was heaving, the canapés were going fast, and tickets were gold dust. No ticket, no entry; on the door, Ian Carvell turned away the MSF boss Roger Lyons. What a man! His girlfriend grinned and came over all mock-swoony. 'My hero. I've *got* to go and see him. For services to mankind.' Later, Carvell would refuse entry to Blair's mum. Whoops.

Blair swept in surrounded by applause, photographers, a TV crew. 'He's so Kennedy-ish,' sighed Alex, 'it's Kennedy all over again.' Yeah, I muttered, that worried me too – but she meant it in an entirely positive way. The speech, she said, was, 'Brilliant, just brilliant. You compare him to John Major, there's no comparison. And I don't care who doesn't like him – we're going to win. And if we don't have him, we're not going to win.'

On the stage Blair's agent introduced him, and again I stood awed at the energy of the man still driving on, 10.30 at night, seven hours after he'd told them Labour was coming home. 'Thanks,' he told them, 'it's been a good week so far. If there's unity and strength and determination here, then those people in Bournemouth next week are really going to have their work cut out.'

In every speech, again and again, there was a constant lecture, a constant reminder on behaviour, on thinking always not of themselves but about the people of this country. 'I'm proud of what I've seen of the Labour Party this week,' he said, 'because it shows we're serious about governing Britain. Seventeen years is a long, long time. There are some people out there who don't have a hope in hell without a change in government, and we should never forget those people right down at the bottom. It's not going to be easy, they'll throw everything at us – but the Tory party above all else is a party that understands the importance of power, and they're not going to hand us the key to Downing Street just like that.'

I was leaning on a pillar, scribbling notes as applause boomed and echoed off the dance floor. Anji Hunter, the head of Blair's private office, swooped past with an eagle eye on my name-tag and Alex said slyly, 'Did you notice how she was scoping you?'

Well, I thought, say hello, get her number. Now people say Blair's ruthless and that's fine, he'd need to be to win, and whatever my doubts I did want him to win – but whether he's ruthless or not, his sidekick scared the pants off me. Hard eyes, quickfire questions, ferocious demeanour . . . I got the number, then backed off quaking before my hair caught fire. After that I took my media pass off. In Labour circles a press badge, after all, is like going about the place saying, Hi! I'm the spawn of Satan. Want to talk?

Blair swept out of the room flashing his smile all about, passing a yard from us as I nibbled a battered prawn, and he gave Alex a nod and said, 'Hiya.'

She said, 'I can tell me grandchildren, Tony Blair said Hiya. But,' she frowned, 'it's 'cause I'm a young person, int'it?'

Walking back to our hotel at one in the morning, we came on a lad with long curly hair and a purple bomber jacket heading the other way towards us. As we passed he said, 'You Labour then?'

We said we were. In our wake he turned and snarled, 'You're all a bunch of fuckin' shite.'

7

Boy X

Med Hughes' screensaver was a copyline from an ad for Berghaus mountain gear: 'Better to live one day as a tiger than a lifetime as a sheep.' He was just back from a weekend in Snowdonia, his coffee mug was from Ben Nevis, and he had a climber's trim, wiry build. A handsome man of thirty-eight with greying hair, sharp grey-blue eyes and a soft but distinct Welsh accent, he was born in St Asaph in North Wales, he'd grown up in Cardiff, he'd joined the police straight from university, and he was now the Divisional Commander for the Calder Valley.

He'd studied politics and economics at Swansea. At first he'd fancied the Royal Air Force but, educated at a comprehensive, coming from what he called 'a middle-class background with working-class origins', he'd looked at the Air Force students – public school people – and thought he'd not fit. Weighing the alternatives, a mate told him one night, 'You like playing rugby, you like kicking people. You should join the police.'

His office was in Sowerby Bridge Police Station, a stone-built house on Station Road among a spread of brick factories, tin barns and old mills; the air hummed with the chunk and clunk of machinery, the coming and going of vans and trucks. On the pinboard in reception there were signs about a minicam facility for the deaf, about road tax and colorado beetles, about a helpline for drug, alcohol and solvent abuse. There was the West Yorkshire force's mission statement, a picture of a missing Asian boy from Bradford, and another of a murder suspect.

From here, Hughes ran a staff of two hundred police and civilians on a budget of £6 million. Mostly affluent, his turf was one of the lowest crime areas in West Yorkshire; among the people he served, the biggest single concern was burglaries. More generally, there was a fear of street crime, of violent crime – but (though they'd soon find guns on a drugs raid in Brighouse) this was not a place under siege from a host of armed criminals.

On the day we met, there hadn't been a burglary for two nights in the entire division. They'd been running higher than average before, around forty a week, but Hughes' people went out the previous week, took out nine suspects, and there'd been only eight break-ins in ten days since. Eight too many, sure – but if you had a relatively small number of offenders who committed a fair few offences each, and you targeted them accurately, you could have an impact. His goal was fewer than sixteen hundred burglaries per annum in the Division – a figure which caused fellow officers from Leeds or Bradford to smile ruefully. But, said Hughes, 'I've to deal with the people here. And ten burglaries in Ripponden, that's an epidemic.'

For violent crime, his target was fewer than four hundred a year. And people think, Four Hundred A Year! *Beneath the civilised veneer of our prosperous community lies a seething tide of brutal pillage and mayhem* . . . but against a backdrop of some 15,000 violent crimes in West Yorkshire overall, it was a drop in the ocean. Moreover, it included people punching each other in the pub, it included domestic violence – and that, he said, was the hardest thing. Officers in their early twenties could find themselves trying to cope with marital strife between people the age of their parents. But, said Hughes, 'I don't care if it's in the home or out of it. A crime is a crime.'

Still, if you lived in Calder Valley and found yourself on the wrong end of one, statistically speaking you were unlucky. He wouldn't for a minute have belittled people's concerns – but if there were places in some cities where the police were stretched to the limit, the fact was that England remained a largely law-abiding country. This was not South Africa; this was not, indeed, England after the Napoleonic Wars, when an embryonic police force had to counter roving gangs of bandits terrorising the countryside, and when large tracts of the country's burgeoning cities were gin-sodden hellholes plagued with violence on a scale unimaginable today. Today, he said – with all our panics, and the press busy stoking them – the majority in this England did not break the law.

With, of course, one glaring exception; one set of laws broken by so many people as to be transparently absurd. Cannabis use in the Calder Valley was, said Hughes, 'Accepted by substantial numbers of people, and that's widely recognised. Nobody's changed the law, so we'll continue to enforce it; I have twenty-five kilograms of cannabis resin in that safe behind you . . .'

There's me thinking, what a waste of good spliff. I asked if the situation wasn't ludicrous, and he trod water carefully; he was a servant of the democratic process, and it wasn't his position to comment. Then we talked about the problems caused by alcohol; we talked about his personal view that a libertarian society was better than a regulated one, and about the need for grey areas, for the police to be able to exercise discretion. Eventually he said (stressing that it was his personal opinion) that throughout history we'd used alcohol, and we'd used nicotine since the seventeenth century. 'So if we can maturely handle that, we can surely maturely handle the question of what other drugs are regularly used by young people, and what status they should have.'

It'd be nice to think so; but from what he said, I'd suspect that on a day-to-day basis alcohol caused him more problems than cannabis by far, and that we weren't handling it with anything approaching maturity. He said, 'If you read the press, we've got gangs of drunken youths wandering the Calder Valley – and they're always somebody else's kids, aren't they? At one community meeting, I was actually told they were being bussed in from another area.' He shook his head, pondering a vision of these teenage sots from afar all boarding their coach – and I was put in mind of my babysitter.

We gave her the keys to feed the kids' fish while we were away on holiday, so of course she had a party, and she didn't muck about. We're talking about a whole load of them carting great boxes of booze down the back lane, cavorting completely slathered in the field behind the house, stopping overnight, making thirty phone calls – mercifully local ones, the good youth of Kirklees not being tuned in just yet to New York or Sydney.

When we got back, it was obvious what had happened; your average burglar doesn't leave alcopop bottle-tops on your kitchen floor and Bernard Matthews sausages in your freezer. He doesn't use all your shampoo; he doesn't make heroic, nerve-raddled and ultimately doomed attempts to clean up the aftermath. So we called her parents and they said, Our little girl wouldn't do a thing like that.

I'm thinking, I'm furious. I'm thinking, next time the fish dies. Our babysitter, by the way, was fourteen. And Med Hughes said, 'We seem to have hit this schism that it's OK to drink when you're eighteen, but that no people under the age of eighteen should ever get hold of any alcohol. Well, we've got to get to grips with that. We have to educate young people about how to use a legal, socially acceptable drug; we have to bring young adults of fourteen or fifteen in, not drive them underground.'

You'd think the same reasoning applied to dope. Understandably, however, Superintendent Hughes (with twenty-five kilos of the stuff in his safe) couldn't possibly comment.

He'd been a police officer for seventeen years, his career coincident with the Conservative government – and all the perspective in the world couldn't change the fact that during those years, by any measure, we'd had a huge increase in crime. He said, 'The rich get richer, the poor get poorer, and in any relationship like that you're going to get tension. If that manifests itself as crime, that's not surprising.'

Solely to blame the Tory government would be too simplistic, however. He said, 'I'd hate to see anybody say that I made a direct causal link between relative poverty and crime, because to do that is an insult to so many poor people who don't commit crime. It's one contributory factor, combined with changes in society's values, changes in the media, changes of all kinds – it's not just one thing. Educational under-achievement, that's very important. Then there are issues of morality; there are statistics, for example, to say that kids who go to Sunday school are ten times less likely to commit crimes than kids who don't.'

He was a Methodist, one who'd recently returned to going to church. He didn't want to make a big thing of it – but he hadn't much time for our more materialistic obsessions, and the phrase 'consumer durables' was delivered with a mild but dismissive distaste. He said, 'You get programmes like 'Through The Keyhole' now, and don't you dare report that I actually watch it – but I understand there you've got the lives of the rich and famous for all to see. Or people have *Hello!* stuffed in their face, and you don't just see the honourable so-and-so but someone who's won the lottery. So it's like, you can have all this, when people will *never* have all this – and if that breeds envy and fear, I'm not surprised.'

If fear and envy helps to spawn more criminals, at least Prison Works. We know it does, because Michael Howard said so. That's why we've got a record number of people banged up, some 60,000 and rising fast, more per head than any other Western European nation – because it works, right?

Hughes didn't think so. He said, 'It's very important that some people go to prison, it really is. There are a number of offenders who are deterred by it, and a number of others who need to be locked away for society's good. But prison does not work for those whose crimes are motivated by survival needs. I worked as a warrants officer in Cardiff Docks serving warrants and fines summons on prostitutes, and on more than one occasion I'd serve a warrant on a young or not-so-young lady and she'd say, I haven't got the money now. Can you come back at nine o'clock? Now what on earth . . . I mean, if she doesn't pay the fine she goes to prison, and how is that supposed to redeem or help her? But if she does, she's further locked in to that life. And I really don't see how prison can help someone like that.' But again it was, he stressed, a complex issue. He said, 'Soundbites don't solve problems.'

Hughes was in training college two months after Margaret Thatcher went to Downing Street, and at first his salary was no great leap from his student grant. A constable with three kids back then was on supplementary benefit; he remembers talk in the station when he joined about how, if they couldn't go on strike, they could paralyse Cardiff with stop-checks on every vehicle.

Thatcher paid up, and she'd needed to. He said, 'If I was to cast my mind back as a political commentator – and police officers are notoriously unreliable political commentators – I think there's no doubt that in her strategy for industrial legislation, she had to ensure that the police were onside.'

He joked that he was known as a Labour infiltrator when he was younger; but today, he said, 'You'd be surprised at the political complexion of the police service.'

His father was a *Telegraph* reader; his mother, in the Fifties, had been a member of the Communist Party. He paused and said, 'I don't think Special Branch know that. Well, they probably don't care. But it was my father who took me to my first political meeting; he said, I don't agree with this guy, but I think you should hear him because he's a fine speaker. It was Ted Rowlands, a Labour man, standing for a safe Conservative seat in Cardiff, and he won it – well, he made an impact. I was ten or eleven, and I loved the idea of someone being able to get up and tell you what they believed in like that.'

Impressed he may have been, but he thought nonetheless that in the past, 'The left in this country have abnegated their responsibilities. I might have my pompous hat on here – but politicians on the left have allowed politicians of other parties to take the moral high ground on policing. As far as I'm concerned, the single biggest issue is that most victims are the poor, the young, the old, the homeless. The fact is, if you're rich you can afford an alarm system, central locking, a house where you don't have to live amid crime. But the people who are most vulnerable . . . in the past, on law and order, those people have not been represented.'

Now, however, Blair talked about responsibilities as well as rights – so was Hughes impressed? Emphatically he said, 'Yes. We've missed that out completely.'

So when Thatcher said there was no such thing as society . . .

'I would personally consider her wrong.'

He wouldn't say how he'd vote; it was a secret ballot. He didn't belong to any party – or, he smiled, to any other secret society – but with the proviso that you couldn't simply blame one government for what had happened, he did believe a change of government could make a difference on crime. 'And,' he said, 'I'd be disappointed if they didn't.'

He was hoping for a change then?

He smiled. 'I think you've gathered my views. But,' he then stated very clearly, 'I will police this election honourably and fairly. And if the Labour Party put out any material that is outside the terms of the Representation of the People Act, I will not tolerate that.'

You will not, I'm sure, be surprised to hear that Chris McCafferty – who chaired the local Police Forum – thought very highly indeed of Med Hughes. Which, when you consider the tense, inimical relationships that have tended to exist between the police and local Labour politicians in the past, seemed to me one of the happier indicators about New Labour.

But if a new government was to make a difference, where did you begin? Throughout the conversation, Hughes returned again and again to education. He said, 'We have an education system that I have a lot of problems with. For five years, I ran an attendance centre for young offenders. They came from a variety of backgrounds, predominantly poor – but overwhelmingly, these people were just incompetent. If you took them out to play football, they were even crap at that. They were intellectually incapable, they were economically incapable, and they had no real excitement or adventure in their lives. I saw hundreds of kids, all boys, from ten to seventeen, and they couldn't succeed at anything. What they could do was get some sort of status or esteem by being the bad guy, because if they couldn't succeed in any mainstream activities they could easily turn to crime. It's too easy to burgle most houses, then they've cash in their pockets and they're hard men. So if we want to reduce our social problems, we have to allow young people some means of succeeding.'

Instead, one outcome of the present education system was more and more ill-equipped losers for whom crime was the easiest, maybe the only direction. He said, 'The uniform feature of virtually every young offender I've ever come into contact with is that they're a poor performer at school, and that we've not provided any alternative, any life skills, any self-esteem. That,' he said, 'is where our system is failing.'

The headmaster was a small, neat man of forty-three years, balding, with a tidy, greying beard. His manner was relaxed – he said he was someone who didn't let things get to him – but there was something a shade wary about him too, as if he were conscious that whatever problem he was dealing with, there'd be another one along soon.

His biggest problem just now was Boy X – and to protect the

privacy of this troubled seven-year-old, he explained the kind of background he came from in general terms. The mother, he said, might be a prostitute, or there was no father, or the father was violent and the mother was in a refuge. Maybe the father was out of prison and looking for them, so the child was constantly on the move. He felt no security, he couldn't form any attachments, and he was disturbed because his father might turn up at any moment, at two or three in the morning, and beat up Mum. Then if Mum was a lady of the night, there'd be callers at all hours who themselves might be drunk or aggressive, and the child was hearing all this day in and day out. With Mum doing what she's doing, he ends up with no care, only sporadically fed; the parent can't cope, maybe doesn't want to cope, and she pushes him out on the street to grow up by himself.

So the child has no ground rules. He does what he wants; he takes what he wants when he wants it. He doesn't co-operate because he doesn't see any need to. He ignores you, because if Mum calls out it usually means she's going to clatter him – and to him, it's no problem to smack another child round the head. When he gets angry, whatever's in his hand he'll hit you with it – be it a rounders bat, whatever. If he wants to throw something, he'll throw it – his dinner, a knife, anything. He'll constantly call out in the classroom; he'll swear. If he's not happy, he'll kick out or bite you – and there's no way you can deal with it. For the teacher trying to cope with this in his or her classroom, it's totally debilitating.

It was October; he'd had Boy X on his hands since February. They'd had to battle with the local authority to get eight hours' emergency help a week from the special needs budget which, for this child, was hopelessly inadequate. It went to fifteen hours a week; he was looked after in the mornings, leaving the head to mind him in the afternoons. It had dented the school's already creaking budget – but the effect was worse than that. This autumn term, they finally had someone to take the boy full-time; but, said the head, 'Until the summer, it was me and his class teacher. I'd be going to that class every few minutes, *every few minutes* – pop my face round the door, is everything OK? D'you need help? D'you want him out? That's how it's been, and it's unacceptable. It should be unacceptable to everyone concerned because it's a drain on that class, that teacher, the whole system.'

Boy X was on the brink of exclusion. The headmaster sighed and said, 'I think, long term, we can help him – but he needs to be in a more secure place. I don't think he poses a threat in terms of him running away, going off and getting run over, because [and maybe this was the saddest comment of all] he's happier here than anywhere he's been in his life. But educationally, he's not receiving a great deal – and he needs to feel emotionally secure before you can even *start* to educate him.'

This was not happening in some inner city sink school. It was happening in a quiet, pleasant village surrounded by rolling fields high on the green tops of the West Yorkshire hills, a little place with a post office, a butcher's shop, a general store, a big old church and a football club; a place where the WI get together once a month in the Methodist schoolroom to hear edifying talks on aromatherapy, salt dough, or Mrs Rushforth's visit to India. It was happening where I live; the class from which Boy X was withdrawn was the class my son had just joined at the start of the new school year. The head sighed and said, 'It's happening in hundreds of schools, hundreds and hundreds. This here – it's just the tip of the iceberg.'

My son's headmaster was from Shirebrook, a pit village by Mansfield; his father, his uncles and his cousins were all miners. When he was still young, his father left the pit to become a minister in the Salvation Army; he himself was a Methodist, and Christianity was a large part of his life. He'd been a teacher for twenty-one years and he said of the job, 'I've always viewed it in terms of service. I'm not in it for ambition's sake, I don't think anybody could be; it's not that sort of job.'

He began at a village primary, then worked for twelve years in an inner-city school; he took on the headship of the school he now ran six years ago. He had 114 children in his care; there were three full-time teachers, one part-time, two non-teaching assistants, a clerical assistant and himself. The budget from the local authority was £170,000 a year.

The catchment wasn't 'difficult'. Between 20 and 30 per cent of the children came from broken homes, and some had emotional difficulties – but day-to-day, they weren't problematic. Managing their parents, on the other hand, was sometimes tricky; compared with the school he'd been at before, their expectations were very different, and they expressed them in different ways. 'My last school,' he said, 'if they wanted to have an argument, they came and thumped you, and you sorted it out afterwards. Here, they make an appointment and tell you what they feel, and they can be more demanding that way. They're more aware of what they feel are their rights; they may be ignorant in some cases of the actual processes of teaching, but they're people with intellect, and very concerned about their children. So,' he shrugged, 'there's a lot of work to do.'

A few had taken their children away; they felt class sizes were too big, and they'd gone private. With a hint of anger, the headmaster said, 'It's exactly what the government wants, of course. And being quite cynical, I've said to those parents, You give me the £4,000, I'll get you an extra teacher.'

The budgetary equation was simple, and ruthless; you had experienced teachers who cost you more, so you had fewer of them and larger classes, or you had smaller classes who didn't get taught so well. He'd opted for the former, which meant he had to do more teaching himself and, he said, 'I want to keep teaching. But how can I run the school as well, with all the paperwork?'

You could spend all week shuffling paper and never be on top of it; with the national curriculum, the new assessments, and the local management of schools so they ran their own budgets, the bureaucracy had mushroomed. He was in favour of management being tightened up, and of children being more thoroughly and systematically assessed – but, he said, 'It's so overloaded. Then they suggest teachers are failing in their job, when what they've set us is far too huge a task. It's caused stress for teachers, and it's raised this perception in parents that schools aren't coping – when they introduced a system that could never be coped with in the first place. But I think it's like the miners' strike. I think it's sinister. I think it was planned this way, to swamp the system, and after that they can do what they want – which is to undermine local government and take central control of the funding and curriculum. Then they're dictating all the moves, aren't they?'

If this were coming from some lefty moaner with naff badges on his lapel and smudged pamphlets in his pockets, you'd dismiss it as alarmist claptrap. But from the head teacher of your village junior school – from a gentle, quietly spoken man who did a spot of lay preaching on a Sunday, who led the children on his guitar in happy-clappy songs about being good and doing right, who clearly cared deeply for the kids in his charge – this seemed to me very disturbing. And sure enough, a couple of weeks later it was revealed that the Funding Agency for Schools – like so many Tory creations, a murky quango that you rarely hear about, but whose power is in inverse proportion to its public accountability – had proposed to education ministers that school spending be taken away from local authorities for good.

The previous year, the local council wanted to borrow £9 million for school repairs and maintenance; they were granted permission for less than a quarter of that. In my son's school, the floor of the school hall is warped; there's rising damp in the walls, and the plaster's beginning to fall off. The head told me with a weary laugh, 'They call it "a skyline priority". What's that? The skyline's in the distance, isn't it?' He sighed and said, 'What a quaint way of saying we haven't got the money. It means sometime, never. But if that floor warps any more, it'll start being a hazard.'

It was getting worse and worse; there'd been real-terms cuts every year he'd been a head. Fewer people did more work, they got more stressed out, and more and more of them gave up. His former deputy was now selling greetings cards on a market stall – and she was, he said, 'An outstanding teacher, outstanding. But she'd had enough. And what a waste. Years of training and experience just gone, just lost.'

Without the money raised by the PTA, the situation would have been even worse. He said, 'You can give of yourself, the staff can – but if you're always cutting back the morale dips, lethargy creeps in, the spark goes out of the teaching, the spark goes out of the children, and it's a downward spiral. And that's the heart of what's wrong with education; without the money to go forward, to improve the environment for the children, so many people just feel they've no control over what's going on any more.'

But who did have control any more? Over the years, he said, 'The government have created this picture of a middle England where everything's nice, when a lot of people don't live like that.

They're struggling week by week just to get something in to feed their kids – and people don't want to think about it, they don't want to know, they *daren't* know. But the fact is, you've got people stressed because they've got no money, they can't reach out, and their children suffer. And it's too difficult, it's too big a problem for most people to tackle, it's much easier just to sit on your backside – but that's what's wrong, after seventeen years. People have no sense of community values left, no sense of responsibility for each other. And it comes back to the Christian ethic; we *have* to be responsible for each other, for the good of everybody.'

It is surely possible that we could get that back; it is surely right that Blair talks about it so much. For too many, however, it may already be too late. My son's headmaster said, 'For a generation of children, I think the damage is irreparable.'

Sometimes at 3.30 I'd see Boy X brought away through the playground from a school that would soon, helplessly, be forced to move him on, and I'd wonder what his future can be. How likely is it that when the teachers are done trying with him, his next port of call will be the police?

I'd moved to Yorkshire to write about the Doncaster Belles; about this time I saw their former manager, Paul Edmunds, who happens coincidentally to be a teacher. Paul's a bright, positive character who, if he's half as good in a classroom as he is in a dressing-room, is surely an inspirational teacher – but I found him utterly disillusioned with his profession.

He had a class of twenty-six eleven-year-olds, eight of whom had a reading age of seven or less. When he gave them homework at the weekend, if ten of them came back with it done on a Monday, that was a good start to the week. I asked what these children's parents did about it and he said, 'Nothing. That's the point.' I remembered then a woman who ran a dental health project in schools in the former mining villages round Doncaster, and who told me she'd come on five-year-olds who'd never seen an apple.

Paul said if he could see something else to do he'd pack in teaching, it was that bad. He said, 'I trained to be a teacher. I didn't train to be a psychiatrist, a social worker, a health care worker, but

nowadays you need to be all that and then some. They don't want
you to be a teacher,' he sighed, 'they want you to be a superhuman
being.'

At the beginning of November, the Ridings School in Halifax
fell apart. The rat-pack descended; a reporter from one of the
tabloids called the *Courier*, and asked about 'these scumbags'. So, a
spot of objective reporting there – and, amid the general fug of
moral hysteria, Gillian Shephard professed herself in favour of cor-
poral punishment. Incredible – in a country desperately concerned
about child abuse, the Secretary of State for Education apparently
thought it was OK to hit children.

Headmaster Peter Clark was sent in from Rastrick to sort out the
Ridings, and Stephen Pearson – the Liberal candidate for Calder
Valley – produced a peculiarly brutalist quote about him. Clark was
not, said Pearson, 'One of your open-toe-sandalled, bushy-bearded,
anorak-wearing seventies-style teachers.' Not a Liberal, then.

Over coffee and a bacon sarnie in a greasy spoon by Halifax
Town Hall, McCafferty pointed out that, when the council had
been hung, it had been the Tories and Liberals who pushed through
the merger of the schools from which the Ridings was formed, and
which lay behind the present breakdown. Labour, she said, had
opposed that move. Then, when the rat-pack descended,
Calderdale had no press officer to field their fevered investigations –
and it had been the Tories and Liberals who'd axed that post too.

But the situation, she said, was too bad to be scoring points
now. Of 600 children at the Ridings, 135 had special needs – yet in
the next spending round, it was projected that Calderdale would
lose another chunk of its special needs budget. Imagine, nearly one
in four of your kids has significant, identified problems – and yet,
when it goes down the pan, people start blaming the teachers. The
quote that struck me most forcibly came from the mother of two
boys, aged thirteen and fifteen, who'd *already* been excluded; it was
terrible, she said, those teachers just couldn't cope. But whose children were they not coping with here?

McCafferty looked very, very tired; she felt, she said, as if she
were living in a tunnel. But with the election not now likely 'til the
spring, she and Tarlo had booked a Christmas holiday in Goa; they
badly needed a recharge. And at least, politically, things were looking up. She'd feared, between the Tory party conference and the

recall of Parliament, that the government were showing glimmers of togetherness, of having a chance – the economy was up, and Labour's lead looked flaky at the edges. Then Major got back to Westminster and produced more U-turns than a drunk in a stock car rally. Stalkers, paedophiles, knives, calling Shephard on her mobile and saying caning wasn't party policy – it was one bungle upon another. McCafferty said, 'The past seven days have been a microcosm of the past seventeen years. And if people can't see that, God help us. God help us.'

There was one thing that bothered me. It was all very well Labour going after the mess the Tories had made – in schools, in debt-ridden hospital trusts, in sardine-packed prisons, in the country all round. But surely everyone knew that sorting out this mess would take money, and that the money would have to be raised in taxes?

She said, 'We may very well find that the cupboard is bare, and raising taxes may very well then be a necessity. But we can't say it.' She sighed and said, 'We can't even *think* it.'

In the months to come, I'd become increasingly enraged at what I considered Labour's pusillanimous failure to confront the electorate with economic reality. Unlike the Liberals, however, who could afford the luxury of claiming honesty about tax because they knew they'd never win, Labour had to behave this way because their first imperative was to get into government – and to get into government, they had to cater for the wilful selfishness of the floating voter in middle England.

In this England, it seemed, we wanted politicians to give us a perfect world; then we howled if they dared tell us we had to pay for it. But were we too blind to see that if we didn't pay for it, all we ended up doing was stuffing prisons full of people who started out like Boy X?

8

THE SHADOW CAVALCADE

All the while, a steady procession of shadow ministers paraded through Calder Valley, hunting pictures and column inches to boost McCafferty in the local papers. It could be pretty thankless. Frank Dobson, a stout, cheerful, fat-fingered little fellow with an earthy tongue and a taste for pork pies, came to berate the privatised utilities for not paying corporation tax, and ended up chewing exhaust fumes on a bleak patch of roadside by the gates of a sewage plant. The *Huddersfield Examiner* turned up, and nobody else.

Nick Raynsford, Labour's housing man, came and got his feet muddy on an estate in Brighouse, and a self-build project in Todmorden. On the estate, they were converting flats back into family homes, but the money to do it was thin – they had 160 houses to restore and at the current rate, sighed a council official, it'd take them twenty years. We stood and peered at a tiny island of renovation amid an ocean of damp. One of the residents said, 'You can wipe it off the walls with your fingers.' The next homes that were due to be done were boarded up; broken glass, beer cans and a rusting bike frame lay in unmowed grass. For £1 billion you spent on housing, said Raynsford, you made 30,000 jobs – and the country's councils had £7 billion just sitting there that the government wouldn't let them spend.

The procession continued. Margaret Beckett came to the Kirklees & Calderdale Training and Enterprise Council – a sharp, polished, attentive little woman spinning through from an elevator manufacturer in Keighley, *en route* to a textile co-op and a paint plant in Batley. The TEC bosses briefed her on what they did in a blizzard of acronyms and management-speak, two tanned women in power suits burbling away about paper-based this and systems-led that, about investing in people and developing champions, about networking with your peer group, benchmarking, and lifelong learning strategies. In my notebook I have someone talking at one point about 'portfolio accessible interview technology', and I've not the faintest notion what it means. I sat thinking, Does anyone here speak English?

One of the TEC people would later say they had a standing joke that the building was crawling with TLAs – Three-Letter Acronyms – but I did understand one thing. The TEC's funding to help unemployed adults, they complained, had been cut during the past two years by fifty per cent.

But this language fog's a feature of the times, isn't it? In the name of efficiency and the market, one area of our life and then another has fallen under the sway of the tribe of accountants. Schools, hospitals, the BBC – public enterprises which cannot ever be businesses must nonetheless, the Tories told us, be run as such. The result is a torrent of needless paperwork, the demoralisation of your staff (three-quarters of the Crown Prosecution Service were reported in a MORI poll at this time to be disillusioned, and overwhelmed with bureaucracy) and it all comes wrapped in an insidious subversion of the language. We end up swamped in mission statements and nursery vouchers. In education, in local government, in all manner of fields we have *choice* now, as *consumers*, when before we didn't know that we needed it – and when (unless we're wealthy) we've not actually got any more choice than we ever had. But Orwell had a thing or two to say about this brand of semantics, didn't he?

Once language is abstracted from concrete reality, you can say what you like. Thus could the Tories claim that Labour's spending commitments would require an extra £30 billion of public spending, when in fact Labour policy (knowing too well what had happened with the 'tax bombshell' in '92) was very deliberately a commitment-free zone. The Tory figures, wrote Donald MacIntyre in the *Independent*, were 'spectacularly creative' – and charges of economic recklessness from a government that had doubled the national debt in six years were rich indeed. But expecting the Tories not to lie, by now, would have been like expecting a skunk not to smell.

★

There was no fog in McCafferty's language. If a thing was done quickly, it was done 'within two shakes of a lamb's tail'. Of her tendency to arrive at events and meetings only barely on time she said, 'I'm always on the death for everything.'

There had been some disagreement with the party's regional office in Wakefield; it was felt she should resign as a councillor in order to get away from her case load. Typically direct, her response to this was, 'Those are my voters I'm dealing with.' She was, she joked, going out leafleting in disguise – but each issue she tackled brought in a few more votes. If the Greave House objectors, for example, seemed to have found a way to stop development there (which they did), or if the Kershaw church shop appeared to be saved (which it was), then a job had been done for the people involved, and the local politician who helped do it came out looking good. And why not? Isn't that what they're there for?

She did agree to come off the waste management board, though not before turning another problem to her advantage. Hollins Hey, a projected waste-disposal site, became the focus of a campaign of objection. A site visit was arranged, with a bus to take the landowner, assorted objectors and officials to inspect it; when they got there, they found Tarlo all but being lynched by other objectors already there, one of them getting hands round his neck. 'I took a deep breath,' said McCafferty, 'and proffered my hand to anybody and everybody.' Subsequently convinced that the site was too small, expensive and short-term to be bothered with, her decision to oppose it enabled her to write to the objectors and show that their case had been met.

Their addresses had been loaded into Tim Swift's growing database – and again and again, I'd hear people say how Labour had never been this efficient before. In the past an election was called, and out they spilt for three weeks' manic canvassing; this time, however, the canvassing (at least in theory) would all be done ahead of time, with endlessly useful results.

Example: McCafferty's anti-handgun petition gathered some 3,000 signatures, all logged in Swift's databank. The petition was presented to Jack Straw in support of Labour's push for a total ban; when Sir Donald (as ever) then toed the government line and voted for a partial ban, McCafferty could write to all the signatories thanking them and pointing out what Sir Donald had done. Now, I say *all* the signatories – except, of course, that the Calder Valley Labour Party couldn't afford 3,000 stamps. But with the database now able to identify which signatures were hard Labour, which floaters, which faltering Tories and so on, in fact only 1,000 or so letters went out – to the floaters and falterers where that letter was most likely to pull a vote.

Thus does the nitty-gritty of politics work, a daily juggle of what you can do with the money and information available. As a PPC, McCafferty got endless invitations – for example, to go to lunch at the BBC in London on budget day. And it was exciting, the idea that people wanted you there at the centre of things – but apart from the fact that she'd probably do herself more good if she stayed up north and went on Radio Leeds, the nub of the matter was that the campaign had better things to do with its limited money than buy her a train fare to London and back.

On one front, at least, there came blissful relief. A wealthy local nabob donated £1,000 to the constituency party; Tarlo and McCafferty matched that sum, using some of the compensation they'd received after Tarlo's father died tragically in an accident caused by poor signposting at some roadworks. The money went to employ help for one day a week at home because, said McCafferty, she was drowning in a sea of paper.

From early morning, the house was chaos. The phone, the fax, press releases, case-work – because, while people may despise and deride politicians, they still need and expect help from them on every front imaginable. I remember one call coming in from the landlady of a pub who was splitting up with her husband, who needed help over finding a place to live. McCafferty gave the best advice she could, and a number to call, then put the phone down and said how sad it was. 'And,' she sighed, 'she was a damn good cook too.'

Her recipe for survival was a sense of humour and a glass of red wine. A friend asked, Did she and David ever have time alone together any more? She said, 'Not very often. Maybe an hour before bed. And maybe this is how you judge a person's relationship, but I wonder how a lot of people survive it. We'll survive it all right. But there's always something to be done, when sometimes you just want to put your feet up. This holiday,' she said, 'it'll be precious.'

Rebecca, the woman who came to help, was manna from heaven. For a couple of years they'd had a software system called Caseload Manager, but they'd not known how to work it. Now Rebecca got it running, loaded ninety-odd standard letters – then you could enter a person's problem, it'd find you the appropriate response, you personalised it and bang, off went the answer. On your own, said McCafferty, you did the quickest thing: a phone call. But people remember letters more than they do a call, and now Rebecca was firing off twenty or thirty every day that she came. So by the time they went to Goa, McCafferty thought she'd have caught up with everything – and as winter kicked in everything, on November 20th, included chairing the Calderdale Domestic Violence Forum in Halifax Town Hall.

This England: according to figures from the Zero Tolerance campaign in Wakefield, two in every five women have been raped or sexually assaulted. The acquittal rate in rape trials is 78 per cent. Almost one-third of women experience some form of domestic violence at some point in their lives, and one in seven women are raped in marriage.

Fifteen people met in a high-ceilinged room, the sky bright outside on the winter's first snowfall. There was a policewoman, a social worker, two councillors, a solicitor, and representatives from a variety of voluntary bodies. A man from the Church of England had brought case studies from research done in Barnsley, and it wasn't pretty reading. There was a sixty-six-year-old woman physically, emotionally and sexually abused through forty-six years of marriage, reduced at one point to six stones of psychiatric wreck. There was a young mother of two imprisoned in her home, not allowed even to go to the local shop without permission, forced always to wear baggy jeans and jumpers, fleeing to a refuge when her children started mimicking their father's violence. There was a woman abandoned at the age of eighteen months, passed round different homes all her childhood and abused in them, married at eighteen to a man who beat her so badly she needed a hundred stitches and nine months for the bones to mend; another assault left her needing a hysterectomy, after splinters of bone were found in her fallopian tubes. She had three sons, who stayed with their father when she fled. One's a drug addict, one's in prison, and the third one's on remand. This third son visits his mother occasionally, to extort money with menaces. The woman has eating disorders, she's emaciated . . .

The Domestic Violence Forum wanted Calderdale to adopt a Zero Tolerance campaign, but persuading the council to find the money was difficult; one of those present described it as 'virtually bankrupt'. There are many concrete ways to make women's lives more secure – better street lighting, better estate design, safer public transport, or innovative tenancy agreements such as that drawn up by Manchester City Council whereby domestic violence can result in the perpetrator's eviction. But it all costs money, and the short-term effect of a campaign is to increase demand on your services. So you have to show that the money spent is, in McCafferty's words, 'a sprat to catch a big mackerel' – because in the longer term you reduce the number of children going into care, the number of women who need rehousing, and all the other costs associated with the distressed and dysfunctional people thrown on the state's mercy in their suffering.

But the long term was a long way away, and in the short term there was no money. The Forum had the room, but it had no tea and biscuits for the meeting because the council these days had to charge for them, and the Forum had no money to buy them with. They were begging from the police, from the Halifax Building Society, from a church printer to get their publicity material produced at cost. They'd thought they might get funds from the health authority, but now it looked as if that was in the red as well.

Afterwards I went to a newsagents, and looked at the row of men all eyeing the top shelf. I thought, what a sorry bloody state we're in.

After Kenneth Clarke's budget Frank Dobson came back, and sat down in Halifax Town Hall with McCafferty, the Halifax MP Alice Mahon and the council's Labour leader Pam Warhurst. Warhurst is a slim, teemingly energetic woman with a striking mane of tawny hair, a ferocious smile full of big sharp teeth and a seriously loud voice – 'not a foot soldier', as one of her colleagues put it, with a kind of vexed admiration. She briefed Dobson on the local impact of the budget, and listening to a Warhurst briefing was like standing by the M4 at rush hour under the Heathrow flight path.

She produced a booming welter of figures and acronyms, pelting through the infamous complexities of local government finance with confident knowledge, at vigorous volume, with undaunted brusque language. I couldn't follow all of it, but the bottom line was clear: Calderdale had the worst settlement in West Yorkshire, council tax would have to go up by seven per cent, the price of council services would rise, and the provision of those services would be cut. All this when they had millions in reserve that they couldn't use, and with the crisis at the Ridings costing an extra £160,000 already. 'So far,' said Warhurst, 'we've not been deflected from any capital programme, which is bloomin' amazing. But what they say is extra for education, that all vanishes in pay and inflation – so we'll probably have to cut the primary school budget, which we'd managed to avoid before. We are,' she concluded, 'fairly knackered.'

That morning, Dobson had already got his press release out for the local media; it compared the way Tory pet Westminster was funded against the grant assessment for Calderdale. Somehow Westminster, under the Conservatives, was deemed to be the fourth most deprived area in Britain, whereas Calderdale ranked only seventy-seventh. If Calderdale were to get the same grant per head that Westminster got, it wouldn't have to levy any council tax at all; it could, on the contrary, give a rebate to every household of £290. Or, if they'd had the same education funding as Westminster, they could in the past year have employed 831 more teachers at no extra cost – and what chance a collapse at the Ridings then?

A bloke from the *Courier* came to get this juice, and Dobson had a handy statistical shocker primed and ready to feed him. As the scale of deprivation in Westminster was deemed to include not only that council's residents but also its visitors, this meant that for the purposes of the government grant twelve per cent of the people staying at the Ritz were regarded as living in grossly overcrowded conditions.

Otherwise, Dobson played out the line – and wherever you went now the line was what you got, and the line never changed.

Tory lies/twenty-two Tory tax rises/they give with one hand and take away with the other – how many times did you hear that? Certainly, several people I know had heard and read it to the extent that if you asked them about the budget, they played the line straight back as if they'd thought of it themselves. What was happening was an endless beat-beat-beating on the message drum, to din it home until it was all but subliminally implanted: an orchestrated, multifaxed repetition tromping down the wire from campaign HQ to every candidate in the land. It was this blunt: a fax would come headed, 'Line to take', and they'd take it. Independent thought? Nah. We've got an election to win here . . .

Which task, I had previously feared, would be made much more difficult by Clarke's budget. The Chancellor, I'd thought, would produce some irresponsible but spectacular bribe, prodding another Pavlovian spurt of satisfaction in the electorate's greed gland – but he didn't, and (with Labour beating the message drum all the while) his penny off income tax was everywhere seen for the con trick it was. Unsalvaged by Clarke, the Tories turned to a new round of self-mutilation over Europe. While Tony Marlow called for Clarke's resignation, Labour's lead climbed to 37 points; they stood on 59 per cent. Dobson shook his head, grinning; the figures, he said, were ludicrous. But then, 'You listen to Bill Cash, some of those other people; they're just not on Planet Earth.'

So Labour sat smugly tight, playing out the line – but where was the outrage? For the seventeenth year, another budget had made the rich yet richer while foreign aid to the world's poorest was pared back yet again, while lone parents had their benefits cut, while one-third of our children in this England grew up on the breadline – while children fell prey to pneumonia because of the damp in their housing and TB, for God's sake, came creeping back amongst us. Where, I ask again, was the outrage? Do we not live in the same country as these cast-off people any more? Are they starving Africans, to have their aid budget cut while they choke on the exhaust fumes of Ken Clarke's passing Rolls-Royce economy?

As local government was no longer given enough money to do what it needed to do, it had instead to go cap-in-hand and beg for it. In the corrupted language of the times this was, presumably, the beneficial business of *competition* – competition with other needy authorities for lump sums dished out by unelected quangos like the Rural Development Commission.

Two days before Dobson came, McCafferty rang in a state of high jubilation. Hebden Bridge, she announced, busting over with local pride, had won £1,000,000 in a Rural Challenge Bid. That in turn would pull in £2,000,000 more of private finance; a host of projects would be set in train in the town, and 150 jobs would come with them.

It related to the recent re-opening of the Rochdale Canal, the renovation of an extraordinary feat of early nineteenth-century engineering – the first trans-Pennine waterway – and it aimed to pull more tourism into Calder Valley. A millpond would be flooded to provide a boatyard and a wildlife sanctuary, and make water levels in the canal more reliable in the process; there'd be a cycleway, and more room for anglers. Canalside buildings would be converted into workspace and new housing; a rubble zone between the marina and the cinema would be cleaned up to give the market a permanent five-day site, freeing the existing site for more car-parking space. The back of the cinema would be cleaned up too – a dingy, litter-strewn patch of dirt and weeds where, at the minute, small-fry dope-dealers and under-age girls did their night-time trade. (In Hebden Bridge? Yes, in Hebden Bridge.)

And that, laughed McCafferty, was one picture of the candidate you'd never see – her standing there inspecting that sorry piece of earth under a huge graffito on a tatty brick wall yelling, 'Free The Weed!'

The following day, the cheque was presented to Pam Warhurst at the marina by Miles Middleton, a quangoman with a fruity accent, a faded blue suit and a fabulously patronising manner. Thirty people came, among them the Mayor of Hebden Royd with tinted specs, a fine floral tie and his chain of office draped over a dashing lilac jacket. Champagne was served on Calder Valley Cruising's pretty narrowboat the *Sarah Siddons*, and trays of coffee were brought over from the Hebden Lodge Hotel. Middleton stood supping with his silver head bent under the boat's low ceiling, and blithely opined that the quality of some of the bids had been simply awful. I tried to imagine the desperately underfunded local politicians and voluntary workers in all the places round the country that hadn't won any money, and all the work they'd done scrabbling for these funds that he'd now so airily dismissed. Seeing me scribble he said, with a hearty, couldn't-give-a-damn chuckle, 'You'll be writing down everything I say and using it in evidence against me. I know what you boys are like.' I'm thinking, Too right, pal.

Snappers snapped and scribes scribed, and Middleton gave his speech. The Minister, he said, had told Warhurst when she'd made their presentation that he hoped she'd not sulk if she didn't win. Haw haw! Himself, he said, he hoped she'd not vault over the table and belt them if she didn't win.

'Not a bad character assessment, actually,' one observer would later remark – but the tone overall was so condescending it made my gorge rise. These were grown people, committed local activists and volunteers, being handed £1,000,000 by some aristo nob as if they were kids at a public school prize day. He praised their enthusiasm – but of course they were enthusiastic, weren't they? They needed the bloody *money*.

There was a cyclist there, a woman who worked for a carers' project whose council funding was almost certain to be killed off by the budget. She told an ugly traffic story she'd seen in the *Courier*, trying to remember what day it had run – then she said, 'It must have been Wednesday. I only get it on Wednesday. For the jobs.'

The carers' group had applied for funds to the National Lottery – just as Hebden Bridge had applied to the Rural Development Commission, winning money that the likes of Marsden and Meltham would therefore have to do without. McCafferty sighed and said, 'Everything's a lottery now, isn't it? This money, we've not had anything this good for ages. But it doesn't mean the budget isn't still megashit, does it?'

Back home, Tarlo was spinning on the spot in anger and frustration. On his first calculations after Clarke's phantom giveaway, he feared the council would have to close five libraries – or, certainly, to cut back their opening hours by a significant amount. This England: I imagined a future of prettified canals, and half the people walking alongside them illiterate.

Not, of course, that you have to go too far to find the ill-educated in England in the present, never mind the future. A few weeks later I was watching Barnsley play Ipswich, and the family in front of me (a crew so fetching as to make the Munsters look like Boyzone) took increasing exception to the style of the visitors' play. Eventually the patriarch of this toothsome crew cried out – referring to Ipswich, remember – 'Can tha' not play football in West Country then?'

9

BLUR PIE

Only Nigel Mansell could say it: 'The proof of the pudding is in the clock.' So he's a dessert chef, then.

Mansell produced this gem on December 11th, the day David Willetts resigned as Paymaster General for 'dissembling' – and I introduce our Nige at this point because only the English could produce a racing driver like Mansell or a Prime Minister like Major. Here were two blokes with two of the more exciting jobs in this world – one went rapidly round and round, clinging barely to control amid a chaos of impenetrable noise, and the other was a racing driver – yet they both succeeded in making their trades seem astonishingly dull. Striving to look on the bright side, I suppose you could say that this peculiarly English brand of whingeing stodginess has something strangely comforting about it. After all, Senna crashed.

But in the first week of December, there was little comfort to be seen on any front for Major, and the Tories were crashing big time. After a characteristically incompetent feed to the *Telegraph* that Major was leaning towards ruling Britain out of the single currency in the next Parliament, Clarke and Heseltine armlocked him definitively into the 'wait-and-see' position. Assorted ministers had garrulous lunches with eager journos; assorted Europhobes went straight bananas. Then Sir John Gorst took his ball away because the government wouldn't give him the casualty unit he wanted – so Major was notionally deprived of his majority by a Tory MP, even before Labour could do it for real in the Barnsley East by-election.

By a picture of the Prime Minister holding his head in his hands, the *Independent*'s lead headline on December 7th said simply, 'The Abyss'. Now *The Abyss* is a film in which a bloke puts on a weird suit, dives into the unfathomable blackness of an ocean trench and meets a bunch of aliens – rather like dealing with the Europhobes, I imagine. Anyway, Major panicked, and went live on TV on Sunday lunchtime to tell us he wasn't panicking.

The next day, Blair came to Yorkshire. So far, every Labour politician I'd met would always stress how close the election was going to be, how there was no way they were twenty or thirty points ahead in any real poll – but now there was a change in them. Among those waiting for Blair at a community centre in Grimethorpe was an MP who said, 'I'm still in the if camp. But if they carry on like this, we'll wipe them out.'

T he winter morning of Monday December 9th was one of those when you can really love England. I drove on back roads round the north of Barnsley, under chill wisps of pale blue sky spread between nacreous sheets of cream and lilac cloud, backlit by a faint gold sun. In the dips of the land, banks of fog hung heavy, luminous grey; across the fields and amid the bare black trees, tendrils of mist crept over the damp green earth. My country.

My country, where once thousands of men went down into the earth to get us coal, and where the pit villages now are battered places, their main streets lined with discount stores, charity shops and boarded windows. In Grimethorpe the community had been pounded, so then they built them a community centre, and a big part of it was the police station. It was called the Acorn Centre, and the literature proudly called it 'a new heart for Grimethorpe'. Once this village had work; now it has a job-search room. They filmed *Brassed Off* here; in three days' time, come the Barnsley East poll, Labour candidate Jeff Ennis was the surest bet for a win since the tide rolled over Canute.

In the Acorn reception, Labour men in smart, rosette-splashed overcoats mingled with a motley of hacks by the counter of the Oak Tree Café. There was a sad notice on the wall: 'We try to keep our prices as low as possible. However it has come to our attention that items of crockery, mainly knives, forks and cups are being removed from the premises. If this continues we will have no choice but to increase our prices considerably to cover these losses.' I fingered earnest PR literature about the 'end vision' for Grimethorpe, and wondered how the nonsense merchants could blithely pen such claptrap, as if Grimethorpe hadn't been deep in a vision of its end for years.

Outside, press officer Mark Covell paced tensely, urgent on his mobile. Blair's train was due in Doncaster at 10.05. At the counter, a man with a broad coalfield accent grinned and said, 'Have you got any Blair pie, love? We'll give some to Tories alreet.' His accent turned Blair into Blur: 'Blur Pie'.

I went outside, and found the Labour boys talking football. The local lads were cockahoop over Barnsley flying high in the First Divison; Kevin Barron, up from Rotherham, was deep in gloom over his lot, lurching around at the wrong end of the Second. 'If we don't get a win before Christmas,' he muttered, 'I'm giving up.'

There was a library, a big parking area, and different buildings for welfare and business advisers, adult education, a crèche, and Labour's campaign HQ. Amid three TV crews and twenty-five scribes and snappers, Covell gestured precisely as he said, 'He'll arrive *here*, he'll go up *there*, he'll go over *there*' – every pace planned out. Then the car turned up, a rented maroon Vauxhall Omega (pulling to a halt just *here*) and Blair got out, shook hands, then piled through to the first band of waiting citizens. As the scrum dived after him Ian Carvell, who'd been driving, watched them go and said, 'Half an hour. I'll have a cigarette. You'll never guess what happened.'

He'd been stood by the Omega's boot in the station car park, holding it open for people to lob in their stuff. As Blair came over, the driver of the follow-up car turned on her ignition, not realising she was in gear, and jumped forward – so there's Carvell meeting the leader of the gang, the next Prime Minister, with a car on his foot. Normally one with a vivid mouth, he said drily now, 'I was very good. I didn't swear. I said nothing.' But the Blair effect, eh? People chuck wine on one another, lose the power of speech, drive cars into each other . . .

He met half a dozen women working laptops in the community college, nattered for five minutes while the cameras snicked and snacked, then whisked on to the little café. The woman who ran the job-search programme was waiting there with two of her more promising young people – a stout lass with a ring through one nostril, and a quiet lad with lank blond hair and the beginnings of a beard. Blair sat to talk with them, and photographers packed in tight round their table, a leaning bank of lenses. A local scribe behind them murmured, 'I don't know how they cope with it. I'd get a picture of his eyebrows and leave, me.'

Explaining what she did, the job-search woman was fluent and stern. 'If someone comes in and says, I'm just a housewife, I say, I'm not having that. These are the skills you've got, now let's put them into a job.'

Blair listened, asked questions, and spoke of similar situations in his own constituency. The lad wanted to go into civil engineering, and said something about how it was a pity they'd scrapped a lot of apprenticeships. Quick as a whip, Blair shot back, 'It's a pity they scrapped half the engineering industry.'

The job-search woman got him to autograph her napkin, then he was gone again, off to a side room to talk to the TV crews. The blond lad said quietly, 'I could have done with a bit longer to talk to him, to ask a few more questions – what he foresees his govern-ment doing. But I were quite surprised on how he were quite a decent bloke to talk to, really.'

Blair came out of the TV room, and another young lad darted through the reception doors – wanting, again, to get his auto-graph. Blair paused to do that, then moved again to another room for the local papers and radio. Asked what Labour could do for a place like Grimethorpe, he fed them Blur Pie – 'hope for young people, skills and work opportunities for young people, we've got a proposal funded by the one-off windfall levy to get more young people into work' – then he segued flawlessly into the five pledges and played out the line. But he was, at least, bru-tally frank on one thing: 'People don't want to have myths peddled. There's absolutely no point me coming here and saying I'll put the mining industry back to where it was forty years ago, because I can't.'

While he talked I passed Anji Hunter a note, asking how many politicians get asked for their autograph. She shrugged and said, 'He gets asked all the time.'

The minders were looking at their watches. 'We've got to go now,' they told him, and off he went.

After dishing out more snacks for the cameras at a primary school, Blair went to the Royal Armouries in Leeds to speak to nearly three hundred business people, these good folk paying £75 a head for the privilege. The Armouries are housed in a large grey box deposited in a baffling post-industrial wilderness; I roamed the convoluted, multi-coned mayhem that passes for a road system in Leeds, found it, and eventually sat for lunch with an accountant who said she'd been born in Leeds, and she'd still got lost on her way there that morning.

When I arrived at 12.15, a small crew of earnest young men and women in suits were talking on mobiles in the airy blankness of the foyer as they handed out badges and programmes. To one side, the restaurant was a large and spartan white room two storeys high, the walls minimally adorned with martial flags, suits of armour and paintings. A four-piece band warmed up, playing jazz lite on drums, bass, sax and electric piano. An empty space before the tables housed display stands from, among others, Torch Telecom, BA Corporate Documents and Yorkshire Electricity. The event's strap line hung along the wall: 'New Opportunities For Business'. I went to the loo, and found a bloke in a suit patting down non-existent hair across his bald patch in the mirror. My own fear at these occasions is always that, all unawares, my flies are undone. And I'll never get the contract then, will I?

Outside, a bloke in day-glo yellow swept invisible dirt off spotless, brick-paved approaches. He said solemnly, 'There's a lot of important folk here today. And one that's more important still to come.' Inside, eight seminars were winding up – eight shadow ministers briefing pinstripes and power dresses on the budget, regulation, competition, energy, regional, legal, training and small business policies, and the superhighway. No use to me, pal – I can't even figure out the road system.

Anji Hunter arrived, fielded requests from photographers and marched into the restaurant – now buzzing with the chatter of early arrivals – to check out Blair's flight path through the room, where his table was, how the podium looked. The way his vanguard went before him like this, it was hard to avoid the impression of a director laying out stage marks for the star. At 12.45 we were told, 'Ladies and gentlemen, if I could ask you to take your seats, please. Mr Blair is five minutes away.'

I sat with David Tarlo, two people from an accountancy firm, a woman from Yorkshire Water, an MP's wife and a couple of others. Teams of waiters fanned out through twenty-seven tables. The starter was a trio of Scottish salmon served with lime mayonnaise. I doubt you get much of that down the Oak Tree Café in Grimethorpe – assuming there's any crockery left to eat it with.

Yorkshire Electricity's Chief Executive introduced Blair – delighted to be sponsoring the lunch, we want to see future prosperity, stakeholder economy, puff puff, blah blah, please come and see us here in Leeds again, *perhaps in a different role . . .*

Blair thanked the sponsors. 'Practically everything I do these days seems to be sponsored by one utility or another,' he said, with a sly grin. 'Perhaps they're trying to tell us something.' Then he joked about the colour of the conference programme – pale blue. 'Some people may say it's an indication of the times. The further sell-out of Tony Blair.'

Some people may say that indeed – and much of what followed could as well have been delivered by Thatcher. He had, he said, addressed 10,000 business people around the country, he'd gone to the equivalents of the CBI in Germany and Japan, he'd gone to the New York Chamber of Commerce – because, he said, 'The Labour Party today is a pro-business, pro-enterprise party.'

So Labour today was about low inflation, a stable macro-economic policy, tough rules for spending and borrowing – and his reason for all this was perfectly defensible: 'It is better to offer what you can credibly deliver, than things which may get you a round of applause, but which you can't do.' In the face of all this fiscal rectitude, however, this kow-tow to the global market, a fellow like me is left hunting for straws.

He did say his basic belief was that a society with ambition and aspiration could still be a society with compassion. He did say that he wanted competition on the basis of quality, not of low skills and low wages. He did defend a minimum wage, and Labour's intention to sign up to the Social Chapter. He did talk about promoting education, referring to his visit earlier that morning to the Acorn Centre.

And he said that if Labour was making tremendous efforts to establish a relationship with business, that was because it was necessary to reassure them, certainly – but also to say that things could be better.

But if, behind all that, lies a refusal to contemplate any increase in spending, or any increase in taxes to fund it, what is any of the above but Blur Pie? As, indeed, were most of the answers he gave when the diners threw him questions, flannelling about a stable economy, about 'setting frameworks and enabling' – and while the audience were quiet and attentive they were also, I suspect, mostly somewhat mistrustful. As one questioner put it, if this event was called 'New Opportunities For Business', 'I have to say I haven't seen many so far.'

The accountants at my table were concerned about the minimum wage, and that it would be set at a disabling level. One of them said she came from a working-class background, she'd worked for what she had – not sat there like some do, expecting it to be put on the doorstep with the milk – and she feared it being taken away from her. It was unlikely this time that she or her colleague would vote Tory again – but whether they could go all the way and vote for Blair, they doubted. She had this nervy image of a bunch of bearded lefties keeping mum 'til they were in, then laying waste the land.

So, a little further to the right, Tone, and you might get them yet. The lunch was a plain illustration of how, in order to get elected, he'd accepted great chunks of the global-capitalist agenda – with the result that we'd have a contest between a party that wanted to cut taxes but had raised them, and a party that needed to raise taxes but couldn't say so. Clear as mud, really.

The main course was roast lamb with a rosemary stuffing. Like the speech it was stodgy and fatty, and like the ideas behind it the veg was undercooked.

Meanwhile, I was beginning to get another image of Blair. With his odd, pointed sprite-ish features, he put me more and more in mind of the Elvenking from *The Hobbit*. Basically a good ruler, but over-fond of treasure (likes his fiscal discipline) and highly suspicious of any itinerant dwarves passing through his murky domain. Tough on dwarves, tough on the causes of dwarves . . .

The lunch wound up. With her right hand numb from signing 2,500 Christmas cards, McCafferty went to Halifax Town Hall to fill in the forms for her candidacy. It would be a bit of a slip, a fretful Tim Swift had told her, if the Tories finally imploded and the election was called while she was away on holiday, so then she raced back to find she'd not done the paperwork and was ineligible to stand.

With that sorted, she and Tarlo flew to Goa – and the next day, Jeff Ennis won Barnsley East. His victory statement declared, 'They think it's all over. It is now.' For any reader who's been on Mars these past thirty years, this was another football line – and that, it seemed, was the level we were down to. It was so glib, so trivial, and I was beginning to wonder why we need bother having a political campaign at all; we might just as well have a penalty shoot-out: Mansell v. the Elvenking, five kicks each.

10

DOG JIBE FURY OF SEX ROMP MODEL

At New Year, a footballer was reported to be playing away with a young woman possessed of unfeasibly large breasts. His wife apparently said she'd have minded less if it weren't that her dog was better-looking than the model in question – hence the headline above. This was, of course, earthshaking stuff (for the footballer, anyway) and it duly bounced back and forth in the tabloids, during which time the banter in the Wimbledon dressing-room doesn't bear thinking about.

In his New Year's Message, meanwhile, Paddy Ashdown ventured the prophecy that the forthcoming election would be the stupidest this country had ever seen. Given the level of public debate, and the kind of subjects deemed worthy of said debate, this was not a remarkable piece of foresight. But what exactly were we thinking about, as the clock ticked down towards this millennial election? Fearless in my quest for the true tone of this England in 1997, I decided I should sally forth into the Siberian wind chill and investigate our popular culture. Feet crunching over the permafrost, I popped out and bought the tabloids.

On January 6th, as we went back to work to the annual soundtrack of shattered resolutions, the main stories adjudged to be concerning the nation were:

CROWN AND OUT!
Agony of Charles and Camilla over devastating poll

I'M SO SORRY
Charles: 'I've let down Diana, Camilla, Queen, and my sons'

SPICE GIRLS GET HITS OUT FOR THE LADS
Pop queens beat blues by flashing

BOY WHO DRAGGED DOWN A TORY MP

TORIES URGE GAY SCANDAL MP TO STAY

FURY AT SOCCER DOG'S DIRTY TRICKS!
Mascot bog-roll stunt stuns fans

This last is from the *Sport*, and concerns Barnsley's mascot Toby Tyke allegedly mooning the crowd, mock-wiping his bum, then lobbing the used roll into the stand – an incident I regret to say I missed. Why is it all the best stuff happens at games you didn't go to? Still, how this is deemed to be front-page news escapes me – except, of course, that the *Sport* isn't really a newspaper anyway, so much as a promotional tool for pornographers with weird jokes on the front.

Nonetheless, I include it because the ugly tone of prurient hypocrisy that characterises the popular press is itself a kind of pornography. Consider, for example, the *Sport*'s centre spread 'news exclusive': FURY OVER DAWN'S SEX TRICK. In reality a mail-order promotion for a top shelf magazine, it included the priceless disclaimer that, 'A responsible newspaper like the *Sport* can't go into any detail about the mind-stretching act' – and the *Sport* absolutely is a responsible newspaper. It said so on the mast-head, 'The Paper That Fights Crime', and on page 2 they were inviting us to shop a rapist. This amid a tumult of ads promising 'Live Bum Action', 'Sex Tart Talks Filth', and 'Hear Me Moan Just For You'. So what paper, you wonder, would a rapist read?

More to the point, where exactly is the difference between this sorry dross and the three-page coverage given by the *Express* to Paul Stone, the young man alleging he'd had an affair with Tory MP Jerry Hayes? Coverage adorned with pictures of Stone lipsticked and bewigged, no less. (The *Star* was less subtle, fetchingly describing Stone in its editorial as 'a teenage wooftah'.) Myself, I cannot see much difference at all between panting guff about what Dawn does with her private parts, and what Hayes does with his private life. You can get your titillation straight, you can get it from the

Spice Girls or Elle Macpherson or a pretty boy in a wig – but otherwise what's the odds? Yet this stuff purports to be middle England; I know this, because one of the editors at the *Express* told me so. He said, 'We *are* middle England.'

So, in middle England, we live in a climate of galloping frivolity; our public discourse is a rancid *bouillabaisse* of feckless, brainless, adulterous royals, models, pop stars, soap characters and footballers, all these sorry fish-heads floating in an overcooked slop of hysteria about money and E and 'morality'. Even fashion designers, for goodness' sake, are deemed these days to be important people. The front pages of both *The Times* and the *Independent* on January 20th, for example, led with the dismaying news that iron man Gordon Brown wanted to maintain the Tories' two-year freeze on public spending – and next to this story they plonked pictures of, respectively, a woman with a two-inch gold bullring through her nose and another wearing a hat as big as a dustbin lid with an animal horn sticking out of it. So do silly hats and scary politics now go hand in hand, as matters of equivalent froth and irrelevance?

I am not against fun (though most of the 'fun' popularly on offer has less punch than instant decaff) any more than I'm in favour of some wild-eyed crew of socialist utopians marching in to recapture the commanding heights of the economy (though it'd be nice, at least, to have our water and our railways back). But in 1984, in a tatty little room on the roof of a hotel in Rabat, I wrote the first draft of my first novel, *The Last Election*, about the direction I feared we were heading in. I didn't set a date in it, but I imagined that the book took place in the mid-Nineties and I predicted, among other things, rave culture, wall-to-wall sport on multi-channel TV, a top football division full of Scandinavians, the dismemberment of the BBC, and a political culture of enraging imbecility driven entirely by PR men. Well, not wanting to crow here – but look where we were now, eh?

Where we were now was both main parties spending exceedingly large sums of money on poster campaigns of the most dubious veracity. Where we were now was Blair succumbing to the nonsense language of the PR people, talking to business about how government should 'set frameworks and enable' – claptrap, really, because governments are there to bloody *do* things. And where we were now was poor old Major trying to kick off the New Year pulling the family values line again, when the next thing you know

Max Clifford's flogging some backbencher's gay love letters to the
gutter sharks.

Still, forget the tabloids; I was going to look into them, but
they're such a stinking sump of smutty, fawning, clamorous, illiterate and generally dispiriting trash that I rapidly abandoned the idea.
And forget Jerry Hayes, too – who he fancies, that's his business.
The really icky thing was the family values stuff – this coming from
a government that had left so many families under so much pressure
that most mothers in the country now had to go out to work
whether they wanted to or not.

I met a social worker, and was depressed to learn that there are
more mothers in this country than you'd care to realise who can't
even cook, never mind find work. They've come out of dysfunctional
backgrounds, had kids themselves, and now those kids are living on
convenience foods and take-outs that are unhealthy and expensive . . .
So the social worker's colleague visits one of these struggling mums,
and teaches her how to make your basic meat pie; she tells her what
cuts of meat are cheap, what veg'll go with it, how to put it
together – then a couple of weeks later she's back to check on things,
and she asks the man of the house how it's going. 'It's great,' he tells
her, 'great. Just one thing, mind. Could you teach her another recipe?
'Cause we've had that meat pie every day since you came.'

The social worker – we'll call her Ann, as she preferred not to be
identified – said that when she heard Conservative politicians talking about family values, 'I find it a bit sick. Because I see the
policies they put forward actually doing the opposite of promoting
family values.' Cuts in benefit to young people still living at home
increased the pressure on those familes. Cuts in benefit to single
parents made it harder and harder for them successfully to bring up
their children. Excessive demands on fathers from the Child
Support Agency put severe strain on families involved in second
marriages. There were examples all round, but the nearest to hand
was the repeated cuts in the social services' own budget. 'We are,'
she said, 'being forced more and more to set thresholds and criteria to limit service, because the funding's just not there. Which
doesn't help us support families, does it?'

The last few years had seen substantial retrenchment; on a

budget in the previous year of £30,000,000, Calderdale Social Services in the current round were looking to lop nearly £2,000,000 away from that. One thing that would probably go, more and more, was the home help service; put simply, more and more old people would be left to live in dirty homes. But then, they weren't the only people to find themselves living scuffed and down at heel.

When you drove into the Social Services' head office, the grass on the verges round the car park was overgrown and untended; there was no sign over the main entrance. The place, Ann readily admitted, looked unkempt and uncared for, and it wasn't the way they wanted it to be – but there wasn't any choice, because the money didn't run to that much maintenance any more. In the field, meanwhile, they were having to employ less qualified people and to prioritise case-loads in a way they'd not seen for years – which obviously risked making it more likely that someone in danger might slip through the net.

Of the hundred or so children in the borough deemed officially to be at risk, the majority were in Halifax, in places like Mixenden and Ovenden. However, the idea that out in middle England all was fine and dandy wouldn't wash; the child care teams in Hebden Bridge and Todmorden were busy people too. Child abuse is not restricted to class; where it occurs in more affluent families it may be better concealed, go on for longer, and actually be worse by the time it's unearthed.

More generally, said Ann, what they'd seen happen over the years – whether or not an area was well off – was a decline in any sense of community. The word she used for what she felt had disappeared was 'neighbourliness'. What kind of country had we become, after all, where old people could die alone behind their doors and lie rotting unnoticed for weeks? What kind of country had we become, where we were now encouraged as much to snitch on our neighbours as to care for them? Where the dole scrounger was a figure of inflated public menace, yet where tax evasion among the wealthy was almost considered good sport?

I wondered, could a Labour government make any difference? She said, 'In the short term, no. They've got to pick up so much, and I think they'd be unwise to commit themselves to doing wonderful things quickly, because they'd just let people down. But with a change of emphasis, I would hope they'd eventually do better, because there's such a lot to do. There's a lot of people struggling out there, and a lot of people closing doors on them.'

Against a background like this, for Honest John Major to talk about family values seems to me the most egregious hypocrisy. But then, in an election market mediated by soundbite news and the lumpen shorthand of the tabloids, was I being hopelessly idealistic to expect any better?

A few days later, Conservative plans to push large tracts of the social services' work into the private sector hit the news. Family values, in other words, did not mean that families were to be valued. They were, instead, to be value for money.

Here's a family for you: there're eight kids and four of them are deaf or, in the jargon, 'substantially hearing-impaired'. The previous house these ten people had been living in had three bedrooms, it was damp, and some of the windows were boarded up where one of the sons had put them in because he didn't want to go to school. To use the jargon again, his was a case of 'school refusal', his model being an older brother whose 'school refusal' got so severe that, to avoid it ending in court, his parents eventually packed him off back to Pakistan for a year. And this older lad might be up watching videos 'til four in the morning; of course he's got younger brothers sharing the room with him so, if they're going to school, when they get there they're half asleep. Not to mention hungry, too, on the days when they didn't get breakfast.

But this is actually a happy story. I found out about it on a visit to Holywell Green Junior and Infants' School, where a ten-year-old boy and two of his younger sisters from this family were being taught in a special unit for children with hearing disabilities. The visit involved Peter Kilfoyle, a rotund Scouser on the shadow education team who was getting coverage with McCafferty in the *Courier* and on Radio Leeds – but, as with all these shadow drop-ins, also learning a little more about the country they hoped soon to be running. It was no trite in-and-out; Kilfoyle was there for two hours, leaving half an hour later than scheduled, and by the end he had the place filed for future use as an example of good practice.

The school had doubled in size in seven years, and was oversubscribed. The special provision for kids with hearing problems had grown up simply because, seven years back, the school had a deaf child with whom they'd been successful, and other parents of similar children had heard about it. At the time, Calderdale's provision in this field had been poor – mostly, deaf kids were sent out of the borough to facilities elsewhere – but with pressure from vociferous and articulate parents provoking a positive response from the council, they'd now built a state-of-the-art, sound-treated unit where a dozen children got intensive teaching help.

Among them were the three children from the family I've mentioned. The boy, moving from one authority to another and back again, had previously been in school only sporadically and hadn't wanted to go at all – but since nine months back the teachers had been visiting him at home, winning him round, so he'd come to the unit and was now a regular attender. His story, and the way the unit worked generally, was described by the woman who ran it, a tall, smiling person with a lovely, gentle Northumbrian accent; while she talked, the boy and his sisters eagerly took to the attention from the visitors, chatting gamely and alertly with the aid of sign language and an interpreter.

Kilfoyle was impressively at ease, telling how he himself came from a giant family – he had four sisters, and a football team's worth of brothers – and when he played a counting game, he kidded at one point that he'd thrown a six when he'd not. His quick joke over that – 'I'm a politician' – may have been over the boy's head, but his manner with him never was. In these circumstances, it was easy to forget the purpose of the visit, and just to become absorbed in watching these clearly very happy children in a place that was helping them forward past significant difficulties. The woman who ran the unit said with warm pride of the boy that, whatever fear of school he might have had in the past, 'You look at him now. He's like a sponge, he soaks everything up.'

The unit's rules were on the wall: 'We work hard. We care for other people. We look after our things.' Some folk, however, don't look after things at all – and the previous spring some maniac vandal had driven a stolen Cavalier down a flight of steps outside the unit, through a metal gate, come to rest by the school's nursery, torched the car, and burnt the nursery to the ground in the process. The nursery had then been less than five years old.

Headmaster Ken Ingwood said, 'It was a tragic event, it upset everybody. But you have to find a silver lining, and we have. We've come out of it better.' Between the insurance payout, the council, Sir Donald pressing ministers for money from the School Renewal Fund, and the school's own efforts – on a project costing over £250,000, they'd raised £40,000 themselves – they'd succeeded in converting the school's old hall into a new nursery, with a new store in the roof space. On the day of our visit – less than a year after the arson – the contractors were officially due to sign off, and decorators were even then slapping on the final touches.

To achieve these things, said McCafferty, 'You have to scratch for every penny in the dirt.' But under the financial constraints, against all the obstacles, people do achieve these things. It doesn't make the news – the Ridings falling apart is news, a new nursery at Holywell Green is not – but it would be an imbalanced picture of this England that said only how everything is broken and battered. Kids with problems *do* get helped, new projects *do* go forward, and good people *do* go home every day from worthwhile work that may go unsung, but which most surely is not unimportant.

All the same, Ingwood still had thirty-five kids in his reception class, a figure he considered to be unacceptably high. So, with an election coming up where we could vote for a Labour Party claiming that education was the peak of its priorities, I asked Ingwood a question: when Labour said they'd cut class sizes, but said also that they'd not raise taxes, didn't that make him scratch his head? He said, with a kind of stern sadness, 'Put it this way. If we had proportional representation, I'd vote Liberal Democrat.'

Kilfoyle's visit picked up a decent report in the *Courier*, but nothing as prominent as another headline in that paper two weeks earlier, a front-page item that raised a rich laugh in the old bakery in Hebden Bridge: COUNCILLOR IN TERROR FLIGHT.

On McCafferty and Tarlo's charter back from Goa, three drunks caused such a ruck that the pilot eventually decided, for the safety of the flight, that he had to put down in Vienna. There followed an hour or more of milling mayhem in which the louts refused to identify their baggage, so the entire planeload of holidaymakers in their shorts and flipflops had to debark into the sub-zero Austrian night and sift through every case until the miscreants' luggage had been separated. They were left behind in a Viennese cell (to make their own way home and, hopefully, to face a large bill from the airline for their pains) while the rest of the passengers wearily reboarded.

Of course, a good politician is not going to let slip a lively story, and the *Courier* duly obliged with a front-page account of their ordeal – relegating Major's visit to the *Emmerdale* set to the inside pages, and prompting one Labour supporter happily to quip that to compete with it, Sir Donald would now have to hijack a plane. On the other hand, of course, the experience was no fun at all, and prompted McCafferty to say that after three weeks in Goa, where the Indians had been smiling and friendly and generally wonderful beyond measure, to meet people like this was a culture shock in reverse.

Welcome back to England – and any refreshment she'd gained from their Christmas R'n' R soon faded. As she went into January and the campaign picked up, she found herself waking up at night and her mind would set to churning, and then she'd not be able to sleep again. Mind you, with Calderdale Council to fret about, who'd sleep? They faced a damning management audit, a damning OFSTED report in the wake of the Ridings business, and the unceremonious dismissal of their chief executive to boot. The Tories, they knew, would be making hay with that lot.

Then there was just the fear, the fear, the fear. At a reception at the Grosvenor in Victoria towards the end of the month, the evening before the PPCs had briefings from Blair, Brown, Mandelson and Prescott, a party worker told me how the last week of the campaign in '92 had been calamitous, how they'd thrown it all away. There was a story, he said, perhaps apocryphal, of Major meeting Kinnock somewhere ahead of that election and, with the polls looking juicy, our boyo couldn't resist the verbal equivalent of a jovial dig in the ribs. He said, or words to this effect, that it wasn't looking good for Major's lot – to which Major said quietly that when it came to the wire, Labour would panic.

Mandelson, said McCafferty, was predicting a surprise election on March 6th. The press were fingering March 20th or April 10th – and fretful Tory MPs were reported to be urging Major to hold off into the year's second quarter, so they could claim another three months' worth of office allowances (about £11,000) before they lost their jobs. Or, said the press, Major might yet hang on to May 1st – but who knew? Politics, in part, is a gigantic gossip factory – but Mandelson was apparently claiming secret information. On the other hand, of course, what he had might just as well have been secret *mis*information.

Two horoscopes – in the *Independent on Sunday*, and in a publicans' trade rag on the bar of my local – both said I was likely to be extremely busy very soon. These were, I suspect, as reliable a guide as anything the press or the politicians said, because the bottom line was that only Major knew, and it was far from certain whether he knew either. It's a ridiculous way to run a country, isn't it? And it led McCafferty to say firmly that she favoured fixed terms, because we all knew the uncertainty did no one any good.

She was now waking up every morning asking herself whether today would be the day that the election would be called and, when it wasn't, going to bed every night wondering if it would kick off the next day – a nerve-racking way to live, I'd have thought, but she seemed to be handling it with a fair degree of equanimity. She said simply, 'I'm quite a laid back person, I don't easily get nervous. I just want to get on with it.'

It was the last week in January; she'd fielded the morning's mail, the faxes and phone calls, and was curled up comfy in an armchair in the living room. She was upbeat; in the wake of the latest muffed ploys from Major and Portillo about cadets and the royal yacht, she said, 'Every time they do something, they shoot themselves in the foot. Or higher and higher up the leg. I'm just hopeful that each shot's more painful, and that they'll end up completely incapacitated.' This was, remember, a government now so hopelessly addled that it could lose a vote by mistake – an education vote, for goodness' sake – because *they couldn't count* . . .

She couldn't believe the things that were happening; she'd ask herself, were they actually *trying* to blow it, so they could have it out with each other in the aftermath? She knew the royal yacht would be a loser the minute she heard it. In Calderdale they'd been waiting for a new hospital for years, and now they'd been told it had to be financed through a PFI (with private money) – when that hospital would cost less of the taxpayers' money by far than Portillo was prepared to dish out so the Queen could have a new boat. It was crazy – and indeed, 'a royal yacht' instantly became a new unit of currency. When someone on the *Today* programme said that eye tests for half a million old people too poor to go and get them – thereby risking blindness – would cost £30,000,000, the interviewer said immediately, 'Half a royal yacht then.'

And yet, and yet . . . McCafferty said, 'There's still that sneaking feeling, always. What if they find something that works for them?' Tax, of course, was the big one – so Brown's announcement that he'd stick to Clarke's spending plans, and that income tax rates would stay unchanged for five years, was widely seen as a potentially decisive vote-winner. For anyone who knew the economic realities, and who wanted money for our schools, our hospitals, our huddled masses, it was also profoundly depressing; McCafferty said that when she first heard the news, she was despondent.

At the PPC's briefing in London, however, she thought Brown was the best of the lot. She said, 'I was very impressed with how he explained himself – and he was explaining himself, because there were a lot of people there with question marks. So perhaps I do want him to be bolder, but I do see that he cares about what I care about, and that he's trying to deal with it. And,' she shrugged, 'he wants to get elected. We all want to get elected.'

So she was much happier now. She said, 'He did talk at length about where he saw money coming from. But he's not prepared to talk about those things publicly, because they're terrified of being nobbled.' The trouble with this, however, was that outside the closed doors of the Grosvenor, it meant Labour was going into the campaign unable even to say to its own people, Psst, it's all right, we're going to get the money. And wasn't that a sorry indictment of the state of us, that they had to behave in that way? She said, 'Absolutely.'

Was she not, then, going to spend the whole campaign biting her tongue? She laughed, 'Ask me afterwards. But yes, I suspect it'll be like that.'

The pressure was on. She said, 'At the end of the day, the responsibility is mine. I feel personally responsible for the outcome of the election in a key marginal. The balance of the government could rest with a place like this, and I'm very conscious of that.'

When I asked how she'd feel if Labour won, but she herself lost, she said, 'I've considered that. Of course I'll feel very, very bad – but not for myself. I know I'll have given my best – but on a personal level I've many other things in my life, things I've not done that I'd like to do, so not being an MP wouldn't be the end of my existence. But on a wider level, I'd still be distraught, because all the people in this constituency who want a change of government have their money on me. It'll not be as distressful to them if there's a Labour government anyway – but they've been hoping to have a more active MP, and the members of the council have been hoping to have a Labour MP they could work with. All that would be lost. So even if we win the country, if we lose here . . . it'd be bitter.'

There were three areas where she felt she might be vulnerable. Firstly, the Tories would go after the council. The council, she stressed, was not badly run; previous management audits had been good and, paradoxically, the government had just decreed that the council had been so successful at selling off assets that it wouldn't be allowed to borrow any more money. But after the Ridings crisis, it would certainly be portrayed as badly run; Calderdale might find itself held up as evidence for a Tory case that education (like everything else) should be taken away from local government. It was an issue she'd discussed with Blunkett and Prescott, and one of which Labour was keenly aware.

Secondly, there was abortion. In 1992, Alice Mahon had been subjected to horrendous barracking by the pro-life people; now the issue was higher up the agenda, and as a woman (who'd worked many years at a women's health centre) McCafferty expected to be put through the same. With a sigh, she described the pro-life groups as, 'A kind of diabolical alliance.'

Thirdly, there was fox-hunting. It just shows how bonkers our electoral system is that a pivotal constituency might swing on whether a few people should be free to chase and kill small animals, but it was certainly a factor. The British Field Sports Society – a loose umbrella group comprising not only hunters but anglers and all sorts – had around 1,500 members in the Calder Valley, of whom maybe 200 might be inclined to vote Labour. Among these people, the hunting lobby was mounting a noisy anti-Labour campaign, and the flavour of some of it wasn't too pleasant.

Example: to avert the threat of 'ever more loonie animal legislation', the editorial of a Dyfed-based magazine called *Earth Dog – Running Dog* point-blank urged its readers to vote Conservative. It went on to concede that, sure, the Tories were all over the place, but under Labour, 'Things will be WORSE!!'

'Morality. At least the Tories, on the whole, conduct their affairs with members of the opposite sex and that's something to be grateful for in this day and age. Its an age-old tendency and it overwhelms red-blooded men of all parties. Europe. Labour will have us licking the boots of Germany and France quicker than you can say "Mais Oui" . . .'

There's plenty more in this vein, and you can fear the bloke's raving but the electoral maths mean you can't dismiss it. If one hundred votes swung to the right because they thought socialist nutters were going to come and put down their dogs, that might just mean Sir Donald kept his job. Equally, however, one hundred votes for Tony Mellor, a former Tory councillor for Ryburn now standing for the Referendum Party, might mean that he lost it. Or he might lose it because he'd supported the government over nursery vouchers. Or BSE might rear its wobbling scary head – Sir Donald had been a junior agriculture minister in the 1980s – or any other issue might come along to blow it one way or the other.

The only thing you could be sure of was that whichever way it swung, you wouldn't get much sense of it in the papers. How different in tone, after all, are the *Star* or the *Sun* from *Earth Dog – Running Dog*?

11

WIRRAL SOUTH

Up the M53, past the chemical plants and oil refineries of Ellesmere Port, the pocket of farmland to the west of Junction 4 was hard-core Tory territory. Here, in Wirral South – Conservative majority 8,183 – a by-election was to be held on the brink of the main event. I drove down a weaving country road, past the substantial red brick houses of Brimstage, to the pleasantly nondescript little town of Heswall; I had coffee in a woody little tea-shop among old ladies with blue rinses and too much make-up. The food was stodgy, and the pace of the service glacial.

If the Tories couldn't hold this, what could they hold? Yet their strategy – or lack of it – had Labour activists as baffled as they were gleeful. Why had they not got it out of the way earlier, so that if they lost it the memory of the loss had that much longer to fade? Why had Heseltine all but conceded they'd lose it, saying he expected the voters of Wirral South to give the government a good kicking? What were they doing?

In the Tory party's office on the main street in Heswall, they weren't doing anything much. There was only one person there: a suave, pleasant fellow with silver hair, a heavy Silk Cut Ultra habit, and one of those very Tory shirts with blue and white stripes and a white collar. True, he was being visited when I arrived by an unshaven, shambolic youth who seemed several votes short of a quorum – but otherwise he was just sitting there.

Blair had been through earlier that day, and a weird tableau took shape in my mind. Here in the Tory heartland, the Labour leader had glad-handed his way down the street with the media swarm in tow, hacks and snappers and even the odd voter clustered about him, while this solitary gent sat watching the triumphal invasion though blank glass windows, wreathed in smoky isolation. The lack of activity spoke of supine surrender; it was almost sad – well, you can imagine my heart bleeding, can't you?

His name was Peter Robinson, and he was a professional agent. Having lived in the Wirral in the past, he knew the place – but could they find no one local to man that office? While we talked, two old gents wandered in and sat down, and one of them idly asked, 'Where's the tea?' Between them they did their best to talk a good fight, but the place seemed flat with indolent resignation. Conceding that they might well lose the by-election (because by-elections are just like that) they affirmed that they'd win the seat back in the general – because, said one of the old gents, 'When you're choosing a government you take a more considered view. You choose the lesser of the available evils.' Which is hardly a ringing endorsement, is it?

Round the corner, two blokes in the Labour office were busy stuffing leaflets into envelopes and bundling them up, while others came and went to fetch them for delivery. In Labour's HQ a few miles away in New Ferry, the contrast was even more marked. The place was heaving with activity, humming with phones, spilling over with leaflets and posters and sweatshirts. I spoke with Martin Liptrot, the party's communications manager for the North-West, and he said, 'It must be very difficult to be a Tory organiser at the minute. It's like Bush in '92 – there's no plan, no vision, no message to rally the workers. No one *believes*.'

We talked in a trim, TV-friendly press centre, a flat grey room with a prominent slogan behind the speaker's desk. Liptrot was the very model of a modern message merchant – young, fluent, clean-cut in a smart blue shirt, a living embodiment of that very Eighties adjective, 'thrusting' – and he rejected the idea of Major calling a surprise election on March 6th. He said, 'Be John Major for ten minutes. For one minute, even, it doesn't take that long. You're getting rejected in a constituency you'd normally consider your own, at a maximum of two and a half months from a general election – and when the picture in the nation is no better, are you going to run away from the Wirral to the nation? No. To lose here will be damaging to morale, but a lot less damaging than losing the country. So he'll go as long as possible. They're waiting for the thunderflash, some bolt of lightning from the sky, and it isn't coming. They have no strategy. They have nothing.'

Whereas Labour were so together he was virtually glowing on it – and when I ventured the suggestion that to get this way they'd become so bland, so middle ground, that they might actually put their own people off, he wouldn't have it for a minute. 'The majority of Labour voters,' he said, 'are overjoyed at what we're doing, because we're *credible*. In the past we spoke about dogma, ideology, altruism, third world aid' (he didn't curl his lip here, but he might as well have done) 'and we expected people to vote Labour just because it was the right thing to do. But now we're addressing the aspirant values that ordinary people have – as Thatcher did.'

To be fair, he did add the proviso that he thought her policies were all wrong – but it was the plainest statement I'd heard yet of where New Labour was coming from. Back in Heswall, in the exhausted stillness of that barren Tory office, Robinson and the old boys had spoken of the opposition regularly, unthinkingly, with a kind of reflex historical tic, as 'socialists'. But if Martin Liptrot, in his media-modern campaign base, was any kind of socialist, then I'm the King of Buganda.

In a metaphor entirely appropriate to the language in which this election was being conducted, Liptrot said winning Wirral South would not be easy. He said, 'It's like a cup-tie. It's not a league game, this – February 27th is our cup-tie. It's all about how it goes on the day.' After which, presumably, given a campaign of two halves, the boys would be over the moon. They'd have done good, held their shape, worked hard as a unit, got the result, and be taking it one seat at a time.

On my way home, I stopped for a cup of tea with some students I know in Liverpool. When I told them what I'd been doing, one of them said bluntly, 'Politics is boring.'

David Tarlo said if it were up to him, he'd not mind doing away with the word Labour altogether. It carried, he suggested, too many old-time implications of confrontation, it was too redolent of a class ethos; he'd have happily settled for a new name altogether, something more objectively descriptive. Social Democrat, basically.

It's hard to see that happening, of course – at least, not without explosions of bulb-eyed rage among traditionalists all round the country. But whatever Labour was now – New, User-Friendly, Social Democrat or Smoked Salmon – politics in Wirral South on February 27th was, for any person of a Labour inclination, not boring at all.

In Heswall, their little office was jumping. The papers were giving Labour a majority of 2–3,000; one man there said he reckoned they'd do better than that. He had, he said, been trying to get a bet on for a Labour win, but he couldn't find a bookie anywhere who'd take his money. Tory lethargy, by contrast, had them both mystified and elated. OK, they said, the Tories have more money, they can do more work in the post and on the phone – but on the ground, where were they? 'In Heswall alone last Sunday,' said one guy, 'we had forty-two people out working – and their office was shut.' Another bloke, I'd guess younger than twenty, said he'd been out leafleting since six-thirty that morning, and he'd hardly seen a Tory all day.

Down the road, three well-turned-out women of a certain age set out from Peter Robinson's office, sporting brave smiles and blue rosettes. When they were gone, he was alone again; two phones were going and by the time he'd answered one, the other caller had rung off. He said, 'Isn't that just the bloody way?'

In Bromborough, the Tory HQ was as listlessly invisible as their campaign, marooned in a cul-de-sac at the far end of a nondescript business park. They had two units of pale tan brick box, windowless and drab; unlike Labour's High Street base, which was open plan and very visibly bustling, anything the Tories were up to was hidden behind grey partitioning. From the quietness of the place, it didn't seem they were up to much.

Tim Collins, a rising young campaign guru who'd been sent to the Wirral to stick his finger in the dyke, came out to talk to me – to spin, as they say. With only two exceptions, he said, since 1979 every single seat the Tories had lost in by-elections had been won back at the next general election. As for the opinion polls, 'They have about as much predictive value as a ouija board. Labour have been forty per cent ahead, and that's ridiculous. Now that's not to say we're covered in roses every time we cross the street – but if there's a late swing, any poll beforehand is useless. And then, there's the so-called "spiral of silence", where people don't admit they'll be voting Tory. Now if you believe in that, it can only have increased, because if we were unfashionable in '92, we must be even more so now. So the real gap is much, much closer.'

It's an interesting phenomenon, this one – the 'shy Tories', the people who don't tell pollsters they'll be voting blue – and it says worlds about the state of us. Imagine, a whole swathe of the electorate feeling, *knowing in their hearts* that there's something sufficiently shameful about what they mean to do that they won't own up to it. It puts voting Tory in the same category as wanking, doesn't it?

Struggling to dispel this choice notion, I asked Collins if the situation wasn't demoralising. Well, he said, they'd been here before, and four times they'd gone on to win. 'That's concrete, indisputable, historical precedent. It's not spin; it's cast-iron fact. So they've got a big uphill battle to fight. They've got to achieve the biggest swing since 1945, and they've got to defeat the incumbent against a good economic background, and that's never been done.'

It was brave talk, but it was only talk – and down the road in New Ferry, Labour's people were too busy winning the election to talk to me at all. Full of beans, spick and span and entirely Clintonesque in their campaign baseball caps, they were working the phones, spilling in and out of the door – people from all across the country come by the busload to turn out the vote. Martin Liptrot's cup-tie, it seemed, was going to be a walkover.

Another sign: all round the constituency, any place where people lived was comprehensively bedecked with Labour posters. Tory posters, by contrast, adorned not buildings or gardens but fields. So if cows voted, the Tories would have been a shoo-in – but cows are mad, right?

The Tories duly lost – not by 2,000 or 3,000 as the papers had predicted, but by 7,888. It was a seventeen-per-cent swing, a wipeout; the Tory vote had imploded. Even if you allowed for the inevitable swing back to the Tories come the main event, any way you looked at these numbers, Blair was heading to win by a landslide.

Ben Chapman, Labour's victorious candidate, gave his acceptance speech quietly, looking flat-out exhausted. The effect was spoilt somewhat by the swaying, gap-toothed presence at his shoulder of a sweaty, gurning individual called Colin Palmer, who'd placed himself before the people of Wirral South as a representative of the twenty-first century – obviously, a man ahead of his time – and he'd duly been rewarded with the votes of forty-four deluded souls. But that, of course, is the great thing about democracy; any old fruit-cake can join in.

February had been a flat, fraught month. Waiting to see whether Major might spring a surprise and go early had been painfully tense – and then, as the days went past and a March poll was written off, the numbing fact set in that there were two more months still to go. 'Keeping us on edge like this,' said Tarlo, 'it's all they've got. And it isn't very nice.' So the result from the Wirral blew into the old bakery in the small hours like an invigorating gust of spring breeze. 'I just squealed with delight,' said McCafferty, 'it was *exquisite.*'

They turned to their campaign massively uplifted – and they needed to be, because things were far from perfect. In theory, Labour HQ had wanted every constituency 80 per cent canvassed by October; in practice, at the end of February some of these West Yorkshire seats had managed only a shade over half that. The problem (as Tim Swift had predicted) was that too many Labour bodies on the ground still tended to think they weren't needed until the campaign was actually called; they thought you went out and did it then. Still, at least McCafferty could reassure herself that they were well ahead of where they'd been five years ago; when the campaign began in 1992, less than 20 per cent of Calder Valley had been canvassed.

Getting further prepared, they'd also spent February moving into the constituency's campaign base in Brighouse. Bang in the middle of town, they'd got three storeys of an old Job Centre that had been empty for three years; three wide slices of airy office with big windows all round the building which, especially on the top floor, amounted to many thousands of pounds' worth of highly visible advertising space. They signed the lease on 'the premises known as Wellington House', moved in and hoovered, got the heating up and running to waft out the cold and damp, put phone lines in and started toting in tables and filing cabinets, faxes and photocopiers.

On the afternoon after Labour took the Wirral, walking about her embryonic headquarters, McCafferty was plainly thrilled and eager to get to it.

She was in the process of sending out 6,500 letters, one to every council tenant in the constituency; the government wanted Calderdale to sell off its remaining housing stock, so she wanted the tenants to tell her what they thought about that. Replies were flooding back, twenty or more every day – way above the response you'd normally expect from a mailing like this – and by a massive margin they were hostile to the government's proposal. What follows is one of the replies, which I reproduce as written:

> Dear Sir
>
> Thank you for giving us the opportunity to have a chance to register our disgust at the suggestion you outlined by the Tories, this band of bastards (John Major's own words) not mine, have had it their way to long, and the day of reckoning is now in site – Please state in your election run up the need for a Labour Gov. to provide a fixed % of Lottery money for the N.H.S. and you are on a winner odds on thats all people are wishing, Radical policy's and a Labour Gov dedicated to looking after their people as the Tories have done so effortlessly with theirs,
>
> May I on behalf of myself and family wish you the very best of Luck in your battle for M.P. and if gut feeling is anything to go by then you are there

That would gee you up, wouldn't it? But that Friday afternoon, while McCafferty smiled and Tarlo took a bottle of Windolene to the ground-floor windows and started putting up posters, and Ian Carvell arrived in a battered old van with more tables, Ann Martin in Bradford was getting ominous faxes. This building had been empty all this time – but even as Labour were moving in, out of the blue a firm of rugby league publishers now turned up and said the top two floors were theirs. Of course, you'd think if you signed for 'the premises', then the premises is what you get – but think again.

Martin got lawyers in, but to no avail. Labour ended up with the ground floor only – and after eighteen years of bewildered, often disorderly opposition, it wasn't hard to find Labour folk inclined to the wilder reaches of paranoia. Much glum muttering now ensued about dark Masonic plots, but it was just an estate agent's cock-up. Labour got £500 compensation for their relocation (which, as 'relocation' mostly involved Tarlo and a few others carrying their stuff downstairs, was very welcome) while the rugby league boys turned out to be very friendly. Besides, the ground floor was plenty big enough – and the way some of them were talking now, you got the impression they thought they'd win if they had to fight the campaign from a bin in a back alley.

That same weekend, Alice Mahon's campaign co-ordinator was knocked off his bike and hospitalised. Again, there was an initial seething of murky suspicion; again, it soon faded. It was a nasty accident and a great inconvenience, but the Tories weren't *that* bad. Indeed, the Tories by now were so out to lunch that if they did try to knock someone down, they'd miss, hit a lamp-post and hospitalise themselves; they didn't seem in a condition to run a cake stall, never mind the country. On the one hand they promised stability; on the other they said they'd privatise the tube, the social services and your pension. They bickered in bilious confusion about the single currency, the Scottish parliament, and scary bugs in your meat; Tebbit laid into Heseltine, everyone laid into Douglas Hogg, and George Gardiner joined the Referendum Party. Then David Evans (presumably remembering that there was an opposition involved here too) called his Labour opponent's children 'bastards', prompting this memorable headline in the *Mirror*: TORY MP GOES MAD.

In West Yorkshire, meanwhile, a telephone canvasser reported back from London that 'Brighouse has gone red.' As the office got up and running, 'switchers' – Tory voters moving over to Labour – came in voluntarily off the street to announce their conversion. In the *Telegraph* on March 7th, a post-Wirral Gallup Poll gave Labour a 26 point lead. There was a sort of tentative euphoria about Labour now – but McCafferty didn't think it was in the bag for a minute. Nor did Edward Riley, the editor of the *Courier*. He said, 'I don't think there'll be any change. It'll be Alice Mahon for Halifax, and Donald Thompson in the Calder Valley.'

12

LIBERAL WITH HIS OPINIONS

About this time, our nursery vouchers dropped through the door. In Kirklees, where my daughter was at an excellent state nursery, this scheme involved taking over £5,000,000 from the council, which they were supposed to recoup by returning the vouchers to central government – a payback they'd never fully receive, because even if every parent involved managed not to lose their vouchers (fat chance) there were now fewer eligible children in the council's area than there'd been in the year used by the government as a template for the scheme's budget in the first place.

One way or another, Kirklees reckoned they'd come out half a million short on primary education. Council after council would lose in this way – especially those with good nursery provision – and that's not counting the costs involved nationwide in the blizzard of paper these vouchers generated. As for the idea that it gave you more choice, this was dream-world. Where else would my daughter go, other than the nursery she was already at? How was our choice enhanced because we now took her there clutching a fistful of coupons? Quite possibly, given the threat to both state and private nurseries as fund-hungry schools hoovered four-year olds into their (often inappropriate) reception classes, we'd find we had less choice, not more.

Either the perpetrators of this folly were alarmingly stupid, or it was the next stage of a conscious agenda. While so much else had been taken from local government, education remained the largest service it provided; it absorbed, in Calderdale, just over half the entire £162,000,000 budget the council had just passed, and was way bigger than anything else they did; over six times bigger, for example, than the highways department. So were the Tories planning to screw up nursery education and blame the mess on the councils, then take that away from them too?

Another attack on this front was aimed specifically at Calderdale, whose education department – in the wake of the Ridings implosion – was now the focus of a report from OFSTED. That Gillian Shephard was playing electoral politics with the council's children was, however, painfully obvious. The report wasn't supposed to be published until June, and the inspectors had promised the council they'd have sight of a draft before it was; that promise wasn't kept, and instead the report was rushed out in early March, heralded by a thoroughly misleading press release from Shephard's department. This claimed that Calderdale was failing its schools – which wasn't what the report said, and which wasn't true. The government's own league tables showed that Calderdale had the highest number of GCSE A–C grades in West Yorkshire – while the report, though critical in some respects, made clear that in many others the council was doing a reasonable job, with standards of achievement generally close to national norms.

Caught on the hop when the Ridings went pear-shaped, the council handled the media rather better this time. At the *Courier*, news editor John Kenneally doubted whether local people would swallow Shephard's assault; they knew their schools were all right, because their children went to them. Even at the Ridings, it wasn't as if children were being stabbed in the street, and the whole business had been inflated out of all proportion; the rat-pack from London had stayed longer than for any local story since the Ripper, which – when schools were in trouble all round the country – hardly demonstrated a sense of perspective. But, shrugged Kenneally, well aware of what Shephard was up to, 'When she holds a press conference about it, that's a story, isn't it?'

In short, Calderdale was being held up to the nation as a Labour horror show – by a Secretary of State for Education plainly unconcerned about the effect of her damaging and inaccurate hyperbole on the children, parents, teachers and local councillors involved. But anyone who could introduce something as barking mad as nursery vouchers was obviously dogma-crazed anyway, weren't they?

On the Monday morning when Shephard let loose her

statement, Pam Warhurst's office was in constant touch with David Blunkett's team. The message came back not to lay into OFSTED and the inspectors, to come over reasonable and co-operative and – said Warhurst's PA with a wry little grin – 'These days, what Blunkett says, you do.'

While the press hovered, and the phones and faxes hummed between the town hall and Westminster, I talked with Helen Rivron, the council's deputy chair of education. Saddened and annoyed, she said, 'I don't suppose we expected them to play by the rules. But it's certainly not in the interests of children in Calderdale.' She readily conceded that, like any other LEA, they had their problems – one of which, she said pointedly, had been the preoccupation of supporting their schools through the introduction of nursery vouchers. As for co-operating with the OFSTED team that Shephard now meant to send in, sure, they'd do it. Hopefully, she said, by the time they reported back Gillian Shephard would be out of office.

There'd been times, said John Foran, when he and his colleagues would sit in the dusty splendour of Halifax Town Hall, they'd look at what the government was doing and they'd throw up their hands in despair.

Foran was the one remaining Conservative councillor for Hipperholme and Lightcliffe. The oldest part of Calderdale, this was the comfortable, mostly well-heeled ward where Sir Donald Thompson lived – and where Foran was chair of the local party – but they'd lost their other two local seats to Labour in the past two years. It was, said Foran, simply a reflection of what had been happening round the country, and he reacted to it with the loyalist's mantra – that the government 'weren't getting their message across'.

But now Shephard was on the electoral warpath, laying into Calderdale, and the plain fact was that he couldn't agree with her. As Sir Donald had said in the autumn, so Foran said now: 'We have very good schools here, extremely good schools. But,' he sighed, 'government ministers, and MPs of any party, are going to make political capital where they can. So you're going to get this, aren't you?'

We were talking in one of the town hall's meeting rooms. Fine old high-backed chairs stood round a distinctive, leather-inlaid table in the shape of a rugby ball; odd little ashtrays, globular glass bottles like inkwells, were set into the table before each chair. Like the town hall altogether, there was something mustily grand about it; it was a place still engraved with the details of a more confident time, when there was something more to civic purpose than just contracting everything out.

In their reduced circumstances, nonetheless, the fact is that the majority of local politicians still try to do their best. When the Ridings had blown up, said Foran very emphatically, 'Politicians on this council – of all parties – tried hard to ensure that it was kept in perspective. We didn't attack each other over it, and we attempted to look after the best interests of the children. The press were on everybody's phone – they've been on mine suggesting the most awful personal things about my opponents, things that were totally untrue, horrid stuff – and the only comment they got from me was a swift goodbye. So we could have played politics over this, but none of us have. We've tried to help each other.'

Yet now Shephard had weighed in with her charge that Calderdale was failing. He said he couldn't agree with it, and he smiled. 'There,' he said. 'You've got what you want, haven't you?'

Foran was fifty-four years old, and had lived in Hipperholme virtually all his life. Like his MP – whom he greatly admired – he was a short, genial man for whom membership of the Conservative Party was simply an article of faith. He'd been seven years at sea as an engineering officer with the Cunard Line, then a director of a local plant hire and construction firm; he'd won his seat on the council in 1990, and he professed 'a basic belief in choice and freedom, in allowing people to make their own decisions'.

But he was a most moderate Conservative. He said, 'The Conservative ethos has always been a caring ethos. There's been a view from some extremes of my party that everybody should go out and help themselves. Well, everybody should do their best, but not everybody's capable of helping themselves. People aren't deliberately needy; it's a fact of life that some people are always going to need an umbrella to cover them.'

Now it happens that some on the left find it impossible to understand how you can be a Conservative and still be a nice person – but there are enough decent souls like John Foran to prove it can be done. You might say that in logical terms it's hard to reconcile the views just expressed with the mean-minded intolerance so often vividly put forward down the past eighteen years of his party in government; you might even unkindly say that for a nice person to be Conservative rather suggests that such a person can't be very bright.

That, however, would be to ignore people's history, their old affiliations of class and family – and in the case of businessmen like John Foran, to ignore also a deep-seated and powerfully felt fear of 'socialism' as they experienced it in the trade unions of the Sixties and Seventies. So never mind that, in 1997, this fear might be wildly misplaced. The fact remained that, however much he might despair of vacillating leadership, turbulent Eurosceptics, or Gillian Shephard politicking with his local schools, his fear was real nonetheless – which meant that continued Conservative rule, however cackhanded, was for John Foran an infinitely preferable alternative to a Labour victory.

He would not for one minute have portrayed Chris McCafferty as a looming red-eyed threat. He said, 'Councillor McCafferty is a very nice person – but with the greatest respect, compared to Sir Donald Thompson, she's a little bit lightweight. And I do believe that behind these nice New Labour candidates like her, behind the media veneer, the left wing of the Labour Party are still there, and they'll be out of the woodwork very rapidly. I could give you quotes from some of their members here about how the first to go will be that Blair, and that Mandelson with him. So if they win, there'll be a honeymoon – but it'll be a very short one.'

And, he said, they might well win. A lot of people, he knew, did feel it was time for a change; he said people felt with the Tories the same mounting tetchiness they felt about Manchester United always winning things. But, he stressed, if Labour might win the country, they'd still not win Calder Valley. In his job he got around, he met people, and he didn't detect this deep shift the papers were all on about. Whether Labour won or not, he said, if McCafferty ousted Thompson, 'I'd be very, very shocked.'

Stephen Pearson, the Liberal Democrat candidate, also believed that Sir Donald would, as he put it, 'crawl back in'. Thompson was, he said, 'Much smarter than people give him credit for. He's a very canny operator, with very sensitive political antennae.'

Just a few minutes later, Pearson told me that Sir Donald was 'over the top and coming backwards in a big way'. Now I don't quite see how those two statements square up; but Stephen Pearson, it was rapidly transpiring, wasn't a candidate who put any normal rein of political caution (or indeed, of simple modesty) on what ran out of his mouth.

He was forty-one, a short, chubby little bloke who ran the engraving and engineering firm started by his father and his uncle in the 1950s. He'd studied engineering in Bradford, European law and politics in Edinburgh, and after a short stint in Brussels and Strasbourg he'd gone to the City. In 1986 he'd been bought out of a commodity broker's, he'd come home with a stash, and he'd gone to work in the family business. Meanwhile, since university, he'd always been a Liberal; he'd got on the council in 1990, and he evidently believed he was rather good at it.

We met in his office on the road from Huddersfield into Halifax; he took me through a plain little foyer – the walls showing samples of signs and doorplates in steel, plastic, brass, aluminium and traffolite – to a bare, scratty room with cheap furniture and a generally colourless air. But if the surroundings were as unpromising as his electoral prospects, this was not a man afflicted (not on the surface, anyway) with the remotest hint of self-doubt.

'I believe,' he said, 'I am clearly the best candidate in this election. I've thought that for a number of months. I've come to that assessment objectively, based on what I believe to be the criteria you need to do the job. You have to be mentally tough, intellectually rigorous, you have to be capable, you have to have a very clear perspective on what you want to do, how you see your role as a representative of the people, and what your abilities are. And on all those bases, I think I'm the best candidate. Most other people probably think that as well. Most people of an independent mind, if they assess Donald Thompson and Chris McCafferty, would recognise that I was head and shoulders above both of them.'

Are you smiling by now? I can tell you, I was. I was having to put my hand over my mouth here. I mean, I'd have thought that among the criteria you need to do the job, being likeable, being

nice, having some restraint in what you say about other people –
that might have figured somewhere too. But, well, maybe not.

I put it to him that he was going to lose, and he agreed that he
almost certainly would. So I asked him, why bother? Since he
thought a Labour government was more desirable than continued
Tory rule, why not get out of the road and let the Labour candidate
in?

'The answer,' he said, 'is because the Labour candidate is
absolutely useless. She is worse than useless. Been on the council
nearly six years and she's made zero impact there, and what do you
want from your MP? You want somebody on the back bench?
Because she will certainly be on the back benches for ever.'

I sat wondering what McCafferty had ever done to this bloke –
and there was more. 'Look,' he said – this of a woman nine years his
senior – 'Chris is a very, very nice girl. A very, very nice girl. But
you could go out and pick any nurse out of the nurses' quarters
tomorrow and put her in as a candidate and she'd know as much
about it. She has no idea what she wants to do. You might just as
well put a donkey in.'

That week, the donkey had been getting herself once more into
the local papers, accepting a petition from a coalition of Green and
disabled activists protesting the withdrawal of concessionary fares by
the local bus company, and promising to get it taken up at council.
Pearson, on the other hand (for all that he was the best candidate)
hadn't talked to formally the *Courier* for over a year. He said they'd
called him a liar; but turning thin-skinned umbrage with the local
press into a drawn-out grudge is not, I would venture, the mark of
a winning politician.

It was his second time standing. The first time, in 1992, the
Liberal vote had fallen from 13,761 to 9,842 – and if what people
(including other Liberals) had to say about him round the valley was
any guide, this time it would drop further yet. But then, it's hell
being a Liberal. As Pearson said, 'You work your balls off night after
night for people who you know will probably, in the main, rat on
you in the general election.'

Voters, eh? Rats . . . and it's time, I think, to pass on from this
edifying fellow. But before we do, let's put him in perspective.
Somewhere along the way, he told me that (among people of an
independent mind) John Foran was one who'd say, privately, that

Stephen Pearson was the best candidate. So, struggling to restrain my merriment as I transcribed the tape, I immediately – privately – rang Foran. When the gales of laughter on the other end of the line had subsided, Foran said, 'How's that for arrogance? That's hilarious. But look, compared to Sir Donald, he's a boy among men. Not in the same league. If you were talking football teams, Donald to Stephen, you're going from the Premier League to the Third Division. He will,' Foran concluded, with rich satisfaction, 'be a poor third.'

Coincidentally, that same Friday afternoon of March 13th, Labour held a seminar in Brighouse on how to cope with the Liberals. Though called at short notice, some fifty key people turned up from seats all through the central Pennine belt – from Oldham and Rochdale, Shipley and Keighley – to hear presentations from John Prescott, Frank Dobson, the Sheffield MP Helen Jackson, and a pair of strategy merchants from Walworth Road.

The office, now fully equipped, was laid out ready, with rows of seats before a table with water and a red rose on it. Prescott arrived in a sleek grey Omega – these people looking ministerial in their suits and saloons already – and the local party workers had the boost of their deputy leader cutting a red ribbon across the door to open the premises formally. A poster in a window by the entrance said, '7 weeks to get rid of the Tories'.

Inside, Alex Powell and another young woman made drinks. 'Not stereotyping here or anything,' smiled Alex, 'but would you like coffee? Tea?'

Helen Jackson started the meeting. 'The Liberals are about in these Pennine seats,' she said, 'and they're good. They get into every little organisation, concentrating on a tree here, a footpath there – they winkle away. But they also have significant weaknesses. They're split all ends up, there's nothing coherent; they've a policy for every street, a policy for every day of the week. So you *can* get at them.'

In what followed, the bile these people felt for the Liberals was patent. They were a runt of a party that said one thing and did another, they were expedient, nebulous, ungraspable, and they never took responsibility. When they got on councils that they didn't control they were, said one speaker, 'Very good at knocking the council, while somehow never letting on that they're actually on it.'

The Liberals wanted compulsory water meters – but when McCafferty had pointed that out in the paper, one Liberal had rung her and said, Look, I respect you, but you shouldn't tell lies. Well, McCafferty told her, I wasn't lying. It's your policy. Didn't you know that?

With United Utilities and Yorkshire Water on either side of the watershed, said Dobson, 'If you can't make capital out of that, you might as well not bother canvassing. So you make clear that we are against compulsory water metering from those thieving bloody rat-bags.'

As to the Liberals' penny on income tax for education, 'They spend it 8,000 times, don't they? Every bit of bother locally, a hospital, the roads, out comes their penny. So get after that. If I may use an inelegant expression, just take the piss out of them.'

Each time that I saw Dobson, I was coming to be more and more impressed with this stout and hale little man – and now he gave an impassioned, impromptu speech. 'When the Liberals say we're the same as the Tories, I'm sorry, but we're not. They say we're pandering to the haute bourgeoisie in Tunbridge Wells – but their kids have nursery places already. Their young children aren't in classes of thirty-five or forty. There aren't many old Etonians aged eighteen to twenty-five who are unemployed. Or the money we'd release from the sale of council houses to build more housing – it'd not be the haute bourgeoisie who'd get that new housing. They've *got* houses. And it'd not be the haute bourgeoisie who'd get jobs building those houses, or in the builders' merchants supplying the materials. So you go out and say, we will do things for our people, for the people who need help. We are,' he said, 'too apologetic sometimes.'

But there were, of course, political niceties here nonetheless. When one speaker said they could use Mandelson Towers giving them a quote from Blair knocking the Liberals, Prescott said, 'If Tony's asked to be hostile to the Liberals, well, we might end up with a majority of one. And we've got to live with these people; it's the same with the Northern Ireland people, he's got to play a careful hand. But,' he smiled, 'if you want an aggro quote, get onto my office.'

Prescott, like all of them, was buzzing, full of energy and promise. On one of his visits to the Wirral, he said, he'd been on Liverpool Lime Street and a Scouse lad came up to him. This lad says, 'Hey. Our John. You've got to win this time. 'Cause I've never had sex under Labour.'

13

I FEEL QUEASY

In May 1979 the *Times* was on strike, and everybody else who wasn't either just had been, or was just about to be. A craftsman in the state sector made a basic weekly wage of £56.35, and the state sector was huge; over half the adult population depended on government as their employer, their customer or their subsidiser.

It was a different world entirely. Somoza was still in power in Nicaragua; in Uganda, the Tanzanians had just ousted Idi Amin. Three Mile Island was a flooded, fizzing heap; if you were crazy, you could fly across the Atlantic to check it out for £157 return. When you got there, your pound would buy you $2.05; in West Germany, you'd get Dm 3.86. Further east, the Soviet Union was deploying SS22s, preparing to sign Salt 2, and freeing Jewish dissidents so we'd not boycott the Moscow Olympics.

Liverpool were winning the league, Wimbledon were promoted from the Fourth Division, and Art Garfunkel was at No.1 with 'Bright Eyes'. The charts featured Supertramp, Wings, Boney M, the Sex Pistols, the Jam, and the Police with 'Roxanne'; Jimmy Savile was doing *Top of the Pops*, and Leo Sayer – dread thought – had a six-show series on ITV. At the cinema you could see *The Deer Hunter*, or *Midnight Express*; on the box there was no Channel 4 or *EastEnders*, and *Coronation Street* topped the ratings ahead of *Blankety Blank*.

The Prince of Wales opened the Jubilee Line; Arthur Scargill tried to organise cut-price holidays for miners in Cuba after meeting Fidel Castro at a youth festival. A computer engineer at Reuters made £6,500 a year; you could buy a new three-bed detached house in Abingdon for £28,450, or an Austin Morris Princess for £3,781. The Princess, said the ad, had 'Comfortable seats of arm-chair proportions, and a choice of 240 driving positions'. Now I don't know about you, but I can't think of any circumstance in which I could contort my body into 240 positions, never mind at the wheel of a car. Could you drive it sitting on your head? In the lotus position? With your ankles round your neck? But there you go; that was the British motor industry. At Leyland, in a workers' poll, the choice of name for the new Mini was narrowed to a short list of three: the Metro, the Maestro, or the Match. Just think, we could all have been driving round in Mini Matches. But who'd ask the workforce what to call their product now?

I was twenty; Thatcher was odds on at the bookies to beat Callaghan. In the closing days of the campaign, the polls (right as ever) started showing a narrow Labour lead; in the *Telegraph*, a car-toon showed Foot, Benn and Heffer as dogs in cages, with Callaghan telling them not to worry – a couple more days and he'd let them out. But on May 3rd, Thatcher won a 43-seat majority – and for the whole of my adult life, the Tories have been in power ever since. Eighteen years – eighteen years of anybody, to be honest – can't be healthy, can it? But what effect have those eigh-teen years had?

The Sunday evening before John Major called the election, I asked a bloke in my local how he'd vote. He had a neat little 'tache, a denim jacket, a flash watch, a business of his own. He said, 'I sup-pose I'm one of Thatcher's children. And I don't want to appear philistine – but the truth is, I don't really give a toss.'

At midday on Monday March 17th, John Major was driving down the Mall to see the Queen, and I was driving over the beau-tiful, narrow, twisting little road from home to Brighouse, green fields and dry-stone walls all about. I dropped off the tops into the jumbled sprawl of West Yorkshire's hard-working towns, paid my parking charge in Calderdale's new meters (shocking – a Labour tax rise, and they hadn't even got in yet), then I ran by Tesco to the new office. Alex and another volunteer, Clare, were watching Michael Brunson in Downing Street on ITV; Major, said Brunson, would 'go to the marketplace' the minute he'd called the vote.

'Ghhnnngg,' growled Alex, 'he's such a *plonker*.'

'You know what'll happen,' said Clare, 'if he goes to the market. He'll get remaindered, is what.'

Then a teacher from Calderdale College turned up, with a dozen folk in tow who had learning difficulties. They milled about, smiling vaguely, eyes wandering behind thick-lensed spectacles – but they were there for a good reason. The teacher, a young man called Jim Whittaker for whom I can only express the most profound admiration, said these people had to spend so much time focused on the basics, on literacy and numeracy, that it could get a bit blinkered – so he was trying to put a current affairs module into their course to get some wider knowledge across, to help them make connections. 'Example,' he said, 'I'm interested in football. So I know where Hartlepool is because of Hartlepool United, right? Same thing here. Just making connections. Because these people are adults, they're more sophisticated than people think – and they've all got the vote.'

Six weeks back, he'd written to all the candidates in Calder Valley and Halifax, asking if they'd meet his class. The incumbents, Mahon and Thompson, with their greater office resources, both wrote back to say they would; but among the other candidates (they'd had six weeks, remember) the only one to respond had been McCafferty. So, by an odd and happy turn of circumstance, the first thing she did in the election campaign of 1997 was to sit down with a dozen mentally disabled souls to talk about dinner fees and bus fares.

She turned up smart, almost austere, in a dark navy suit; no more chilling in her tracksuit now. She said hello, and immediately one of them remembered her from when she'd visited a day-care centre. Struck, she said, 'You *have* got a good memory. Now, would you all like a brew?' But she was a bit nervous, not wholly sure what level to pitch it at. 'It's the worst thing,' she muttered by the kettle, 'to underestimate people's intelligence.'

They sat in a square round two desks pushed together; the group nodded and swayed, and often answered questions in a gleeful chorus. 'This is Christine McCafferty,' said Jim. 'She wants to be the MP for where?'

'Calder Valley!'

'So she wants to beat who?'

'Donald Thompson!'

'My bus fare to college,' said one of them, 'on May 1st it goes up from 20p to 60p . . .'

McCafferty took a deep breath, and plunged into trying to explain local government finance. I'm thinking, you couldn't explain it to Einstein if you hot-wired him into a supercomputer, but she had a brave crack. She said, 'If I gave you £20 and said, You will spend it on this and this and this, well, you might have ideas of your own, yes?'

'Yes!'

But, she said, it was no good having ideas of your own, because nowadays central government told you where you could and could not spend the money, and they didn't give you enough money anyway. So, said Jim, 'What's the follow-up question?'

There was a long pause. They sat with open mouths, sloped shoulders and nodding heads, some with their attention fading in and out, eager slurred voices spitting little blurts and spurts of words. 'The follow-up question,' said Jim, 'is what will the Labour Party do?'

'Yes!'

McCafferty told them about her mother. She'd looked after her until she was eighty-seven; she'd had arthritis, she couldn't use her hands, her feet were so bad that it was difficult to walk, towards the end she was deaf and blind. 'So I know what it's like. And I'd like to see more funds and support for carers, for your families, so people can live in their own homes wherever that's possible, and get out and about and not be locked in four walls. I was on the social services committee, I used to visit all the centres . . .'

'Yes! Lovely!'

'Well,' said Jim, 'one of the things we're going to learn about is the privatisation of day-care centres.'

The idea that anybody should be let loose to make money out of these people struck me, forcibly, as utterly grotesque – and McCafferty said, 'We're *totally* opposed to that.'

Jim asked, 'What does opposed mean, folks?'

There was a bout of murmuring and twitching and then a voice cried out, 'Don't agree with it!'

I wondered how Donald Thompson would deal with them. He'd be kind and hearty, I suppose, and assure them all was right with the world. Jim said, 'OK, folks. You've done very well here. It's very good of one of the candidates to meet you . . .'

'Yes!'

'So thank you for your time . . .'

'Time!'

'And thanks for the cup of tea . . .'

'Thank you!'

They milled about in a happy, burbling heap. They came up to me, to Alex and Clare, full of confidence – saying who they were, asking what we were doing. Alex and Clare were sticking addresses on envelopes; I was taking notes, living in my own little world of complications. As I shook hands I felt sheepish, nervous of my inability to be easy with them, wanting to talk and not knowing how – so I was truly surprised when McCafferty said afterwards that she felt she'd not done well, that she'd not been wholly easy with them herself. It hadn't looked that way to me.

She'd heard the news on the car radio; she felt, she said, 'A mix of excitement and relief, a tingle down the spine.' But even as she was driving in, a fax was coming from London headed, 'Now John Major Has Gone To The Palace'. The message contained long, detailed and immediate instructions about mail-shots, posters, postal and proxy votes, voter contacts and canvassing, what to do in the first forty-eight hours – and once Whittaker's class left, she fell in a chair holding the fax and said, 'I'm a nervous wreck now this has come. I realise it's real. There's such a lot riding on this – people's hopes and dreams, literally. This is the future we're talking about.'

There was still an uncertainty as to whether it had actually begun; was it now, or did it start after parliament packed in? If they started now, and posters went up in people's windows, did election expenses start clocking up? The fax said to get going, so presumably they were off – but she wanted to hear someone say it to her.

Labour was immediately sending 400,000 mailshots to every member round the country; the Calder Valley party was putting out 10,000 letters to their core support locally. Every week it was planned that more material would come in to them from London for delivery, targeted letters to waverers and believers, to people who were switching, to others who needed squeezing. It was more than Labour had ever done before, more by far. There'd be 2,500 videos for first-time voters; McCafferty sighed at the enormity of it, and said they'd have to hire a van for those. She said, 'It's going to be a nightmare,' and then she read out from the fax a reminder that they'd have to pace their campaign. Six whole weeks . . .

'Nah,' grinned Alex. 'Let's do it all in the first week and go home.'

'Right,' said McCafferty firmly. 'Let's go.'

Before the campaign began, the posters in the windows had all been national party posters, images of Blair, the five pledges. Now, however, David Tarlo picked up a poster that said, 'Chris McCafferty. Labour.' As he went to the window with it she burst out laughing, a great hooting peal as she realised it was finally happening. 'Ooh,' she said, putting a hand over a wide, excited smile, 'I don't know if I can handle this. I feel queasy.'

I stuck the poster in the window myself, with Tarlo outside to see how it looked. Three more volunteers had come in already, getting double-sided sticky tape on to more posters so they could be stuffed into envelopes and sent out. 'Tomorrow,' said McCafferty, 'the world starts turning red.'

At six that first evening, more helpers came in from the Regional Women's Committee to do some phone canvassing. Ann Martin said sternly, 'We'll not have women out canvassing alone, not after it's getting dark.' There were, indeed, four drunks toppling raucously about outside the Black Bull already.

People tend to react better to a phone call than a knock on the door; besides, you can get round a lot more homes on the phone and, of course, apart from being safer, you can still do it when it's raining. Moreover – as Labour now had a marketing machine of unprecedented efficiency – you could do it even better when the party gave you a script.

It was set out on a laminated card and it read, 'Hello. Can I speak to (voter's name) please? Good evening (voter's name), my name is . . . and I'm calling from the Labour Party. We're calling because we want to identify people's voting intentions at the next General Election. Could you tell me which of the main parties you most closely identify with?'

Depending on the response, there was a bunch of arrows heading off to the different ways that you coped with it. McCafferty said she'd do some, but she hadn't got a voter list. She said to Martin that she needed some voters and Martin retorted, grinning, 'You certainly do.'

I could imagine people sitting at home thinking, Cripes. He's only gone to the palace today, and the buggers are on my phone already. Still, I fancied a crack at it. I got a voter list, and made nine calls to a road in Brighouse. I got one out of order, two answering machines, a Liberal Democrat and two Tories. One of these said, 'No thanks. We were just on about you lot now. I'm *very* Conservative.' To which the script's assigned response was a polite thank you and goodbye.

I got another bloke who said, 'Is there an anti-abortionist candidate?'

I was sorry to tell him there wasn't . . .

'Is there a Socialist Workers' Party candidate then?'

Well, that was an intriguing mix. I was sorry to say there wasn't one of those either . . .

'I'm struggling then, aren't I? I want to vote for a left-wing party, but there isn't one.'

He would, he conceded grudgingly, most likely vote Labour – as would the other two people I called. Both were women, and both had voted Tory last time. So on this representative sample (four Tories in '92, and two of them switching) I can authoritatively report that the Tory vote in Brighouse had halved. There's polling for you.

Life goes on. While they worked the phones in Brighouse, the pool team in my local was setting off to play the Crown in Scissett. When they'd gone, there were three women left and one bloke. So, I said, how did they feel now they knew there was going to be an election?

One was a nurse. She'd voted Tory last time, but would go Labour now. She was trying to get out of the health service after sixteen years – because, she said, 'The NHS these days is not a good place to be. I'm sad to say it, but it just isn't a good place to be.'

Another woman said, 'I'll not vote. 'Cause I've not a clue what they're on about.'

'How any woman can not vote I don't know,' said the third woman sternly, 'when people have *died* so you can vote. How can you not?'

The bloke said, 'I know what my reaction is.' The women turned to him, and waited. He held their attention for a minute, as if thinking deeply; then he shrugged and said, 'My reaction is, there's going to be an election.'

The third woman groaned. Was that all? She was, unsurprisingly, going to vote Labour herself, but she said, 'It's sad to say it, but it's not an earth-shaking thing, is it? You pay a bit more tax, whatever. It's not like it'll make much difference.'

The next morning, Gallup in the *Telegraph* had Labour up three to 28 points ahead, and the *Sun* came out for Blair. In the afternoon, driving over to Brighouse, I was listening to Nicky Campbell and he said, 'So, John Major's going to the country. *Gonna eat a lot of peaches . . .*'

'But look,' he says, 'have you seen the *Sun*? Shocking news. I'm shocked. All the political parties are shocked. Darren Day's split up with Anna Friel.'

14

EXTRAPOLATION

A year back when I started on this, I was leaving my house to follow the local elections in Calderdale and I found two sad blokes coming down my lane with Tory leaflets. I said, No thanks, I didn't want any of that in my house – and one of them told me, 'Neither do I. But I'm getting paid to do it, aren't I?'

Since that day I'd not been canvassed, leafleted or otherwise solicited by a single soul until, on March 19th, I received a highly amusing video from the Referendum Party, full of wild-eyed people making apocalyptic threats. Horrors! Germany's run by a fat man who wants to eat all my fish! Still, Stephen Pearson thought the Referendum man might get 8 or 9 per cent in Calder Valley. Referendum Man – sounds like something you'd find in a peat bog.

I went to see what the Tories were up to, and on the face of it they weren't up to much. Their HQ was a lovely old house in Hebden Bridge, on a tree-shaded hillside by the turning for Keighley; the best part of two hundred years old, it was a classic stone-built place with black iron railings and a cobbled parking spot. The door was tatty, painted a faint, long-faded lilac; you entered into a small, unlit, bare stone hall. There was a tiny dim kitchen, a loo, and a sign rather vaguely directing you upstairs. I stumbled about a bit in the gloom, turned off a light switch by mistake trying to find where I was going, and heard a faint cry from above. Up the shadowy stairs there were two rooms, and two souls occupying them: a receptionist, and Donald Thompson's agent. And here I was plunging them into darkness.

The contrast between this place and the quiet, chatty enterprise of Labour's office in Brighouse was marked. It would be wrong, of course, to infer from it that the Tories were entirely, dolefully inactive; they had their computers there, their piles of mail-shot. But where was the zing, the oomph, the sense of folk busy about a purpose? The campaign had started, and this place had all the buzz of a morgue. I thought, you couldn't *pay* a volunteer to go to work in a dusty cul-de-sac like this.

Thompson's agent was paid to be there by Central Office – and he was a thoroughly likeable young man. Basically, anyone who describes the BNP as 'the dickhead vote' can't be all bad. Twenty-five years old, his name was James Davidson; the son of an accountant from Bradford, he'd come to work in the valley nine months ago after getting his Masters in international politics. He was a large, heavily built fellow – a rugby union man – with a strong square head, an honest manner, an appealing readiness to laugh and a firm belief in his party. The Tories were, he said, 'The right option for Britain. Other parties or ideologies might be right for France or Germany, because of their own political histories – but we're right for Britain. It's just the way we are.'

All the same, I said, there weren't many people twenty-five years old in the Conservative Party – the average age of whose membership was now sixty-two. He laughed and said, 'Fair point. It's hard to find friends of your own age. But maybe as there's been New Labour, we need a reform of our party too. Whether we win or lose, there'll have to be changes. Of course, we're going to win . . .'

As he said this, he grimaced. It was just a shy, momentary, almost affecting little grimace – but it spoke volumes, as if the magnitude of the task, the unavoidable reality of it, had forced this little wince on to his face. I pressed him and he said, 'It's going to be very close. The overriding feeling is that we need a change. So what we have to stress is, a change to what?'

The prospect of a Labour government galled him – and he agreed, the way things were going, it could get demoralising. You had people working hard, voluntarily, and hard work meant chewing away at Labour's lead, 26, 23, 21 . . . then Edwina Currie comes out and asks for a quick leadership contest if and when they lose, and Labour say thank you very much, and there they are back to 26 again. As for the Europhobes . . .

Davidson was opposed to Britain joining the single currency; he believed the great majority of Conservatives were too. But he understood why Major had taken the wait-and-see line and, he said, 'Unity has to be a primary factor in this election, it's been stressed for a year. But these . . . well. How can you describe them?'

Bastards?

He laughed and said, 'These people that were voted in to support this party, this ideology, this leader . . .'

And they don't.

'They could support him a lot more. And I can say that it does-n't affect me personally, I've still got a job – but it bothers me more for the volunteers. All their hard work just niggled away.'

Among 350 members of the local association there were, he said, a hard core of 150 who'd work; a lot of them would do it at home. He described them with a smile as, 'Old ladies, old men, packing and stuffing for Britain. With the Glenn Miller on.' Now if you ask me, this was a vision that conjured up zimmer frames; but he said, if they did their job, and if James Davidson worked his socks off, then whatever the outcome nationally, Donald Thompson would win here. His advantage, said Davidson, was that people were loyal to the man; he was well liked, he was experienced, and he was very astute. Yes, he conceded, 'In any election you contemplate defeat. But my feeling is, from the 4,800 majority he's got now, I'd like to see 3,000. That's my target. And we'll get it.'

He said, 'I'm a Yorkshireman. I'm not going to invest twelve months in this place and lose.'

John Wheelwright was a natural Conservative. He described himself as born and brought up that way, very much your typical middle-class businessman who'd left school at fifteen, made a bob or two, and now travelled the world exporting to South America, China, Japan, Vietnam and South Korea. Nearing fifty, he was a man of middle height who looked in good shape for his age; he was dressed casually in a sleeveless cardigan, with reading glasses on a cord round his neck. And when he said a bob or two, he was in fact (if he were to realise his assets) a man worth seven figures.

He was also a man who'd voted Labour in '92, who meant to do so again now, and who was preparing to hang a whopping great banner across the top of his mill saying, 'Sowerby Bridge Loves Labour'. He said, 'I'm a basic sort of person, I'm comfortable, not earning what I call corruption money – the million-pound bonuses, nobody's worth that, are they? And OK, I don't *want* to pay a lot of tax – but I really do want to see a socialist government. I might not have as much money, but we'd be happier.'

His company was J. & C. Joel Ltd, based in a grand old mill on Corporation Street in Sowerby Bridge. They made drapes, curtains, banners and backdrops for theatres, TV studios, gigs and sports arenas; he employed forty people, and turned over somewhere between £5 and £6 million. The mill was five solid storeys of pale Yorkshire stone with a square turret on one end, a Union Jack on top of it, and a towering blackened chimney to the side. Wheelwright showed me round, past giant rolls of fabric – gauze, serge, velvet, canvas, material for cinema screens, fabrics flame-proofed and light-fast – and we came to the floor where the products were made up.

They had orders from Belfast, Doncaster, Kuala Lumpur; purple velvet curtains with gold tassels for the Blackpool Grand lay on one vast table, and on another were banners to cover the pitch at Wembley for the Coca Cola Cup Final. Another order was for Puma in Sweden, who wanted a T-shirt fifty foot by sixty foot. The bloke in charge said, 'That's a big T-shirt. I wouldn't want to see the lad who'll be wearing it.'

One of Wheelwright's colleagues said, 'We're stupid busy. From where we've started six years back, it's beyond my wildest dreams.' But Wheelwright hoped they'd grow more yet, and be employing sixty people before too long; people getting better than any pro-jected minimum wage, with good bonuses and a health scheme, and among them a few lads that other companies wouldn't have looked at. There was one who'd been brought to them, he'd been in and out of secure homes, and the people who brought him said he'd not stay long. 'Well,' said Wheelwright, 'that was six years ago, and that lad's still here. Because we've talked with him. You lean against the wall with him, you listen. And now he'll say, What if we do this, or this? People, see – they only need to have respect.'

I asked about the threat (if you wanted to see it that way) of the social chapter. He said, 'Look, we live in Western Europe. We should be able to manage, shouldn't we? We shouldn't exploit people, we're not Dickensian. OK, I like good wine, I've got season tickets at Blackburn Rovers, I drive a Mercedes – but if I have all that and my people are working in purgatory, that's corrupt, isn't it?'

Corporation Mill was a piece of the living, working history of England. Some people down south might still think about satanic mills, but part of what makes West Yorkshire so fine is precisely the industry of the place, the feeling of how the landscape has been shaped, of how there've been centuries of toil, of how builders, engineers and businessmen have moulded the old pale stone into bridges, tunnels, canals and places of work along the valley floors. The Huddersfield skyline as you come over Chapel Hill has a rugged beauty of its own, just as the moors do; this is an England veined through with a quiet, proud, determined and productive energy.

In this England, John Wheelwright's story was the story of the last eighteen years in microcosm. His father had a small weaving firm; at fifteen he'd gone to work there. They employed around fifty people, and they weren't mighty wealthy like the dynasties, like Crossley Carpets; among a lot of other smaller firms, they fed off and around the big boys. As Wheelwright put it, 'If there's a cart full of muck going along, some of it'll fall off.'

To begin with, the way you did then, he thought he had a life laid out before him. He'd work, he'd take over – but after a while he could see the sun was setting. In the 1970s, in his early twenties, he started striking out on the side; he became a dealer, buying and selling shirts, coats, women's tights. There were arguments in his family; they'd always made things, and here he was buying up cheap fabric in Italy, Portugal, further afield in the third world, bringing it in and making money while mills were closing all about. Somewhere behind him as he went off on his own, the family firm was one of those that went under – but he was in with the asset strippers by then, the people he called 'the funeral directors of the textile trade'. As the mills shut, he went in and bought the stock.

He loved Thatcher. He said, 'You haven't a conscience when you're starting out, have you? And I enjoyed the environment when she came in, it was perfect for a young man like me.' Still, there must have been something nagging; he remembers meeting Donald Thompson with John Wakeham at some local do in the early Eighties and asking them, Look, I'm doing this, but shouldn't we be making our cloth here in England? And they said to him, Are you making money?

Sure.

So what are you worrying about?

But it isn't creating jobs . . .

That's not your problem. That's the government's problem.

'To be honest,' he said, 'it was music to my ears. So I continued on this way, and it went up astronomically. I just generated cash.' Then the honeypot deal came; he bought a derelict mill for a sum in the low five figures, and sold it to developers for lottery money. That meant he could buy Corporation Mill – and to begin with, back in '88, he'd just seen it as a cash cow. He had no mortgage, he rented it out in pieces to all the little guys that were starting up, and for the first twelve months it was dandy, he filled it.

Then the recession came, and with it came Wheelwright's turning until he'd gone full circle. He said, 'They wanted everybody to be entrepreneurs, and not everybody can be. All these little companies started disappearing, it was just sad. I had printers, photographers, the banks had lent them money, it was signed against their houses and they weren't business people, they didn't know how to cope. The banks were giving billions to developers and losing it on things like Canary Wharf – but they didn't help the little people, did they? Thatcher changed from liking millionaires to liking billionaires, and here I was with these good honest people, and they were terrified. I didn't chase their arrears, I could see how it was – if they paid the rent, they didn't eat. So don't get me wrong, I'm not an angry young man – and when you've made a bob or two you can have a social conscience, OK – but I'm looking at the next generation here, and that's why I want a socialist government.'

The only business left in the mill from his renting days was a gym at one end, and a rag-and-bone man with some space in the top. Wheelwright, meanwhile, had gone back to manufacturing, to a very Nineties, specialist, bespoke form of it; but if you made things, he said, you worked more with people, and then you went more to Labour.

We had lunch at the Old Bridge in Ripponden; a pub dating back to 1307, down a cobbled lane by the banks of the Ryburn. The sun was shining, the place was a picture postcard, and the food was a cold buffet of beef and ham off huge, succulent joints. As we ate he said, 'Donald's very uptight with me now, but I'll only tell him what I'm telling you. I don't like the sleaze, I don't want a totalitarian state, and I'm proud that I manufacture things. There are too many people not working, not producing – and if the Tories get back in it'll be worse than ever. They're past their sell-by date, and I'd be devastated. Whereas a change now will be exciting, it'll create opportunity. And if they take a bit more off you, well – taxation keeps you working, doesn't it? If there wasn't taxation, we'd all be sat about doing bloody nothing.'

From a man originally Conservative, this was the rankest heresy. And back in Hebden Bridge, James Davidson had conceded that, yes, a few people were switching – just one or two. But if a man like John Wheelwright could switch (and switch so firmly, so passionately) and if you could sit and hear him tell you about it over cold roast beef in the heart of Tory Ripponden, then you'd have to suspect that come May 1st, middle England would be switching in droves.

I do my photocopying in a portakabin on a ramshackle little business park half a mile from my village, where the pit used to be. The company makes agricultural chemicals, and exports to the Far East. The woman who runs it has been out there twice, and she loves it. The people work hard, they educate their children, they have wonderful manners, they can't do enough for you – and you talk about muggers in Japan, she said, they had to look up in a dictionary what you meant. She was a strong, cheerful character, married to a policeman; they were people who worried about crime, and illegal immigrants, and who'd always voted Tory. But this time, she said, she might well go to Labour.

Or there's Paul and Leslie, the people I bought my house from. They were Tories; they'd moved to Brighouse but they'd come back for a pint with their mates, and I'd nag them. It became a running joke – bloody Pete's going to talk about politics again. But during that first week of the campaign, I was coming out of Labour's office in Brighouse and they were parked across the street. They waved, I went to say hello, and Leslie leaned across to the window; knowing what I'd been doing, there was something she specifically wanted to tell me. She said, 'I've always voted Conservative, but I'll not be voting for them this time. I can't vote Labour, so I'll just not use my vote. Because the Tories, they've *let us all down*.'

Paul was nodding thoughtfully, as if he'd come to a conclusion and meant to stick by it. 'Your lot,' he said, 'they should have a chance at five years.'

People vote the way they do, of course, for many strange and wondrous reasons. I met a man who'd vote Labour because the candidate was a Libran, and a woman who thought Labour would be better for her cats – but my favourite came during the council elections a year back, when an old lady rang Labour and asked if they could drive her to the polling station. When the driver got there, she told him she'd always voted Tory; but she'd been watching the lunchtime news and Michael Howard was on it, and there was something about him that stirred so great a revulsion in her that she had to act there and then.

But if you added all this up it was still no more than hearsay, no more than just a feeling that the tide was running Labour's way – and there were many odd rocks out there that this tide had to flow by. A girl who cut my hair in Brighouse said she thought John Major was a total waste of space, so I asked her who she thought she'd vote for and she said, 'Conservative.' She didn't know why; it was just something her Dad had told her.

People, eh? James Davidson said, 'There are lifelong Tories who may not vote for us this time. If they were machines, they would. But they're not, are they?'

He'd set his target of keeping Thompson in with a majority of 3,000. Labour, on the other hand, weren't thinking what their majority might be; they'd simply set themselves a target of getting 26,000 votes because they figured if they got that, McCafferty was in. According to their canvassing, by the first week of the campaign they had 44 per cent of that figure pledged – so, said Tim Swift, his gut feeling was good. By any extrapolation, on the numbers they had, McCafferty was coming home.

I went home myself, and told my wife what I'd heard. She said, 'Oh, *don't*. Don't give me extrapolation. There's six weeks to go, and how many times have we been disappointed before?'

15

MONEY & BODIES

Val Watts, the reporter assigned by the *Courier* to follow McCafferty, thought the first week was an anti-climax. 'The comet,' she said, 'has provoked more interest than the election.' But while Hale-Bopp flew high and bright above us, the Tories sank low into the sleaze pit. On Friday March 21st, the *Guardian* ran damning extracts from Sir Gordon Downey's report; Major was bolting from Westminster with unprecedented rapidity, so the verdict on those Tories who'd been lining their pockets could be kept under wraps.

Yet they came before us with the bare-faced arrogance to proclaim they'd done nothing wrong. As we approached the end of March, here were Tim Smith and Neil Hamilton, plainly unfit for office, still standing to be returned to it – and these human oil-slicks were backed in this shameless effrontery by their local Conservative associations. It was a putrid spectacle – and a spectacle, I strongly suspect, of the iceberg variety. As one Labour MP told me, 'They're not all bad. But don't you go believing there was only half a dozen of them at it. It was just the way they did business.'

On Sunday March 23rd, McCafferty addressed forty volunteers in the Brighouse office. She told them, 'This is the most important election since 1964. So we've got to squeeze the Liberals, we've got to get all ours out, and we've got to get hold of the switchers and look after them. But to do that, we need a lot of bodies. We have the ammunition to change hearts and minds but we have to earn their respect, we have to *deserve* their votes. If we just expect them to vote for us 'cause they're fed up with the Tories, we'll lose.

'Cause Sir Donald will be coming back now, they'll start with their nonsense, they'll tell all their lies – so I can go out and work my socks off, but I need help. Now I know you're committed. You wouldn't be here, you wouldn't have got up at the crack on a Sunday morning – but please, give all the time you've got, bring all the friends you can get. Because this is *so* important.'

It was 10.30; more people were coming in as she spoke. They weren't just locals; they came from Barnsley and Bradford, one old boy came all the way from Cumbria. From seats where Labour had a shoo-in majority, or where the Tories were unassailable, workers were diverted to the marginals – and there was plenty for them to do when they got there.

Ten thousand letters to the hard-core Labour vote had been pre-printed at ISCO5, a sheltered workshop in Halifax. Now three computers in Brighouse were running them through printers, adding names and addresses; they'd been running Friday night, most of Saturday, and the last three wards were going through now. All these had to be folded, stuffed into envelopes with a poster and hand-delivered; you couldn't post them, that'd be £2,000, and that way your election expenses would be gone in no time.

Ann Martin organised the volunteers. They had five phone lines; five people were set to canvassing on them. A few more went out in pairs to deliver *The Rose*, Labour's newsletter, a hundred issues per bundle. The rest got round desks to get the letters into envelopes. The room got a hum and chatter about it; to one side, Tarlo tried to work out with a friend how they could rig up an illuminated sign saying 'Labour' on the friend's balcony. He lived way up on a dark hillside over Mytholmroyd, and the balcony was fifteen feet long; if they had 100 pygmy bulbs, 25 watts . . . they scribbled on a pad, calculating amps. Tarlo's mate wondered how much a hundred bulb-holders would cost; Tarlo grinned. 'Are you making a donation then?'

Mick Clapham, Labour's MP for Barnsley West and Penistone, turned up with his wife Yvonne and went canvassing outside Tesco across the street. At first they were worried about canvassing in the supermarket's doorway; they didn't want to get in bother for being in people's way so, to begin with, they kept themselves away around the corner. Then the manageress came out in her suit and asked for a badge; one of the check-out girls, a university student, came to get some leaflets and said she'd think about joining. After that, they moved into full view. As they did so, a young man went by; Clapham collared him, and this lad said he didn't vote. Clapham said, 'Well, you really should use your vote, you know.'

He gave a cynical snort. 'For Labour, right?'

'If it's for Labour, well and good. But you should use it however you decide, because people have died for the right to vote. In South Africa they queued for two days so they could vote. If you don't use it, you're negating your democratic rights.' The lad took a leaflet and said he'd think about it. As he moved, on Clapham said sadly, 'People that don't vote – it's incredible to me.'

A few yards away, his wife was meeting a woman who looked at Labour's leaflets and then asked, 'Who's in now then?'

Yvonne Clapham took a deep breath and said, 'The Conservatives.'

'Oh. When did they gerrin then?' And you hear people complaining about politicians, but Jesus – it's only a wonder politicians don't complain about us more.

Clapham was a handsome figure, trim and swarthy with black hair just starting to go grey, a pricy-looking overcoat and a deep strong voice. He boomed his way up to people, hand out, and most stopped to listen. It was sadly noticeable that most of those who ducked away looking sheepish and uninterested were young. After half an hour, he'd only met two Tories; one woman who said Labour would let all the Pakistanis in, and another who looked as if her life was all sunbeds and hairdressers, and she found the idea of having to think about this (of having to think about anything at all, probably) too fearful to be contemplated.

At 1 o'clock, a message came from the office that if they didn't go back for lunch there'd be nothing left. Clapham said the response had been good; he reckoned 70 per cent Labour.

With David Tarlo on the case, the Buffet Theory of English politics was holding good. Beside the sandwiches, he'd organised a spread of crudités and dips – cheese and chives, garlic and onion. But then, he grinned, with carrots only twenty pence a pound you weren't denting your expenses much, were you?

At 2 o'clock, five of us crammed into Clapham's diesel BMW

(red, of course) to canvass some old folks at a community centre. It was their monthly activity group, a day of music and reminiscing, of prayers and quizzes and armchair aerobics; transport to the centre, and the day itself, were organised by voluntary groups part-funded by the council and the health authority. It was their open day, with a bring-and-buy, a cake-stall, a raffle; amongst the material by the doorway I noticed a 1913 version of *Aladdin*, a 1952 *Telegraph* reporting the funeral of King George and a 1961 issue of *Nursery World*. One of the helpers said, 'Some of them like to look back.'

There were a dozen women and one man, one or two in wheelchairs, gathered in a spartan room with a piano and a pack of armchairs. The raffle prizes were a box of Rose's chocolates, a bottle of Peach Fizz, and a box of tissues with an embroidered cover. On a long table along one wall there was a Ruth Rendell with a torn cover, a pair of plimsolls, a couple of crocheted shawls, tinned food, fading jigsaws, cushion covers, old crockery, a load of cakes and iced buns; they were raising money for a day trip in the summer. Maybe Southport or Fleetwood, said one of the helpers, it depended on the bus fare. Of course they had to plan it carefully, they had to think about wheelchairs, toilets, the fact that there weren't many who could walk a long way. Another helper smiled and said, 'We can't tek 'em to Southport if the tide's out, we'd be there a month. Mind, after today, mebbe we'll tek 'em to Paris.'

McCafferty and the Claphams went round the room, touching hands, leaning over chairs to listen. One of the helpers was called Betty; she said, 'It's nice they've come to see us. But they'll have a job to sort it out, won't they? I've been a nurse fifty years, and the state of it – it just makes me sad. Still, they've brought some postal votes, that's good. 'Cause it's the old ones that *want* to vote.'

One lady in a wheelchair told McCafferty how her Dad had been brought up a Tory, until the day he went to a hustings and had a Damascene conversion. He ended up the first Labour Mayor of Jarrow, she said, and she was near to tears as she told it. McCafferty came away moved, and said how much she liked canvassing with the elderly, how much they thought about it, how much they had to say.

Betty said they'd been talking about schools, about class sizes rising, and one of the old ladies said when she was in school, class sizes were thirty-five or forty then. I thought, great – our primary schools are back to where they were seventy years ago.

Back in the office, the guy running the last letters through the printer said it had been a good day. They'd started with 7,000 empty envelopes; now he told me, 'We're going to run out. That's how good a day it's been.' But one good day doesn't make a good week, and in reality Labour were not as together as they looked, while the Tories were more on the ball than their ramshackle appearance would have you believe. In Hebden Bridge, they had a third big room against whose walls fat piles of Sir Donald's literature lay stacked up ready to go; they weren't officially starting, said James Davidson, until after Easter. During the week, meanwhile, Labour's office rarely had more than three or four people in it; usually Ann Martin, Alex Powell and a cheerful bloke in denims and trainers called Tony who described himself as 'an unemployed geezer', and who'd stuffed and sorted so many envelopes that he must have known every street in the bottom of the valley off by heart. They were keen and positive, and there was a long way to go, but they weren't exactly a teeming host.

The true state of the Labour campaign in Calder Valley became apparent on Wednesday March 26th. At 5.30 that evening, Nick Brown from the whips' office came to Brighouse, and he was there to offer McCafferty two things. He was there to offer help and advice on the business of moving to Westminster, and he was there to offer help and advice on how to get there in the first place.

After polling day, the election of the Speaker would be on May 7th, and they'd take the oath of allegiance then too. (If you ever wondered about the redder shades of MP all stood there swearing allegiance to a monarchy they don't believe in, it's simple; you don't take the oath, you don't get paid.) Then, said Brown, the Queen's Speech would be on May 14th. To help McCafferty prepare for this he'd sent her a list of hotels, and he asked now whether she wanted any help with the grim business of elbowing her way into the Commons to find an office; but talking about this felt just a little bit hubristic. McCafferty said she'd looked at the hotel list and thought, 'That's a bit too existential for me. I'll look at it on May 2nd. I've got to win first.'

Brown asked how he could help her do that and she told him, 'We need money and bodies.' With Tarlo, Martin and Ian Carvell, she explained how difficult the constituency was; how it was near thirty miles long, how it was a jumble of places blurring one into the other, how you could go three miles out in the wilds and come on a terrace of fifteen houses where the people had never been canvassed in their lives – and how short of cash and manpower they were to cover all that.

Brown said he'd try to find some union money for them – and for all you hear from the Tories about the unions bankrolling Labour, and how undemocratic it is (unlike their own entirely open and squeaky-clean funding) I can tell you that at this level we were not talking lottery money. The money Brown was talking about – and he couldn't promise he'd get it – would buy you a few thousand stamps, nothing more.

As for bodies, he said he'd try to get a busload down for the weekend from his own patch in Tyne and Wear; maybe they could get some young ones over, set them working, give them some beer money and a bed for the night. Alternatively, he could set them to telephone canvassing up there. They could e-mail up the voter lists – but either way, in his part of the world there were bodies aplenty. There then followed a discussion of where else help might be found, with much intricate tribal detail of which local Labour parties had people to spare, and where those people were inclined to give their help.

I began to get an impression of the Calder Valley as a kind of electoral black hole. Here we were at the heart of the country, centred on the bar of the H at the hub of the nation's motorway network – and yet no one seemed to know it was there. If you asked them to travel to a marginal from Bradford, say, they'd most likely go to Keighley – when Keighley, said Carvell, would probably go with the national swing, whereas Calder Valley was much, much tighter.

'People here,' said McCafferty, 'like to think of themselves as free-thinking, and Donald's been very clever with that down the years; he's a cunning old fox, and he's played on it.' In other words, the nation might swing – but that didn't mean Calder Valley would. So they agreed they'd have to do something; plainly, said Brown, this was a very key key seat, a key seat among key seats. And maybe he says that to all the girls, but he did promise he'd try to help.

When he was gone McCafferty said, 'That's reassuring. If I had £1,000 and 10,000 phone calls, I'd be a lot happier. If I had half that, I'd be a lot happier.' She looked tense, not standing still, working an elastic band round and round in her hands – because the truth was, while they were better organised than they'd ever been before, they still didn't know how fully half the people of Calder Valley meant to vote. All the anecdotal stuff felt good, but it wasn't hard knowledge – and after eighteen years, how much of that did Sir Donald have?

I'd seen him the day before in Hebden Bridge, and he'd been in good heart. He'd left Westminster the previous Friday, and he hadn't finished packing up there – but that didn't matter, 'Seeing I'm going back there.' He said he'd never been ahead in the polls; on the eve of the vote last time, he'd been 7 per cent behind. Then he won, and afterwards one of the pollsters told him Calder Valley would be engraved on his heart – and so it should be, said Sir Donald. 'I could have told him where the votes were, couldn't I?'

He had his reasons to be confident. Never mind what went on nationally; here in Calder Valley, he'd simply tell people to look out of their doors. This was a place where people had jobs, in stable communities with good schools – he admitted he'd not been best pleased when Gillian Shephard said otherwise – but it didn't change the facts on the ground. So it would be a hard fight but he'd prevail, because he believed he had only to remind people that for the most part they were comfortable, and it was the Tories they had to thank for that. Besides, in the words of his slogan, he was 'tried and tested', wasn't he? Whereas, he said, 'My Labour lady will promise to do the same but better – and that's a funny sort of position, isn't it?'

By the end of the second week, however, it looked as if the Tories were being tried and tested to destruction; it looked as if Sir Donald was whistling in the face of a hurricane. In Scotland on the Tuesday, Allan Stewart stepped down as MP for Eastwood, the Tories' safest seat north of the border, amid allegations concerning a married woman he'd supposedly met at an alcohol clinic; two days later he went into hospital, reportedly having a nervous breakdown. On the Wednesday, Tim Smith bowed out as Tory MP for Beaconsfield; evidently his local association had decided that if he'd put eighteen grand in his pocket (or was it twenty-five?) that wasn't the sort of behaviour they expected after all.

Then, on the Thursday morning, the *Sun* shafted Piers Merchant across six soaraway of pages of sex romp with a seventeen-year-old Soho nightclub hostess. The Tory MP for Beckenham had, it was pantingly alleged, 'shared nights of passion' tied to a bed with her stockings, stuck his hands up her skirt in Trafalgar Square, and otherwise been a perfect gentleman because, when they had a bath together, he sat at the end with the taps. The sting involved tailing Merchant with his totty to a park bench where, this modest soul reported, she felt unable to go all the way with him in public and had instead to cool his ardour by (in the gloriously evasive weasel-speak of the tabloids) 'performing a sex act on him until he was satisfied'. So there we have it; didn't I tell you voting Tory was like wanking?

Merchant denied it all – and it was funny, but it was also grotesque. It had set-up written all over it and the girl, the appropriately monikered Anna Cox, was soon reported to be £25,000 better off for her pains. Which leaves you to wonder which is the easier money, to get it from Al Fayed or the *Sun*? But it speaks volumes that the Tory high command could almost instantly be demanding Merchant's head on a platter for behaving like an idiot with a dolly-bird, while Neil Hamilton still remained in place as the candidate for Tatton, *with their backing*. Here was a man who'd taken commissions from the lobbyist Ian Greer, who'd declared them to no one, who'd denied that he had a financial arrangement with Greer, who'd lived high on the hog in the Paris Ritz at Al Fayed's expense – and he could still stand for parliament?

While the *Sun* was stiffing Merchant, Al Fayed in the *Mirror* was dishing more dirt on Hamilton. Hamilton said his stay in the Ritz would have cost Al Fayed no more than £500; the Harrods boss responded with receipts pointing to a total nearer £4,000. Hamilton said the wine was over-priced; Al Fayed retorted that, 'The Ritz cellar is the best in the world and Field Marshal Goering tried to loot it during World War Two. Mr Hamilton thought he would try and finish the job . . . it was as if he was determined to break every record for conspicuous consumption.'

Amid this frenzy of allegation and denial what were we to think? When you've made every allowance for the prurient hype of the tabloids, the fact remains that they do what they do because they're chasing readers, that they chase readers by trying to chime with their beliefs, and that right now they plainly felt those beliefs were arriving at a pitch of terminal revulsion with the Tories – in which case, no amount of looking out of your door in Calder Valley was going to persuade you that Donald Thompson deserved five more years.

He'd said to me, 'The trouble with elections is that people never say thank you. They always say, What's next? They only say thank you at your memorial service – and I won't be at that, will I?'

But with five weeks to go, for what precisely were we supposed to be saying thank you? Were we supposed to thank the Tories for filling parliament with drunks, creeps, shysters, adulterers and a bloke who'd gone after a bunch of anti-motorway protestors with a pick-axe?

16

TOD JOBS

While the Tories floundered in the media riptide, the daily business of fighting an election on the ground went largely unreported. For Chris McCafferty, that business mostly involved winning hearts and minds at the bottom of the valley, in Brighouse and Elland and Rastrick where there were more people, and more of them undecided – because at the top of the valley, the Labour vote in Todmorden was maximised and solid, near 60 per cent. This was council leader Pam Warhurst's base; and if there was a Labour voter up here that the party hadn't found and nailed down, that voter had to be living in a cave on the moors.

It hadn't always been this way. Fifteen years back, Tod was largely a Liberal place, on the back of a strong Methodist tradition; but as that faded, and incoming hippy and/or middle-class activists boosted the local Labour party, so the political disposition of the place changed. But then, Tod always had a pretty offbeat sort of disposition anyway.

Tod people, one policeman told me, were known as 'numpties' – 'numpt' being a term which once appeared on 'Call My Bluff' and denoted a person of strange character. This quirkiness arose from geography; on the border between two counties and at the head of three valleys, Tod was a place in the middle of everywhere and nowhere. It voted in Calderdale but it had an Oldham post code, a Rochdale phone exchange, if you were sick the ambulance took you to Burnley, and the cricket club played in the Lancashire league. It was apocryphally claimed that on the cricket pitch you could stand with one foot in each county; the local joke had it that Lancashire and Yorkshire had been fighting over Tod for ages, and just now Lancashire was winning – because Tod was in Yorkshire.

This disorientating borderline ran through every aspect of the town. Historically, while the Calder Valley was in the woollen trade, Tod was Lancashire's last cotton town; the Fielden dynasty made their money in cotton here, and sent John Fielden to Parliament as the MP for Oldham in the 1830s. Fielden secured the passage of the Ten Hour Act, limiting the hours children worked and the age at which they started, and it was typical of Tod that it should produce a wealthy millowner who'd pursue that kind of progress.

Todmorden remains eccentrically radical today. Behind the splendid Town Hall there's a CND rose garden neatly laid out, but when I remarked on this to a local he told me it wasn't CND, it was TND – Tod being the kind of town that if there's a campaign going on all around the world, it still has to have a campaign of its own.

The old and new faces of progressive Tod stood side by side in the façade of the Bear health-food store and café. The shop retained most of its original frontage, and it was gorgeous: big, curving windows set in a modestly ornate green frame, topped with the legend 'Todmorden Industrial & Co-Operative Society Limited' in fine gold lettering on blue glass. Some of what was on offer on the handbills in the doorway would, on the other hand, have had the weavers and dyers of old scratching their heads in utter bafflement.

There was gritstone sculpture, poetry and creative writing courses, meditation, massage and reflexology. There was Menstrual Lingerie (sea sponges) because, 'In the past few years wimmin have been searching for an alternative to our present sanitary protection dilemma.' And there were Changing Times – 'Stimulating and Transformative ways to work with the body, mind, spirit, and soul in effective therapeutic sessions'. Courses included Personal Growth & the Tao, The Dilemma of Romantic Love, and My Life's Questions. I suspect that my own life's questions – like, how come Kristin Scott Thomas came out of that plane crash with nary a mark upon her? – somehow didn't fall into the rubric.

It wasn't surprising to learn that Tod was much visited by aliens; this was a place low on light pollution and high on weirdness. The most noted case involved a policeman who claimed in the early Eighties to have been abducted from outside the Ukrainian Club and experimented upon in a spaceship; an incident loosely used since in an episode of *Heartbeat*. Another policeman told me he'd drunk some of the white spirit they served in that club and, he said, 'You'd see anything after that. Pink elephants would be the least of your problems.' But the abductee, who's now retired, has stood by his story, and his former colleagues weren't going to mock. If that was what the man said happened, who were they to deny it?

Constable Philip Sanderson told me that as recently as February, he'd taken a report from another bloke who said he'd seen a UFO. The man was rational, he felt an idiot reporting it – but he'd seen an object in the sky, it wasn't a shooting star, it carried lights, and it travelled at phenomenal speed. So, Sanderson shrugged, you took him at his word. There was a form for sightings; you filled it in, you filed it with the MOD, you waited for the next visitation – and why not? After all, if aliens were going to visit anywhere, they'd visit Tod. They'd fit in, right? All of which explains why, when things went off in Todmorden, the police called them 'Tod jobs'.

On Easter Friday night I went out with Sanderson and another constable, Dave Mayes, in the back of their patrol car. Sanderson's collar number was 3030, so they called him Dirty Gertie; he was the Calder Valley's Environmental Protection Officer, working on badger baiters or the theft of rare birds' eggs. At 10.30 that evening, outside the Tod station, he was talking about the bat-handling course he was about to go on when the radio crackled into life, and Mayes and Sanderson scrambled for the Astra.

On the Burnley Road, another unit had found a car parked and spilling petrol down the kerb, with two lads scarpering away up the wooded hillside; the officer reporting in said he'd caught a glimpse of a Yamaha jacket. We were there in a few minutes, shot up a side track to where the railway line ran through a cutting above the road, and Mayes and Sanderson set to poking through the dark with their flashlights. The lads were gone, of course; the rail-track, said Sanderson, was 'a criminals' road', and they'd be back along it into town in no time.

All the same, the response was impressive. Within twenty minutes they had the car's owner identified and collected, a helicopter had been to scan the woods, a fire tender had hosed down the fuel spillage and another unit in town had spotted a bloke in a Yamaha jacket. He was fifteen or sixteen, he had gloves, a torch and an attitude, and so did his parents; why, they complained, were the police always picking on their lad? Well, why indeed? They couldn't nail him – obviously, said Sanderson, there'd been a few thousand Yamaha jackets made – but they'd be keeping an eye.

It was, he said, a war of attrition – but in a small place like Tod, at least you knew the majority of the criminals; some of them you could virtually arrest by appointment. He said wearily, 'You'll see them grow up from kids into thieving toe-rags and the sad thing is, some of them when they're kids, you just know that's how it'll go.'

Back up the road, the stolen car was an old Cavalier. It had a window put in, and the fuel line was split; they'd probably bottomed it on one of the woodland tracks. The car's owner lived in a terrace off the main road a quarter of a mile away – and while Mayes was rousing him, Sanderson talked about his wildlife work. A fair-haired man with glasses and a slow, dry wit, he was a country boy who'd grown up on the hillside over Rishworth, so when the environment job came up three years back, it seemed a natural thing to do. He worked with the RSPCA and with private enthusiasts – he had a merlin man, a peregrine falcon man, a badger man – and the people who went after those animals, in his heart he couldn't understand them. He said, 'It's something in their psyche, they've no conscience. You try and stay objective, but I can get quite angry about it. What's the pleasure in killing an animal like that?' Still, wildlife criminals tended by and large to be criminals otherwise, so targeting them was worth it; he could get them a stiffer sentence for badger-baiting than he could for stealing a car.

They helped the owner of the car they were dealing with now to push it back down the road – and, in three hours through closing time on a Friday night, this was the only incident we were called to. We swung by the Blue Note from time to time – a night-club that gets good DJs, puts flyers all over Manchester and Lancashire, pulls crowds, gets packed, and then you see them walking in circles round the marketplace, chugging water and chilling out. The policemen talked about it in a matter-of-fact way, informed, unfazed, unprejudiced; it was clear that drunk people generally caused them more problems than drugged ones.

Away from town, we roamed the moortops past the maggot

farm to an old Coal Board track where stolen cars were sometimes dumped. From Lad Law Hill up there, on a good day you can see Blackpool Tower, or miles and miles east to the power station at Ferrybridge by Pontefract. The policemen spoke of how beautiful it was; they were decent, steady men with a quiet fund of local pride and a string of comic Tod tales involving green men, large stuffed dogs, 'Saucy Cyril and the Succulent Sausage' – which last, I regret to say, was off the record.

That night in Calder Valley, thirty miles end to end, Inspector Ian Samson had three sergeants, seventeen constables, two traffic officers, a night detective and a dog. He told me they had the same crime everybody else had – just less of it. And of the current travails of his political masters, he remarked with a wry grin that, if the government was representative of the people, then 5 per cent of them would be criminals, wouldn't they? Then he added, with a hint of sadness, 'I think honesty would be nice. General human failings I don't mind, but honesty . . . oh well. Maybe that's wishful thinking.'

He was going to vote Tory for (he readily admitted), 'Purely personal selfish reasons.' As to Mayes and Sanderson, they were undecided. Sanderson said, 'If I thought I could trust any of them, that's the thing. This Piers Merchant – oh, but they make me smile, these people.'

At noon the next day, the Mayors of Todmorden and Calderdale formally opened the town's new petanque terrain in Centre Vale Park. The park was a grand open space with tennis courts and an astroturf five-a-side pitch, a roller-blading track, a crazy golf circuit and four bowling greens. Petanque, said Tod's Mayor, 'Can be played in almost any weather, which is an advantage in Todmorden.' From which, one infers, Todmordians in future will be chucking boules about while the rain's coming down on them in stair-rods.

Today it was sunny; trees and railings were festooned with balloons and pennants in merry red, white and blue. Two guys played sax and electric banjo: one had a pink beret and a Gallic striped T-shirt; the other wore red shoes, a black beret and a black tailcoat with silver-embroidered lapels and a big snake on the back. Two couples from the Pye Nest Petanque Club in Sowerby Bridge, smartly turned out in uniform black sweatshirts, played an inaugural challenge match with the locals.

McCafferty was there – the petanque terrain was the work of her husband's Leisure Services Department – and she was worrying about Stephen Pearson, wondering why the Liberals didn't seem to be campaigning. She wanted Pearson out wooing Tories away from Sir Donald, not heading off to help his party in other seats they had better chances of winning.

She was worried about other things, too. On Hebden Royd Parish Council, they'd struck an impasse over the election of a new mayor; the council split seven-seven between Labour and Liberal so the incumbent mayor, a Labour man called Les Siddall, used his casting vote to re-elect himself. Now you may think this is small fry; voting for yourself to remain Mayor of Hebden Royd hardly constitutes a lustful grab for big-time power. It was just an act of rather crass small-town vanity; the bloke gets to wear a chain for another year, and to see his mug in the local paper now and then. But in small towns these things ruffle feathers, in the rumpus Siddall was obliged to withdraw, and Sir Donald took his chance to say sagely how that was Labour for you – voting for themselves in cosy corners. So be afraid, be *very* afraid – one minute Hebden Royd, tomorrow the world.

Daft, I know, but the smallest thing can do for you. That week, Walworth Road had been phone-canvassing squeeze votes in Rastrick – and one voter gave the caller a hard time. So after the voter hung up, the canvasser muttered to himself, 'Bastard.' Unfortunately, while the voter had hung up, his wife was still listening on the extension and she heard that. Naturally, she was more than a shade upset, and so was McCafferty. What if they wrote to the *Courier*? It could be the smallest thing . . .

While we talked, the boys with the sax and banjo led a conga of oldsters away from the petanque terrain towards lunch; they kicked off with an impro version of 'Swingin' Safari', then segued neatly into the 'Pink Panther'. Lunch was in a clubhouse run by the town's four bowling clubs; one of the women serving it had babysat for McCafferty when (in another life) she'd lived way up in the hamlet of Colden by Blackshaw Head. They talked a while and then McCafferty put herself round the room, chatting to the bowlers. While she did that I spoke with Alan Turner, the secretary of one of the clubs, and he was justifiably proud of his immaculate four greens. Other places got vandalised, he said, but here in Tod they kept an eye; himself, he'd cycle by every day, sometimes four or five times. It was a John Major image if ever I heard one, this nice old boy on his bike minding his bowling greens in this tucked-away little town under sturdy Pennine rises – and he had, indeed, been a Tory all his life.

Now, however, he said it was difficult. 'I don't appreciate some of the things that have gone on, but as yet I've not found another party I prefer. So I'm undecided. I shall finish up voting Tory, but I'm not satisfied; I'm especially dead against what they've done in Europe. Now I've had that Referendum video, I like that, I fully agree with every word of it. 'Cause Europe to me, I've had enough of it. I didn't fight in a war to be governed by Europe.'

So I told him he ought to vote for the Referendum Party. Sly creep that I am.

'These are they who being peaceable citizens of Todmorden at the call of king and country and in defence of their native land left all that was dear to them, endured hardship, faced danger, and finally passed out of the sight of man by the path of duty and self-sacrifice, giving up their own lives that others might live in freedom. Their name liveth for evermore.'

So said the inscription on the war memorial at Centre Vale, in a well-tended square of ornamental gardens. It was engraved on a wall behind an attractive Art Deco statue of a helmeted figure with a sword, standing on a sphere borne aloft by sorrowing maidens. To either side ran all the names: thirty-two plaques with a maximum of thirty names apiece. So in the First World War, Todmorden – which had a population of maybe 30,000 then, a good deal more than today – lost some 700 of its sons, and 200 more in the Second World War. In the light of which it's not hard to see how some people, especially older people, might think the Referendum tape made sense.

Lunch was over. There was a chilly wind, and grey clouds drifting in a blue sky sporadically obscured the sun. McCafferty lay back on a bench in the memorial gardens, gathering energy for the next Tod job; I had a peek round a little aviary and aquarium. There were cockatiels and java sparrows, peach-faced lovebirds and zebra finches; there were banjo catfish and rummy nose tetras, clown loaches and pink kissing gourami. I was taken with the idea that a fish could be called a tiger oscar or a filament barb, and I was taken too with the civilised oddity of their presence in a park in Todmorden. It's the sort of place no one goes to, and more people should – because you never know. You might, of an afternoon, be staring entranced at a filament barb when the strains of a popular tune will waft your way, and you'll look across the floral gardens to see two men in berets strolling past playing sax and banjo. This England – it has all manner of unexpected moments.

It also has things that make you want to spit blood. In the middle of the garden stood two plinths which, until six or eight months earlier, had been home to two cherubs that matched the main statue – cherubs bearing the Lamp of Memory and the Shield of Honour. The council estimated their worth at around £7,000, and someone had stolen them – so now they'll be adorning some rich bastard's garden, when before they'd belonged to Todmorden in honour of their dead.

We walked into town to the market, under the shadow of the giant arches of the railway viaduct. On the way we were joined by two other Labour women, and one of them said to McCafferty, 'I hope you win soon. It's too much of a shock to the system seeing David in a suit all the time.'

John Prescott was coming on his key seat tour; a bus stop was coned off ready for him. His advance guard, a big Geordie called Phil Wilson, said in three days of the previous week they'd done nine seats: Falmouth, Plymouth, Exeter, Vale of Glamorgan, Monmouth, Forest of Dean, Kingswood in Bristol, Swindon and Edmonton. This week, from Tuesday to Thursday morning, they'd hit seven more: Welwyn Hatfield, Milton Keynes, Northampton North, Luton North and South, Lincoln and Cleethorpes. Today they'd been to High Peak, Rochdale and Oldham; after Tod, they were racing on to Keighley. He looked about him and said, 'I've been places in this country I didn't even know existed.'

A Tod parish councillor called Steve Martin turned up, and Tarlo asked him why he wasn't wearing a badge. Martin said, 'Badges are for children, not grown-ups. I wear a sharp suit now. New Labour, see? Haven't you been on your training courses?'

At 3.15 on the dot the Prescott Express arrived, a luxury grey coach emblazoned with the Labour rose and the slogan, 'It's good to vote.' It pulled into the bus stop, a little speaker warbling that 'Things can only get better' – and what happened next was quite the Toddest job I ever saw. Out stepped Prescott, sternly smiling and shaking hands, and instantly a fan of youthful aides spread out through the market before him, pressing red and yellow stickers and posters on anyone who'd have them, and handing flags to bewildered children. Was this the Deputy Leader of the Labour Party? Or Ronald MacDonald?

Prescott steamed into the crowd like a rugby player with McCafferty in tow, a *Courier* boy frantically scribing beside him, half a dozen snappers in scurrying orbit round this electoral nucleus, and a Hale-Bopp tail of minders with mobiles apparently surgically attached to their ears. Prescott had a supply of credit-sized cards with Labour's five pledges on it, and he distributed them into every hand he could shake. He was particularly good with old ladies, to all of whom he invariably said, 'Here's my telephone number, give me a ring sometime,' leaving them tickled and clucking jelly-kneed in his wake.

'Can I say hello? Let me give you my card.' Another shake of the hand, a smile, a laugh, a question, an answer, admiring this stallholder's floral hat, this other one's display of greeting cards, but always moving, round and round through the indoor market and the outdoor, past stalls and through the people, a fizzing packet of energy, a jostling ruck drawing every eye in the place. As he passed, people gaped and stared at his cheery bundling passage, and behind him there rippled little echoes of reaction. 'Well,' said one voice at a butcher's stall, 'they can't do any worse than the lot we've got now, can they?'

'Sure you can shake my hand,' muttered a woman by the bus shelter, 'but I'll still not be voting for you.'

A woman told her husband she needed some money and he answered, 'Let's tap these chaps. They look like they've plenty.'

'Ooh,' swooned an old lady, 'he looks just like he does on TV.'

In amongst it, I heard a minder in a grey suit tell someone on his mobile, 'We want to try and avoid a picture of that if we can.' Dear me, but I'm naïve. I thought that was up to the picture editor.

On Prezza pressed, McCafferty introducing herself beside him to anyone she could catch with a wide-eyed and rather frantic smile. You could see her telling people she was the candidate, and all the while you could see her thinking, Christ, which way's he's heading off now?

To a rack of flower seeds. 'Delphiniums. Lovely. Only once they're in they start taking over, don't they?' The girl looks baffled. Do they? Prescott smiles, shakes another hand, gives out another card, moves on. And let's hope he's better at helping Blair run the country than he is in the garden because (an expert writes) delphiniums don't take over much at all.

Making more sense on the political than the horticultural front, forcefully Prescott tells the *Courier*, 'We don't take people for granted. We've got to earn every vote. That's why I'm doing 10,000 miles.'

I'm thinking, five more minutes, you'll have done 10,000 miles round this market, never mind the rest of England.

The reporter says, 'Do you like being in Todmorden?'

What a silly question; he's only been here five minutes. But Prescott copes easily. He says, 'I've been here before and it's always got a fresh wind, hasn't it? But if you come from Hull you know all about a fresh wind.'

It's 3.30 and somebody's asking where we're going, and somebody else is saying, 'Back to the bus.' What, already? Prescott crams in one more circuit of the outdoor stalls, and this time he's stopped by a woman in a bright red jacket who wants to know what he's going to do about her pension. He tells her, 'Soon as you've got one, ring me up.'

Stoutly she retorts, 'Flattery will get you nowhere, Mr Prescott,' then launches into explaining her situation. Again he copes, then abruptly she's switching horses and now she's on about her hundred pounds' worth of shares in the electricity company. She's had a letter from John Major, she says, and I'm thinking, Uh-oh. Windfall tax, scared small shareholder.

'That letter,' she says, 'there's that many mistakes in it. There's sentences beginning with And, there's sentences beginning with But. I've thought, I'll write to that John Major and I'll tell him, oi! Back to Basics!'

I'm thinking, Brilliant. She's going to vote Labour because the Tories have bad grammar? Mind you, I'm done for, aren't I? I start sentences with And and But all the time . . .

And Prescott's away. A guy at the last stall calls out, 'You off then?'

He grins and tells him, 'Half an hour in each. Keep running.'

Heading back to the bus, there's a BBC camera waiting to catch a shot of him clearing the market, in better light on open ground. Ann Martin grabs McCafferty by the shoulder, shunts her forward to make sure she's right there by Prescott's side, in step with him for the shot. Smart thinking — because in the end that is, of course, what every minute of this is about. Arrive, colour the place red, run round and round in it, shake lots of hands, dish out some cards, get pictured doing it and then — precisely twenty-three minutes after you arrived — get back on the bus and zoom off to do it all again on a steam train in Keighley.

As the bus pulled off, a little gaggle of local Labour folk came to a stunned halt by the shelter, gasping and bemused, as if they'd been abruptly picked up in a tornado, whirled about for twenty minutes and just as abruptly set down again. As one, four of us reached for cigarettes, lit them and stood dimly contemplating this rapid and mysterious event. McCafferty breathed out hard, grinning. She said, 'He moves at a pace for a short tubby fella, doesn't he? My goodness, he's hard to keep up with.'

We went to get our breath back over a brew at the Bear. Now you're not supposed to smoke there — of course — but Cherie Blair's dad Tony Booth was in the party and, I rather got the impression, this was a raffish bloke who'd cheerfully smoke anywhere and to hell with it. So we sat there sipping and puffing, and the news came in that the Scottish Tory chairman Sir Michael Hirst had just resigned. Stewart, Smith, Hirst, three in a week.

Someone asked, 'Sir Michael who?'

McCafferty shrugged and said, 'Who cares? It's another one down, isn't it?'

17

LESS WIND UNDER LABOUR

Sir Michael Hirst stood down, but Neil Hamilton didn't. The Tory leadership backed him; then they tried to get him to go; then they admitted that they couldn't. Still, Neil Hamilton was innocent. I know this, because his agent told me so. He told me on April Fool's Day.

The Tatton constituency headquarters was a grand old pile of red brick in Knutsford. There was a little entrance foyer in which you were invited to smile, because you were on video while you pressed the buzzer. Cautious folk, evidently. To one side, amid a litter of press releases about the wicked propaganda campaign being conducted against Hamilton by the *Guardian*, was an announcement that all communication with the media would be handled exclusively by written press statement from the constituency chairman. So I went in and asked Hamilton's agent, would he talk to me? Sure he would.

His name was Peter McDowell and, to be fair, he did ask for ID. Trouble is, I'm a shabby fat bloke who doesn't work for anybody – so look, I said, all I've got is my credit card. After all, Neil Hamilton doesn't take cash, does he?

He readily accepted this perfunctory identification, then we talked at length about how hideous it was to be at the centre of the media glare – and to a point, I had some sympathy. He told how they checked every call to be sure it was genuine, and the other day they had a call from a woman claiming to be a Conservative voter in the constituency. They said they'd get back to her, checked the call on 1471 – and it came from London. So McDowell rang back, and got an ad agency. Thinking on his feet, he asked, Can you put me through to whoever's handling Mr Fayed's account?

The response came, Sure. I'll put you through to X. So X picks up, McDowell says he's Hamilton's agent and X hangs up. It would make you pretty paranoid, yes? Then you're getting the anonymous stuff through the door, like a photocopied image of Hamilton with the message underneath: 'Vote Tory. Vote Hamilton. A Liar and a Cheat.' A second page added, in outline capitals blocked in with pink felt-tip: 'AND ANOTHER THING . . . HAVE YOU SEEN HIS *WIFE*? SUCH *GREED* ETCHED IN THAT WOMAN'S FACE! YOU ALMOST FEEL SORRY FOR HAMILTON!'

Almost . . . and there's no call for this. But the bottom line is – when the man looks as bent as a fish hook, what do you expect? And OK, McDowell conceded, 'If the press carry on, it'll go on looking bad all round the country. But what would you have us do? If we get rid of Neil, or Neil goes, it just moves on to somebody else – so that doesn't solve the party's problem. And anyway, what's the right thing to do? The chairman and I and most people here feel the right thing is, you don't dump an innocent man.'

Fair enough – and Hamilton did indeed continue to protest his innocence – but there weren't many people left who believed him. All that mattered to Hamilton now, however, was that the voters of Tatton should believe him. He'd therefore given a full explanation of his case to the *Knutsford Guardian*. It was long, confusing, blustersome, and informed throughout with the blindly arrogant belief that he'd never done the slightest thing wrong. The basis of his defence was that since Fayed couldn't remember precisely the amounts he'd given him, or precisely where or when he'd given them, then obviously he hadn't given him anything at all and was making it all up. I was left, to say the least, unconvinced.

But back to McDowell. He told me the media were voracious, they didn't want to hear Neil's side of things, and they had this deadline-dictated attitude: 'All they want is the next development in the story, and generally that's the next scalp.' So why, against the express policy of his embattled association, was he now talking to me? Blithely he showed me a ten-point advice sheet he'd written for other constituencies who might find themselves in the sleaze mill, titled, 'When the Rat-Pack attack'. Point 7 was, 'Always deal with the national press pleasantly, as though they were real human beings.' From one through to ten, it was a case study in escalating panic management – and Point 10 said that even if you did everything right, you'd probably be let down by someone in London. 'Expect this and be ready to stand firm regardless.'

It looked as if McDowell had recently faxed these wise words to a colleague under similar pressure, because across the bottom he'd scribbled a note: 'Tony. I think we are at stage 10! Don't weaken! The only way the Tory party wins this is if Neil wins!'

When we finished talking, he asked if my word was good. I told him it was. As I'd explained, I was writing a book, and he could read it when it came out in July. So, he asked, I'm not going to read this in the *Sun* tomorrow? I told him, absolutely not. And I went away thinking, This was *so* incompetent. He didn't know me from Adam; I could have had this guy panicked at Point 10 in the *Sun* the next day as easy as crossing the street.

McDowell said the rat-pack at Hamilton's house had diminished to just three or four people, which he took as a good sign. So I drove through the wholesome villages of this moneyed part of Cheshire to Nether Alderley, and found that the rat-pack at Hamilton's gate actually remained rather larger than McDowell had told me.

Bought about the start of the Nineties (and how much did an MP earn in those days anyway?) the house was very large indeed, a grand old vicarage cosily situated down a secluded lane by the Alderley church. Around the gate loitered three TV cameramen, a clutch of photographers and Jojo Moyes from the *Independent*. I asked what they were doing; they said they were bored out of their gourds, eating sausage rolls, kipping in their cars and generally just hanging about. One of them said, 'We don't want to be here, do we? But whose fault is it that we are?'

A car engine started up by the house and one of the snappers said, 'Driver's side, here she comes.' They fanned out ready to get pictures of Christine Hamilton coming out of the drive; she shot through the pack and me, innocent soul that I am, I just stood there in the middle of the lane. Did she brake? Forget it. I had to dive for the verge double-quick. How many points do you get for a hack then? 'Maybe,' said one of the snappers, 'she's had enough.

Maybe she's bashed him over the head with a hammer and now she's doing a runner.'

'Oh,' said one of the others, 'I *wish.*'

As it happens, I have relatives in Tatton. They're wealthy people, and Conservative to the soles of their odor-eaters. There was, they said, no way they could vote Labour or Liberal – but they were angered and confused to find themselves put in a situation where they couldn't vote Conservative either, when it appeared to them that the candidate for that interest was a venal, obdurate and shameless liar.

They were not politically-minded people; they were, however, the kind of people who feel it's incumbent upon you to vote because that's your duty as a citizen. Yet now they were effectively disenfranchised, and wanted Hamilton taken from them so they could vote as they wished to – and I think, myself, this is the worst of Hamilton's failings. Politicians have been bent before, and they'll be so again – but here was a man who, having let everybody else down, was now prepared to let his own people down too.

At the constituency headquarters in Knutsford, they had a brass plate on the wall by the door announcing what the building was, and that Tatton's MP was Neil Hamilton. To which all I can say is, brass plate, brass neck.

Over the next three days, the main parties issued their manifestos. The Conservatives employed a man to dress up as a chicken and follow Tony Blair about, the *Mirror* responded with a headless chicken and a pair of foxes – high-minded stuff – while Labour breathlessly let it be known that our Tone had hand-written his contract with the nation with a fountain pen in his garden. So what? I don't care if he dictated it standing on his head in his boxer shorts. But this was a campaign that so far looked to be nothing but dumb and dumber, conducted in a sump of sleaze, a confetti of fabrications and a cascade of gimmicks.

I particularly liked the Tory idea of tax breaks for conventional married couples. What could be more symbolic of their family values than the offer of a bribe to people prepared to fit in with their antique vision of society? I can see the vicar now: 'Do you,

Peter Richard, take this woman Rebecca Louise and her personal allowance . . .'

Blair, meanwhile, went on the *Today* programme to trail Labour's manifesto, and said he'd confront any uppity unions with implacable toughness. He wanted anyone listening to be absolutely clear about that, whether they were 'a trade unionist, a member of the public, or somebody else.' So, members of the public aside, presumably he was pitching for the alien vote in Tod here.

Meanwhile, Alex Powell and her mum filled envelopes in Brighouse. With Easter passed and four weeks to go, this was supposed to be Labour's 'second forty-eight hours'. Alex spread her hands and said, 'The next big push, eh? Me and my mum.'

Perhaps I'd been naïve. I'd expected people knocking on doors, talking to voters, putting themselves about – but so far a modern election, it appeared, basically consisted of a large amount of media management, a gigantic string of mail-shots, and Peter Snow doing the butterfly crawl through a shiny soup of computer graphics. The latter, however, were no kind of guide. ICM in the *Guardian* had Labour 18 points ahead; MORI in the *Times* had them leading by 27. Take your pick.

David Tarlo said he preferred the smaller figure; he wanted people kicked out of their complacency and off their butts and he felt, he admitted, pretty glum that it wasn't happening. Yes, the letters were getting delivered, Todmorden and Hebden Bridge had people working in them, Elland was OK – but around Brighouse and too much of the lower valley, they didn't have the bodies. The New Model Labour Army, on this evidence, was a lot of people who'd succumbed to a marketing campaign and sent Walworth Road a cheque. But actually going out and doing something – nah. So they were, said Tarlo, becoming uncomfortably reliant on the people from Barnsley, who'd turned up again over the Easter weekend. In short, it was as if the campaign had started two weeks ago in the media, but in the real world it had barely started at all.

There was also a left hand/right hand problem all the time. With hundreds of paid staff hacking away around the country, and thousands more volunteers, that wasn't surprising, but it could get folk tetchy. On Thursday April 3rd Labour launched their manifesto, and Jack Straw was due to come and puff it in Halifax that evening. McCafferty only found out that morning; in Brighouse at midday, vexed about that, Tarlo cried out at Ian Carvell, 'We need more visits!'

Trouble was, said Carvell, the big guns were mostly shying away from the Calderdale seats because the Tories had the council for a target – and just that week, two Labour councillors hadn't exactly helped. 'Councillors in Love Tangle,' yelled the *Courier*. Michelle Mayers had been cautioned for criminal damage at the property of her former lover Stewart Brown, after (allegedly) bashing his door down with a rock. McCafferty muttered darkly that she really didn't need this. So what can I tell you? Vote Labour, and you'll get some reet hard women.

Still, Carvell thought they'd be all right. Life lately had been a regular string of lessons in crisis management, and they'd coped with them all. They'd had Alice Mahon's campaign co-ordinator knocked off his bike, they'd had a fire in the office in Keighley, they'd had a nightmarishly sensitive selection process in Bradford West, with branches suspended over membership irregularities and a tinglingly complex racial angle – all that, and he hadn't had a car.

He'd packed in the Kent–Yorkshire commute, left the Granada down south and finally persuaded the party to let him rent a car locally for the final month. Before that he'd been racketing about in trains and cabs, or begging lifts from volunteers. But at least, where he was based in Keighley, they had volunteers who could give him those lifts. Whereas here in Calder Valley . . . he shrugged, and laughed. 'Well, you can see I'm chain-smoking.'

But he was not, he assured me, stressed out. In the autumn, he'd thought if there'd been a November election, Labour would lose in Calder Valley; now, he thought they'd win. He didn't believe the polls (who did?) but the fact was, in all this time they hadn't changed – and in the meantime, he simply couldn't understand what the Tories were doing. They'd called it, so two weeks ago Labour came out of the blocks – whereas all round the country, Conservative associations were only holding their adoption meetings this week. It was as if they'd planned for a three- or four-week campaign all along, and Major opting for six had surprised them as much as anybody else.

He said, 'It's as if they're trying to dislodge us, it's as if *they're* the opposition. So you have to ask, why did Major do it? You have to assume there's something really rotten in the Downey report, I can't see any other reason. Either that, or they're just terminally disorganised – and my heart can't believe that. They've been a phenomenal electoral machine – and that's why I'm working so hard. I can't believe there isn't something up their sleeve, I can't believe it's going to be a walkover. But you keep waiting for the onslaught and it doesn't come. They just don't look like a party that's trying to win. So we might not be completely together here, but the world doesn't know that. Whereas the world knows the Tories are all over the place. I mean, if Merchant or Hamilton or any of these other guys had been Labour MPs, they'd have been deselected overnight.'

So he was calm; it was going to be OK. Yes, Calder Valley lacked bodies – but he'd still opted to base himself in Keighley because he thought they needed more help there. He said, 'You can't teach Ann Martin to suck eggs, she's been playing this game too long. Then Tim's clever, Alex runs the office fine – so the people that matter here don't need me. Besides, it's not a sprint, it's a 1500 metres. It's the finish to the tape that matters.'

I'd had it put to me, I said, that at the eye of all this McCafferty might lack the necessary ruthlessness – and Carvell smiled. He said, 'She's turned on me a couple of times, I'll tell you.' He made an abrupt little gesture, sweeping one hand back across the top of his head, expressively indicating how a man might feel if he found himself abruptly deposited in a wind tunnel. So, no problem there then.

He shrugged and said, 'That's OK. I'm the bogeyman, aren't I? You don't want them hating each other – so if they've got to hate someone, let them all hate me.' He grinned his shatter-toothed grin and said cheerfully that it was his job to be, 'A professional sneaky bastard.' Whereas David Tarlo, 'He's got a bit of a naïve side. He thinks the world should always be fair. And it's not, is it?'

We were eating lunch in the Black Bull over the road from the office, where the fish butties are as big as your head. We were there an hour and during that time, besides eating a gigantic hot beef baguette, he smoked five cigarettes. He had to light them off my lighter, he'd lost his – then, fumbling round his pockets, he found it in his top pocket, and it had been there all the while. I watched him as he lit his fifth cigarette and I said mildly, 'You're telling me you're not stressed out?'

Back in the office Alex was taking calls, a man from the MSF was canvassing on the phone, and the bloke who'd wanted to stick an electric sign on his balcony in Mytholmroyd (a plan sadly ditched – it was too expensive) had come in with his daughters to do an envelope blitz. By another desk Tarlo was flapping, with Tony the Denim Geezer in faintly baffled attendance. Tarlo said he had to get these garden posters out round Elland, but he had to go to Ovenden too to pick up more letters from ISCO5 . . .

I said, What's going on?

Tony said, 'Fucked if I know.'

Tarlo said, 'So if I go to ISCO5 . . .'

Tony started jumping up and down on the spot. 'Will somebody tell me,' he wailed, 'what *is* ISCO5?'

I said I'd go get the letters, and asked how to get there. There followed much confused poring over maps. Tony grinned and said, 'The economy's safe with us. We're just not too good at giving directions.'

Then I needed to know how to find Alice Mahon's offices in Halifax afterwards. 'Right,' said Alex, 'you want the car park behind the Beehive and Crossed Keys . . .'

'By the time you get there,' said Tony, 'it'll have changed its name.'

Amid the bustle, the union man canvassing on the phone gave us his best reply of the day so far. 'Some years ago,' this voter told him, 'we voted once and for all time. We voted for Jesus Christ our Lord who, when he returns to earth – which he'll be doing very soon – will solve all the world's problems. And we won't need a government then, will we?'

The union man looked at the canvass forms and said, 'I don't think we have a code for that.'

When I got back from the printers, Alex was entering canvass returns into the Elpack electoral register system. Unfortunately, there was a gremlin about; you stuck an ident code by a voter – and the voter disappeared. Not quite the idea, that.

Ann Martin pitched up, fraught. Aside from the computer playing up (it would take 'til ten that evening for their boffin to fix it) she was still running the MEP's office in Bradford, and they'd taken on the party's candidate for Shipley to help out. Now this candidate was twenty-four, he looked about fourteen, he needed a swing of over 11 per cent to unseat Sir Marcus Fox and he was, said Martin, just a tad worked up about it. 'He's saying he's going to lose by fifty votes *and then they'll be sorry*, and as he's saying it he's going white as a sheet. I had to get him to lie down. Poor lamb.'

I went to Halifax to see Jack Straw launch the manifesto. Straw said he'd been in London for the launch, he'd done Wakefield and Batley, now he was here, then it was up to Beacon Hill for the local TV. In Batley, he said, it was so windy that he'd made a new pledge – uncosted, of course – that there would be less wind under Labour.

Well – it's a personal opinion that the Labour manifesto was less windy than the Tory one, concentrating as it did on such deliberately modest promises. But the thing that really mattered was its plea for trust. This was a party proclaiming that government needed to be made respectable again – and in the age of the Hamiltons, this was no bad thing to hope for.

Alice Mahon thought Hamilton would be forced to quit. When the *Courier* had gone she asked Straw, 'Do you think Hamilton will go?'

Straw's deaf in one ear, and she'd asked the question on that side. Mishearing her, he answered, 'No, I don't believe the polls either.'

18

ONE STEP TOO FAR?

Stephen Pearson challenged Sir Donald to a public debate. Sir Donald sagely declined; he tended to avoid platforms. He would not, after all, want to risk his voters getting the impression (entirely false, of course) that their MP was an inarticulate pudding.

McCafferty's diary filled with B-list shadow visits, meetings, openings, launches and lunches. She fretted that somewhere in amongst it she had to write at least five speeches: for the World Development Movement, the churches, the police, the NFU, and a mock election at Brighouse High. The teachers and the Charter 88 people would probably want something too. They were, she said, all different and specific, 'So unfortunately Sir Donald's little thing that he pulls out of his pocket won't do.'

She was getting up earlier every day and, she laughed wearily, it wasn't making a blind bit of difference. She wanted to put herself about the markets at Elland or Brighouse – but you'd look a bit stupid doing it on your own, wouldn't you? So she worked the phone, stroking switchers, fielding queries and complaints. Mostly people wanted to know about health, education or pensions; she sent out several policy documents every day.

A teacher in a grant-maintained school told her she was unde-cided, but she couldn't vote Labour because they were going to close grant-maintained schools, and then she'd lose her job. McCafferty told her they weren't, that it was absolutely not Labour's policy to be sending teachers down the road, that on the contrary they'd be employing more teachers to get primary class sizes down. 'But look,' she said, 'I'm just a politician. I'll send you the policy, then you can see it in black and white. And here's my home phone number if you want to talk about it some more.' Another note, another address, another document copied and posted.

A switcher in Hipperholme said, 'I'm voting Labour 'cause it's time for a change.'

So he'd voted Tory in '92?

'No,' he said gloomily, 'I voted Labour in '92 'cause it was time for a change then too.'

But they lost in '92, so Blair turned the party upside down to make it electable. Now a man in Ryburn said, 'I'll be voting for your position.' He laughed and said, 'Conservative.'

A policeman told me (neutrally) that Hebden Bridge was a place where you saw a lot of middle-aged men with ponytails. If, however, Hebden Bridge had grown too twee for you, too snuggled up to the mainstream, you could always bunk off beyond Todmorden to the wild far tops of the valley. Up in the village of Cornholme on the constituency's western rim, you could carry on being as alternative as you liked.

It was a grey little place; the valley was steep and dark, with only a thin ribbon of pale sky above you. Barely fifty yards long, stubby cobbled streets of terraced houses ran off either side of the main road, like the teeth of a double-sided comb, until they bumped abruptly into the sharply rising hillsides. They had a big mill and a bobbin works here once, half a dozen weaving sheds, a dyeworks and a tannery, branches of Lloyds and the Halifax, and thirty-six shops. Now there were three shops left. One of the Baptist chapels had closed, and the Methodists were gone too.

Red Water Arts, on the other hand, looked to be doing pretty well. Recently registered as a charity, it organised activity weeks for kids, music courses for people who worked with the disabled, local festivals and 'creative camps'. They'd had an exchange trip to Hungary for fifteen local kids, they'd had some people come up from Birmingham to stage a re-enactment of the Peasants' Revolt when the poll tax came in, and another time a local anthropologist who'd worked in Central Asia got everyone busy building yurts. The inclination to mock is irresistible – on top of the

Pennines, how handy is a yurt? – but nonetheless, these were people getting things done in a place that didn't have much else going for it.

On Saturday April 5th, they had a fund-raising day; it was in the hall of what had previously been St Michael and All the Angels' church school, but which was now a community centre. At three that afternoon, the place was packed with the best part of a hundred people, half of them kids. There were bits and bobs of jumble, a cake-stall, a woman dressed as a Napoleonic brigand doing face-painting, and a three-piece band playing meandering, dozy, vaguely jazzy rock music. Half a dozen big canvases hung on the walls, the paintings bland and dreamy-spooky, like bad record covers from the 1970s. Ethnic-type pennants hung in the rafters. This was henna'd hair country, a post-hippy gathering of woolly jumpers and Indian necklaces.

A spot of Reiki healing was also available. Now Reiki, it says in the brochure, 'Is the vital, universal life energy flowing around and through all living things' – so obviously, if you can get hold of a force like that, the sky's the limit. Aches and pains, back trouble, arthritis, rheumatism, sciatica, menstrual and menopausal problems, constipation, migraine, asthma, stress, anxiety, depression, ME, no problem. Get Reiki'd, you'll be shipshape.

You could go to Red Water's Back Rough Farm and get taught all this stuff in a weekend. Your teacher would be Dr John Armitage, 'Also known by his spiritual name Haridas. He is a Batchelor (sic) of Homeopathic Medicine and a Master Healer. He is a pioneer in crystal technologies in the UK for personal and planetary healing and ascension . . . John works with energy of unconditional love and compassion. Haridas facilitates workshops around the planet channeling (sic) from the Ascended Masters.'

The course cost £175 (but you did get a manual and a certificate) and dear God, don't people fall for some hogwash? These were, however, McCafferty's people – albeit the wackier fringe of them. These were the off cumdens who, whatever you think of their dafter notions, had moved to the top of the valley in the Sixties and Seventies when it was a remote place, fading away to the point of moribund, and boosted it up with a bit of new energy. With a bit of Reiki, even. And she had to be sure that these people, on May 1st, would come out – because while you'd think they'd be

Labour (more or less) they did need stroking. As she said, 'It wouldn't be the biggest thing in their lives, would it?'

So she ended up in a plastic chair in her politician's overcoat with the red rosette on it, while a blonde hippy plonked her Reiki-channelling hands on her head and her neck. And I had to ask, didn't I? How was it for you? She laughed and said, 'I didn't feel anything. But I was sat in a chair for ten minutes with my eyes shut, so it was very calming.'

We drove back on single-track roads along the misty tops, on the high terraces before the moors begin where the upland farmers first settled to produce wool. There were people eking out a life up here long before the valley bottom was settled; the wool came first, when the valley below was still swamp and royal hunting forest. At remote farmhouses, in little hamlets and the cobbled village of Heptonstall, gates and windows sported McCafferty posters – but still she worried there weren't enough of them. Tarlo said it was all right and she told him, 'You have to remember I'm the candidate, I'm fragile. I want to see posters *everywhere*.'

We talked about a woman who'd been at the Red Water party. She and her husband had been active Labour people once, but they'd left the party now and might well not even vote for it. McCafferty and Tarlo knew a few like that, who felt Blair had gone too far to the right. McCafferty said she could understand it up to a point but, she went on with not a small hint of anger, 'There's a propensity to be holier than thou in people like that. It's almost namby-pamby to the point of unforgivable. Do they prefer John Major?' That afternoon she'd met a young man who was so far to the left he was all but a revolutionary communist, 'But come May 1st he'll be voting, won't he? Because *he knows his duty*.'

Voters falling away from Labour at the left end of the spectrum was, however, a fear I'd heard voiced more and more. Between complacency and a disgruntled resentment over the move to the centre, would the old Labour vote bother turning out at all? Yet the following morning (when you got past the IRA wrecking the Grand National) the Sunday papers brought news that Blair was now accepting privatisation. He would, we were told, go to the City to tell them, 'The test is not public ownership but the public

interest . . . where there is no over-riding reason for preferring the
public provision of goods and services, the presumption should be
that economic activity is best left to the private sector.' So maybe
Parcelforce might be sold after all, or the air traffic control system –
which news, I can assure you, was about as welcome to the Calder
Valley Labour Party as a lemonade enema.

At the Trades Club in Hebden Bridge, a folk-singer called Joe
Stead gave a benefit for McCafferty's campaign. Built in 1924,
adorned with fetching stained-glass windows over the doorways,
the club belonged to the local branches of the Labour Party, and it
was a thriving place. Near lifeless twenty years back, its current
vigour was testament to a more useful energy among the off cumdens than Reiki; they'd borrowed money from a brewery, put in a
lot of work and time, done the place up, paid the loan off, and now
they hosted three or four gigs a week, with jazz on Sunday
lunchtimes.

The club was upstairs, above a community centre and the Labour
Party's local campaign office. At the top of the stairs, big notice-
boards had pictures of artists who'd performed here, with ads and
leaflets promoting local activities. A band called Owterzeds had a
handwritten notice looking for 'a guitarist with a sense of humour',
to which someone had added the inevitable graffito, 'You'd need
one with them.'

The club had two rooms: a larger one for the gigs, and a smaller
one with a pool table. Both were comfortable and smartly done up.
On the walls of the latter hung pictures of Keir Hardie, and the
Trades and Labour Club Commitee in 1918. On the bar-top a
large collection bottle was labelled, 'The Donald Thompson
Retirement Fund.' In the main room, Joe Stead filled the little
stage, a big man with a banjo for some songs and a bandolin for
others; he'd had this specially made – it had a banjo's neck and a
mandolin's body. 'We thought about calling it a manjo,' he said, 'but
we were worried someone might try and eat it during the interval.'

His act had a nice twist to it; in the programme he'd printed a list
of seventy-five subjects and songs, and rather than getting up and
playing what he wanted, the audience got to call out what they
wanted to hear. His repertoire included songs having a go at

(among others) British Nuclear Fuels, the French, the Tories, Bob Dylan, Paul Simon and the royal family. He wanted the audience joining in; he said, 'Let's get our tonsils ready for this election. 'Cause one thing we mustn't be is complacent. If we're complacent, we won't win it.'

Spots of light span round the room from a mirror globe turning in the ceiling's iron girders. In one corner McCafferty sat with Tarlo and Ann Martin, sipping orange juice. She was exhausted and wanted to go to bed, but she wanted to thank Stead for his money-raising efforts at the interval, and to try and gee up the forty or so people there to come out and do some work. When the time came she gave a short speech, urging, pleading for assistance – but how many of these people would we see coming to Brighouse in the next few weeks, to help where help was most needed? In truth, very few. They'd vote, they'd put money in the bottle, they might drop some letters or leaflets where they lived – but their enthusiasm was limited. This wasn't Sierra Man here; Tony Blair didn't hit many buttons for this lot.

On our way out, I was waiting in the street with David Tarlo for his wife when a bloke with cropped blond hair and an earring turned up at the door. He asked, 'How's Chris' campaign doing then? Got to beat the singing butcher, eh? Mind, she's gone all weird now, hasn't she? Straight hair, pearls and twinset. It's kinky, that is.'

It was Labour's problem in microcosm. Like her party, she had made herself presentable – and the people she'd started out with in that party didn't know what to make of it.

Ann Martin left about eleven that night; the next Sunday morning she was up early, getting in to the office to prepare for the arrival of the Barnsley crew. I found her alone there, churning canvassing sheets off the printers, organising blown-up photocopies of street maps on clipboards, muttering at the computer when it jammed, leafing through the latest instructions from HQ. This woman was working like a slave – and if you ask me, her leadership was taking her (and how many like her?) for granted. When I read from my newspaper what Blair was going to say to the City about privatisation, she sighed and said wearily, 'God save us and preserve us.'

About 11 o'clock, fifteen or more started pitching up from Barnsley. Martin organised half a dozen into a canvassing gang, and sent them out to hit a patch of suburban Brighouse up the road. They were Mick and Yvonne Clapham, the MP and his wife; Philip Lofts, a community educationalist; John Ryan, a self-employed caravan servicer; Lawrence Sheppard, unemployed, a voluntary welfare rights worker; and Colin Harker from Brighouse to show them around.

The area they'd targeted was a modestly smart estate of bunga-lows and semis, some in brick and stucco, some in Yorkshire stone; lawns were tidy, flowerbeds neat, small trees stood in blossom, there were a fair few Sky dishes about, and at least half the cars were shiny-clean, with L-reg plates or newer. With Harker in charge of the electoral register on a clipboard, they fanned out cheerfully through a faint fine drizzle, knocking door to door, greeting each occupant by name. Astonishingly, this was a place Labour had never been to; it was, as the Barnsley men saw it, artisan working-class transformed in the Thatcher years to aspirational lower middle, and in Barnsley it would have been solid Labour. Here, it had until recently been solid Tory – but it wasn't any more, and perhaps a third of those they spoke to said this time they'd be Labour. I'd say what summed it up was the woman who said she'd vote for McCafferty, but she'd not take a poster. 'I don't want to spoil the windows, I've just cleaned 'em.'

As we went, I asked Mick Clapham how he felt over this latest news about Blair and Brown accepting privatisation, and he said it caused him a real problem. His was a traditional constituency, and he'd already had several activists saying that this time they'd not be coming out to work. So far he'd persuaded them to stick with it, but he said now, 'I can see people saying they'll not work after this. My agent teaches trade union studies, he saw the *Sunday Times* this morning and he was going berserk. And personally,' he said firmly, 'I couldn't bring myself to vote for any privatisation.'

He moved on, past a friendly old woman in her drive who said the Tories didn't have a cat's chance; I told John Ryan this and he said grimly, 'I thought so too, 'til I saw the papers this morning. Thing is, they're telling all the party members to keep their mouths shut, then they run off at theirs and it's us who cop it on the doorstep, isn't it? Oh well,' he sighed, 'you get some laughs, don't

you? Going down the streets.' He told of the door he'd knocked on
and the voice came back at him, 'We're not in.' Well, he says mildly,
he's having trouble believing that. 'I'm telling yer,' the voice wails,
'we're not in.'

Lawrence went by muttering under his breath, 'Some people.
They get a BMW, all of a sudden they're fucking Tories, aren't
they?'

They handed out pledge cards or popped them through letterboxes. One woman took one and grinned at it as if it was an
Instant. 'Scratch Labour, eh?'

People worked on their gardens, tinkered in their garages or
washed their cars. One man was putting up a security light; one had
laid three stars of pebbles into his concrete drive, and another had
put up a little lamp-post and a carriage wheel over a florid name-
plate. The house was called Blarn Lee Deigh. The estate was a
pocket of little English castles, individualised at B & Q and the
garden centre – but still a dozen of them took posters, and a lot of
those who were undecided were swaying to Blair. And then – it was
bound to come – John Ryan got the man with the caravan who
told him, 'What's the point in voting Labour? You're same as
Tories.'

He came away laughing sadly and he said, 'The trouble is, I
agree with him.'

Back in the office, McCafferty was on the phone stroking switchers, and she wasn't too happy. The good news was that some of
them had seen Major on Frost laying into Blair that morning,
saying you couldn't trust him, saying he was slippery and slithery,
and the switchers didn't like that; they found it nasty and negative.
The bad news was, she was worried how many Labour people
might agree with Major – so the privatisation story didn't please her
at all. In response to queries from some voters lately, she'd written
to the local papers saying the Post Office was safe with Labour.
Well, for goodness' sake, was it or wasn't it?

She said, 'All it's doing is responding to the Tory agenda. They've
gone Yah Boo Sucks, there's a hole in your spending plans – which
has come up because Gordon Brown's tied himself to *their* spending
plans, which he should never have done in the first place. So I'm

very irritated about it. It's one step too far, all the time, and with every step we risk losing more of our people.'

Like Clapham, she said if she were in the Commons she couldn't see herself voting for it – and this, bear in mind, was a most moderate Labour candidate, a Blairite from her heels to her new haircut, a woman who'd howled with outrage when she'd found herself described on a website as left-wing. And yet, she said, 'It's really ironic, 'cause all these switchers I'm calling – they love it, don't they?'

It left her feeling deeply uncomfortable. She said, 'All the time that I'm talking to them, there's a tiny little voice in the back of my head that says, You two-faced . . .'

Complete the sentence as you wish – and a few days later, shadow transport spokesman Andrew Smith came through. This was the man who'd ringingly declared at conference that our air traffic control system was not for sale; yet now, apparently, it might be. Like any good politician he was able, for the benefit of the *Courier*, to state smoothly that the position this week was the same as the diametrically opposite position last week. But, subsequently pressed by myself and Tarlo as to what was going on here – Tarlo all but jumping up and down on the spot with indignation – he could only say, 'We're examining it.' He said this with all the enthusiasm of a man who sounded like he'd never expected to find himself examining it at all.

It had been a steady theme of the campaign so far that a whole swathe of the electorate, when asked, would numbly mutter back that, 'They're all the same.' Myself, I found this vexingly stupid. I wanted to go down the street with a sandwich board and a megaphone screaming, 'Wake up! They're *not* all the same! Politics *does* matter!'

However, apart from the fact that most people would dismiss me if I did this as an irritating nutter, it was now beginning to feel (as Labour wobbled first over devolution and now privatisation) that to all intents and purposes, they might very well be the same. Certainly, from the New Agers of Cornholme to the boys from the battered pit villages of Barnsley, that was how it looked to them. And what was the point of winning all the switchers, if you so thoroughly pissed off all the people up and down the country who'd always been there for Labour when no one even knew what a switcher was?

There could be no doubt that a major factor in the Calder Valley's body shortage was disillusioned people not coming out and working any more for a party they felt had abandoned them. Council leader Pam Warhurst attributed the turn-round of Todmorden from Liberal to Labour in the past fifteen years to the ceaseless work of three individuals in particular – one local, two off cumdens – and two of these, she now told me, weren't bothering any more.

Interviewing Warhurst was a treat. In her high-ceiling office in Halifax Town Hall, her voice boomed and echoed like an artillery barrage, and I felt for my poor little dictaphone as it juddered and trembled on the table between us – a scientific instrument built of tinfoil and chewing gum trying to record and analyse a major land-slide. As for her laugh, it was a volcanic eruption; the woman was a force of nature all round.

She was forty-six (though she didn't look it) and she'd moved to the top of the valley from Lancashire in 1980. She'd been an animal rights activist back then, but she got fed up with jumping over fences and picketing people; she decided if you wanted to get any-where, you had to get into politics and work to change the law. She joined Labour in the mid-1980s; they saw her coming, she said, so now she was chief cook and bottlewasher – a typically pithy way of saying she ran a council with an annual budget of £162,000,000.

That council was one of Donald Thompson's principal targets. To this she answered, 'Any council that's had its budget cut for the past eight years cannot possibly be operating at optimum strength in its front-line delivery areas. It cannot *possibly*. So it cannot possibly stand up to the sort of scrutiny they want to subject us to, because for eight years we've been operating damage limitation.'

With the Ridings being rescued with cross-party support, they were in less trouble on that issue than they might have been. A cut of £1,100,000 in primary education, however, was a clear target – and all Labour could say was, what would the others have done? Where else would they have found the money, and still kept doing everything else they had to do?

Both the Liberal and Tory budgets – produced late in the day,

once they'd seen where the council was vulnerable – were back-of-
fag-packet efforts designed only to score political points. The
Liberals said they'd save money for primary education by cutting the
funds going to the Ridings, and by charging kids a fee to be looked
after while they ate their sandwiches at lunchtime – an untested
notion of questionable legality. The Tories, meanwhile, said they'd
save the money by selling off the council's remaining stock of residential care places for the elderly – which one of them described as
a gift from the elderly to the young people of this community.
Fine, said Labour, you go tell our old people they're making that
gift.

Neither were budgets that the Director of Finance could sign up
to – but the voters don't see all that, do they? All they see is the cut
in funding for primary schools and, unless they're well on the ball,
they don't see that it's central government forcing that cut to be
made. All of which, of course, Donald Thompson knew perfectly
well.

Thompson's greatest strength, said Warhurst, was that people
dismissed him as a fool – and he wasn't. She said, 'He's a strong
grass-roots politician. He'll have a drink in the pub, he'll have a
coffee at the coffee morning – and when push comes to shove,
people will vote for him because he's the local chap, the local
butcher made good. So he's a hard man to beat, 'cause he *understands* – you keep it simple, you be personable and smile, and you
talk about the loony left council.'

As a result of which, she said, Calder Valley was too tight for
comfort – and all those people not turning out to help was a major,
major pain. She said, 'They ought to know better. They say they're
not prepared to go on the streets any more because there's no difference – and all I say is, aren't you *lucky* to have been so *sheltered* all
these years? 'Cause are you really telling me there's no difference
between a Labour government coming in and these Tories carrying
on? Have you any *idea* how they've decimated our budgets? Have
you any *idea* of the stress and strain they've put on people in the
front line? Have you any *idea* what they've done to old people
when their home help charges go up, or to kids when their classes
are overcrowded? 'Cause that's what we're fighting. It's beyond
comprehension what'll happen if the Tories get in again – housing'll
go, education'll go, social services'll go – and I have to believe that

a socialist party of any shade, pink or red or whatever, will at least put a stop to some of those things.

'So I understand the difficulty Blair's got. We haven't seen the books for eighteen years, we don't know what the *fuck* they're going to look like – and the last thing we want is not to have a second term, 'cause that's exactly what the Tories are after. That's why Portillo's getting his profile up now. 'Cause we're up shit creek and they want us to have it for five years, then they'll come charging over the hill and we'll be *knackered*. So I can see Blair thinking, we have to have two terms, we can't promise what we can't deliver – so what do I do? I create an image and I say, Trust me. Thatcher did it, I can do it. Then I'll get power, and *then* I'll work on it.'

None of which, right now, helped Chris McCafferty. Warhurst said, 'I have to believe we're going to win, but I'd prefer to see it nailed down – 'cause, look, there's nothing more insecure than a bloody politician. We all need to be loved, we all need to be told we're going to win – and I'm not sure Chris is going to. I hope she is; she's worked really hard, she's done her damnedest, she's fought the old "You're-a-female" thing, she's fought the "You're-New-Labour-I'm-having-nothing-to-do-with-it" thing – it's been really difficult for her, and I feel for her. Because,' she sighed, 'this has been the *longest* fucking pregnancy . . .'

I turned my dictaphone off before the poor wee thing imploded under the weight of Warhust's passion. Then I went away wondering how many times in the next few weeks I'd wake up in a cold sweat after terrible nightmares about May 2nd dawning, and the Conservatives winning yet again.

19

BANANAS

Viv Smith certainly thought the main parties were all the same. They were, she said, all controlled by the banks. She was therefore standing as the Green Party's candidate for Calder Valley.

She was fifty-three years old; she lived with her husband and their twenty-eight-year-old son in a big, roomy house near the Halifax Royal Infirmary. Her husband had taken early retirement from what she quaintly called 'the gas board'; herself, she was a family worker for the council's social services department. She was a stout, cheerful woman with a ruddy face, bright white hair and a large, horsey and all-but-permanent grin. She was also quite the vaguest person I've ever met.

She didn't know how many candidates the Green Party had, she didn't appear to know a great deal about what they were proposing to do, and she didn't have much of a notion as to what would happen if they actually tried to do it. She told me they had a policy (as far as I could understand her) of merging the tax and benefit systems, and giving everyone 'a basic income'. There were no numbers involved here (or in the manifesto either) so how basic was this income going to be? Could I still afford football tickets on a Saturday? Could I rent a video now and then? Was there a beer allowance? Or did I have to stay at home eating vegetables?

The idea was that no one should be poor any more; an admirable ambition. In the absence of numbers, however, I suggested that the only way this herculean redistribution of wealth could be achieved would be to take a considerable amount of money not just from the very wealthy but from everyone who was moderately comfortable too – and that this, apart from bankrupting the country overnight, wasn't likely to make those people very happy.

She said, 'I don't know whether it'll make them unhappy or not. But it isn't how much money you've got, it's the quality of your life, surely? I mean, what is this money? The amount of money you've got written down in your bank account, it's just a figure.'

I was having trouble not collapsing in gales of laughter here. I mean, what is this money? It is, I believe, the stuff we work for so we can live in big houses in pleasant streets like those to be found in the rather desirable area around the Royal Infirmary – and if you take that stuff away from folk in large bundles, I said, I really don't think they'll be happy.

'I disagree. I think they will. There's just as much stress at the top; they're like hamsters on a wheel, aren't they?'

I love it, really, I love it. Take my awful job away, please, take away my money so I don't have to buy all those things I don't need any more, and then I'll be chuffed as punch.

It said in the Green Party manifesto that 'Greens are realistic'. Evidently the folk who wrote this document hadn't met their candidate for Calder Valley.

Viv Smith had a problem. She was standing in Calder Valley because most of Calderdale's Greens lived there – so in Halifax where she lived herself, there wasn't a Green candidate. Consequently, she didn't know who to vote for, but she confronted this dilemma with her customary analytical rigour. She said, 'I could be a socialist. I'm a Unison shop steward – but I couldn't vote for this Labour Party. So I don't know what to do. I like Alice Mahon, but . . . well, I might spoil my paper. No, I think I'd probably vote for Alice. Who knows?'

Then she said, if she lived in Calder Valley, she'd probably vote Liberal. I said, you'd vote for Stephen Pearson? She said, 'Isn't that a funny thing? Why would I vote for him rather than Chris McCafferty? I don't know where that thought came from.'

I don't know where any of her thoughts came from. This was a woman so spectacularly unsuited to win the trust of the public as their representative in parliament that my gast was utterly flabbered at her gall in standing in the first place. For goodness' sake, she said she didn't really want to win anyway.

Basically, she was standing because she was a nice person who was upset about what she saw on the news. She had a daughter who'd come in one day, at the age of fourteen, and announced that she was a vegetarian; she'd subsequently got herself arrested at Greenham Common. This had set Viv Smith to thinking – and quite right too – but it hadn't set her to thinking very deeply. When I put it to her that what she was proposing was pure dream-world, she said, 'Yes, it is. But if it isn't on offer it isn't there, is it?'

I said this all struck me as vague beyond belief.

'Well, it is, isn't it? Oh dear. Perhaps it would be better if I was more assertive. It's not vague in what I want, it's vague in how to get there. And maybe that's something we need to address.'

No kidding. And look, I'm not against the Green Party, not by any means; the world would be a paler place without them, and the major parties wouldn't be so pressed to address this crucial aspect of the contemporary agenda if the Greens weren't out there. Being troubled about the world's injustices, however, is not of itself sufficient justification to stand for election – and in its terminal woolliness of mind, I'd say Viv Smith's candidacy was reprehensibly frivolous. I'd say this because, in 1992, she'd won 622 votes; if she were to score something along those lines again, and Sir Donald Thompson were returned to parliament as a result, she'd have helped to achieve the outcome most directly inimical to her own interests.

For this reason the Green Party did in fact have a policy (not an absolute one, but a 'preferential' one) of not standing in marginals. Viv Smith, however, had ignored that – or, quite possibly, wasn't even aware of it. She asked me, 'Would you say it's a marginal?'

Even to raise the question suggests a wilful blindness to reality. But then, as McCafferty said with tart exasperation, 'It's not the Green Party here, is it? It's the Viv Smith party.'

The Calder Valley had two other fringe candidates. One of these, Christian Jackson, was standing for the British National Party. As people of warped and odious views go, he was oddly personable: a fresh-faced lad in his twenties with a rather fetching goatee. His opinions, however, were beyond logic and beneath contempt, and all his efforts to present them as reasonable or legitimate couldn't mask the fact that this looked to me like a young man in urgent need of therapy.

He lived in Todmorden, and had done so all his life. He'd already stood twice in council elections, securing between three and four per cent of the vote on each occasion; in the process he'd had his phone line cut by the anti-Nazis, and the door of his flat was heavily bolted, with a security light on the steps outside. Inside, the place was polished and dusted to a positively anal degree of spotlessness, and on the coffee table lay copies of a magazine called *Resistance*. This, said the masthead, was 'the music magazine of the true alternative', offering '68 pages of pure white power'.

Jackson's arms were entirely covered in tattoos; my tea was served in a Union Jack mug. He told me that he'd acquired his views following Leeds United, in which pursuit he'd been charged with (and acquitted of) conspiring to cause an affray in 1987. In 1993 he'd been in court again, after being arrested at an anti-IRA demo; he'd been fined £200, with £100 costs, but he maintained that this was a police fit-up. He did not, he said, espouse violence.

However, he had recently been sacked from his job as a foundry-man at Warman International – allegedly for threatening one of the company's managers. With a tribunal pending, the company would say only that they viewed Jackson's offence as 'gross misconduct'. Draw your own conclusions. My conclusion is, Jackson doesn't espouse violence, and I'm Dick van Dyke.

So, I said, you're a racist.

'What's a racist? OK, I'm a racist. I'm proud to be a racist.'

He said we were being swamped. 'Go to Birmingham,' he told me, 'go to London. There's no white people left.'

I said this might come as a surprise to all the white people currently resident in Birmingham and London. I then said that he was sick, and needed help to wash all this crap out of his head. He laughed.

On Sky News, Blair was on a podium with a Union Jack on it. Jackson said, 'How dare they?'

He tried to argue that we didn't live in a democracy. I said, well, he was allowed to stand in an election. He said, 'Yeah. Then we're exposed to the red filth, we get people like you come and tell us we're sick – we're under the cosh. And this is Britain. We're defending Britain.'

Not any kind of Britain I know, pal – and most people I knew in Todmorden said they were embarrassed to have this person among them. The police said he was 'a resource implication', partly because of the threats made against him – but they weren't going to go posting him twenty-four-hour protection. When I asked if they'd want to do that, one said grimly, 'Only if it was at Her Majesty's pleasure.'

Tony Mellor probably thought he was defending Britain too, though in an incomparably less offensive manner. He lived in a modern house he'd had built for himself up a small, tight little valley on the edge of Ripponden; it was a delightful spot, with the Ryburn flowing past the patio, and in this wooded seclusion he had until recently run a trout farm. He'd also been a Conservative councillor for ten years; but sadly, three years back his wife had died, and he'd packed all that in.

He wouldn't say how old he was – I'd guess about fifty – but he wasn't working any more. After losing his wife he thought he'd do more tranquil things – a bit of picture restoration, a counselling course – but over time he'd become more and more concerned about Europe, so now he was standing for the Referendum Party.

He was, he said, still a Conservative really; but his membership of the local association had lapsed. His dissatisfaction wasn't initially to do with Europe, it was more an accumulation of things: VAT on fuel, the pit closures, negative equity. The general crux of it, he said, was that while those who have nothing are looked after by the system, and those who have everything don't need the system, the true Tories in the middle, the backbone of the party – those who've been prudent, saved a bit, bought a modest house – those people were being penalised more and more.

Then, more recently, he'd started worrying over Europe. We were, he said, being taken by stealth into a federal union; a handful of politicians were making decisions of a historic nature, decisions as big as any we'd faced in seven centuries of parliamentary democracy, without first securing the consent of the people.

Personally, I think this is drivel. We could use more debate on this subject, no doubt – but then, we could use more debate on everything. To say we had no debate at all, however, was preposterous; the Tory party had nearly fallen to bits talking about it. Moreover, the parties all had clear positions and were all offering a referendum – so what was the point of the Referendum referendum?

He said the other referenda were only about a single currency, and that wasn't good enough. So, leaving aside the fact that you can't have a federal Europe without a single currency, let's address instead the questions that Mr Goldsmith's merry crew wanted to put to us: 'Do you want the United Kingdom to be part of a federal Europe? Or do you want the United Kingdom to return to an association of sovereign nations that are part of a common trading market?'

It is screamingly obvious that the only possible purpose of this is to secure a 'Yes' answer to the second part of it; to enforce thereby a re-negotiation of our relationship with Europe; and thus, since the other European principals are going ahead with or without us, effectively to remove ourselves from the European Union. Anything else these people were saying was smokescreen. So either Tony Mellor was lying when he said he was pro-Europe, or he was seriously deluding himself about what the party he now stood for was up to.

I put it to him that his party was the plaything of an egomaniac billionaire, under whose umbrella he was now allying himself with all manner of basket-cases. He answered that if Goldsmith wanted to put his money into this cause, why should he be criticised for that? And as for the basket-cases, yes, the Referendum Party had its share of them. 'But there's plenty of them in the Tory party too, aren't there?'

Such is the rich soup of democracy. Simmering away in the Calder Valley it was flavoured, beside the three main parties, with two pleasant nitwits with bees in their bonnets and one paranoid racist jerk. And, given the A to Z of alternative possibilities – that is, Albania to Zaire – I'd say it suggests that we're most fortunate to live in this eccentrically tolerant country.

★

Back in the real world, I popped in to visit Thompson one after-noon and found him looking tired, walking with some difficulty; he said he'd been out and about, knocking on doors, talking to people in their gardens, and it had left him stiff in his bones. Still, he said, 'I'm plodding along. And without any bullshit, I'm being well received.'

His dusty little offices still seemed dolefully quiet – indeed, on two occasions when I went there they were shut – but I was wary of reading too much into that. All the things Labour were now doing – the targeted mail, the phone canvassing – the Tories had been doing for years. In the past, said McCafferty, 'They must have thought we were off the Ark, they must have been laughing their socks down. We'd be out there knocking on doors in the pouring rain in the dark of the night, patting ourselves on the back 'cause there weren't any Tories about – and they're sat in the warm on the phone, aren't they?'

So maybe they were all busy as bees in some secret lair – but Labour was certainly busy, and busy for all to see. Nick Brown came good, and sent two of his staff and three students into the Brighouse office for three days' work. The candidate, meanwhile, got herself in the *Todmorden News* checking out a housing estate and rebutting the impression previously given in that paper by Stephen Pearson that the place was awash with litter, condoms and excreta. (It wasn't.) From there, she went up to Blackshaw Head to meet a group of wind-farm objectors, and got herself in the *Courier* while she was at it.

The next day she got in the *Courier* again, meeting shadow trans-port spokesman Andrew Smith with Alice Mahon at the site of a ghastly lorry accident. The day after that, she chaired the Halifax launch of the West Yorkshire Policing Plan for 1997–98 at the Shay Stadium. She sat between a magistrate and the Chief Constable, impressively austere in her dark navy suit and her half-lensed read-ing glasses, and she ran the show: a show concerning the public expenditure of £275,000,000. And people say Labour have no experience?

The policing presentation lasted ninety minutes; when it was done, she shot across town for the opening of a centre to help young people start out on their own when they left council or foster care. I watched all this, and I wondered how many things a person can wrap her head around. Housing, wind-farms, transport, policing – if you think politicians are useless layabouts, could you do all this?

But the high point of the week was a public meeting held by the World Development Movement in the Tourist Information Centre in Hebden Bridge. McCafferty, Pearson and Viv Smith had all agreed to speak; at the last minute, to general surprise, Sir Donald agreed to do so too. On the night, he and McCafferty greeted each other with amiable civility; each joked that the other was always getting in the paper. Well, said Sir Donald expansively, you could only watch your own campaign; you couldn't always be watching the others, 'Otherwise you get possessed.'

About twenty people came; the meeting was chaired by Geoff Tansey, a local writer on agricultural and development issues. Pearson sat at the left end of the table, next to Viv Smith; Tansey was in the middle, with Thompson and McCafferty to his right. He called the meeting to order, and asked the candidates to stick to their own policies; having thus been mildly requested for a spot of decorum, Pearson stood up and immediately laid into his opponents. It was appropriate, he said, that they were both sitting on the right; they were Tweedledum and Tweedledee, and you couldn't tell them apart. Then he started in on a standard stump speech about how wonderful the Liberal Party was, until one of the audience said, 'Excuse me, but international issues don't get much coverage, and that's what this meeting's about . . .'

Pearson said sharply, 'I'm just giving you a picture, if I may. I hope you'll take the opportunity to interrupt the other candidates as well.'

When he got to the matter in hand, he was impressively well-briefed; he spoke fluently, without notes. He was also remorseless; his speaking manner had the charm and efficiency of a power drill.

Viv Smith, by contrast, was simply hopeless. Woefully unsuited to public performance, her hands shook violently over her notes as she stumbled and bumbled along; as to what she said, I can't tell you, because she was mostly inaudible.

McCafferty was rather better; as well-briefed as Pearson but less jackhammer in her manner. She knew all her conventions and her treaties and her acronyms, her sustainable this and her departmental t'other – so, like Pearson, she made a good case for her party's policies on the various issues of the night, on debt, on human rights, on arms sales and aid programmes. Then Sir Donald stood up, portly in his pinstripe, and what followed was priceless.

'Good evening, ladies and gentlemen. I've represented you for some time and I've been lucky enough to be involved with the Commonwealth, which is much underrated. I was delighted when Nelson Mandela joined . . .'

There was a bit more praise for the splendours of the Commonwealth, then he segued flawlessly into the following: 'I was lucky enough to take a million pounds to the West Indies for their banana trade. We've a commitment to support West Indian bananas, which the Germans are against. If we do not grow bananas, the alternative in the West Indies would be drugs. We must keep the West Indian economy going with bananas.'

I regret to say that things now became a bit blurred, basically because I was struggling to affect a spot of smoker's cough in order to prevent myself falling out of my chair in hysterics. The remainder of his speech, however – so far as I can make sense of it from my notes – was a splendidly logic-free ramble, a masterpiece of inconsequence, a performance that took the *non sequitur* and raised it to an art form.

There was something about the Council of Europe and NGOs, and a conference in Vilnius. Then there was something about manmade natural disasters, and how whenever there's a disaster, 'The European Union always want to get their flag there first. Now I've met some East Europeans, and they were very good chaps. And as you'll be aware, most natural disasters lately have been around Russia, the Caspian, all that.'

They have? While I pondered this news, Sir Donald travelled impenetrably via the Fire Brigade and biscuit stockpiles to his membership of a committee 'for disarmament and all of that'. He then issued a few large and baffling numbers, praised free markets, and arrived for no clear reason at an abrupt halt. It was completely surreal – and the only firm policy I could draw from it was a commitment to keep the West Indian economy going on bananas.

What this man had been doing in Parliament these past eighteen years, God knows – raising a fair bit of money for charity, I'll give him that – but it was impossible to dislike him. Towards the end of a question-and-answer session marked principally by the sharp criticism and peculiar moral absolutism of Stephen Pearson, Sir Donald sighed at Pearson's latest bit of unnecessarily unpleasant invective (about Tony Mellor 'coming out of his hidey-hole in Ripponden') and he said wearily, 'Do you lie awake at night thinking how to be rude to people, Stephen?'

20

AMONG THE UNDEAD

A fter the meeting, Pearson told McCafferty she was a dead cert. If he was in her place, he said, he'd keep his head below the parapet; he'd stop at home, keep mum and quietly let it happen. To which the only response has to be, You would? Sure you would.

There were three weeks to go. Depending which poll you looked at, Labour remained ahead by anything from 12 to 23 points − despite their gutless about-turn on privatisation and the icky sight of Blair wriggling like a bug on a pin when David Dimbleby went after him on BBC1. True, one or two polls had slipped a shade (and a rogue MORI in *The Times* had tumbled out of the twenties to a mere 15-point lead) so the media duly declared that the Tories had scented blood; but they probably had to say that because, apart from Christine Hamilton handbagging Martin Bell on Knutsford Heath, there really wasn't much else to write about. (And if you spend your life in press conferences, what do you expect?) But even on the lower lead, we were still looking at a landslide.

Indeed, poll analysis in the *Guardian* suggested that the swing in the marginals was greater than that in areas where Labour was traditionally strong − which I'd have thought stood to reason, as in the latter areas there'd be fewer folk available to do the swinging − but anyway, on this reading you could predict a Labour majority of 300. On the other hand, a rolling poll in the *Sunday Telegraph* had Labour's lead steadily declining at such a rate that, if it continued on trend, come May 1st John Major would get back into Downing

Street. To all of which I can only say, why does anybody waste their money on the pollsters at all?

McCafferty never thought she was on a landslide. She was tired, laying on the stuff that covers the black bags under your eyes with a trowel – and evidently the Calder Valley's body shortage was beginning to worry people higher up, too. Word came down that Mandelson had been talking about this seat; as if by magic, more visits started materialising in the diary.

Meanwhile, on Friday April 11th, she talked to a group of General Studies students at Brighouse High – mostly seventeen- and eighteen-year-olds who wanted to know about employment, Europe, sleaze and why (if they were old enough) they should vote for Labour, and why specifically for her.

Before she spoke, she handed out a brief questionnaire; when it came back, it showed Labour first equal with None Of The Above on 8 points apiece. Otherwise the Tories had 7, the Lib Dems 4, there was one undecided, one voter for Sinn Fein who didn't know how to spell it, and one sticker of Tony Yeboah.

It would have been interesting to re-run the poll when she'd finished, because the reaction of these kids was surprisingly strong. I talked with half a dozen of them; they'd been spoken to by Thompson and Pearson already, and they didn't mince their words. One lad said, 'She was certainly the best. Thompson seemed very defeatist about his own party – when we asked if he'd win, he didn't give any definite answer. And Pearson was big-headed; he got shirty, he got really het-up. But both him and Thompson, they were very condescending. You asked a question and they did what you expect politicians to do, they went all around the houses. Whereas she seemed human, and she was honest from the start. She didn't pretend to know everything about every policy.'

Another chipped in, laughing, 'Thompson looked like he was going to die. He was sweating, he didn't give you much hope. I thought, this is the face of the future?'

Only one of these kids was old enough to vote; he'd be voting Labour. Another said, 'I've said that even if I could vote, I wouldn't. But after today I would, because of the candidate. I'd always thought they were all the same, and after the first two I thought my nightmare was coming true. But she was completely different.'

This reaction was all the more interesting because, by her own standards, she'd performed pretty poorly; she'd not been succinct, she'd repeated herself and she'd wandered. So what would they have thought if she'd been on form?

I asked why so many of them had raised Europe as an issue. One of them laughed and said, 'It's because people have been booking their holidays.'

Back in the office, the phones were ringing off the hook. There was regional office, the photocopier man, people wanting postal votes, the secretaries of the new slate of visiting MPs all wanting directions. And while you're at it, do you support the application of the Baltic states for EU and NATO membership?

Ann Martin had told her to buy a new suit for when she won. Now McCafferty said, 'I'm beginning to think that if I lose, I shall be very, very pissed off.'

At this point, however, Labour privately believed that she was leading Sir Donald by less than one percentage point.

According to their party-supplied six-week election planner, switcher mailings were supposed to go out every Friday – but on the last two Fridays, they hadn't. Waking up to the situation, Labour high-ups told her to start treating it like a by-election; they said she'd get an MP coming in every day. As for herself, all she had to do now was smile, smile, smile and shake as many voters' hands as was physically possible. Oh, and one other thing – she wasn't to worry. So the Saturday night after the meeting when they told her that, she was awake worrying 'til 4 in the morning.

The next day, Sunday April 13th, the Barnsley crew rolled in to Brighouse again. Labels had to be stuck on 74,891 election addresses – one for every Calder Valley voter – so the first women through the door sat straight down at the tables and set to peeling and sticking. A big, smiling man came in behind them and said, 'C'mon, mek tea then.'

One of the women told him, 'Get brew on yersen, yer doing nowt.'

He said, 'That's what women's for, mekkin' tea and sandwiches. Why have a dog and bark yersen?'

There were twenty of them, give or take, with kids in tow. The room filled with cheerful chat and a dense fug of smoke. Tony the

Denim Geezer, whose knowledge of Elland was encyclopaedically detailed, was deputed to get a mob of them out knocking on doors, with McCafferty tagged along to be introduced to every voter who wanted to meet her. They stocked up on pledge cards ('Tony's flexible friends', Lawrence called them; me, I found them very useful for cutting sponge cake) and we set off to a spanking-new housing estate off Elland Lane.

The houses were spotless replicas off a production line, clad in Yorkshire stone, with trim little gardens and shiny cars; the place had all the character of a cardboard box. At the estate's entrance, a man was moving in to this nirvana-by-numbers with a local removals firm. He'd been in two rentals before he'd found this place, and you know what moving house is like. He said, 'I'll be voting, sure. I'll decide how when I've got five minutes.'

A big bloke lugging an armchair out of the van said, 'I'm Labour, me. Got to get that rubberface man out, eh? And another thing. Can you send all them ethnics home?'

One of the houses was called Witt's End. I felt like I was at it, and I was.

The Barnsley boys fanned out and hit door-knockers, and McCafferty talked to three voters in their wake. After she'd finished with them, they all professed themselves more likely to vote Labour. Three down, 74,888 to go.

In one house, a young couple – a self-employed plasterer and the manageress of a Boots opticians' practice – said they were undecided, it was difficult. 'It's all squabbling and sleaze, isn't it? What are they going to *do*?' The woman said, 'I'd be happy to have a Labour MP locally. I'm less sure I want Tony Blair for Prime Minister, though.' I asked why and she said, ''Cause he's a smarmy git, isn't he?'

Across the road lay an old, run-down estate of red-brick terraced houses; they were all Labour here, if you could only get them out of their doors and down the road to the polling station. Tony the Geezer's plan was to test the Tory water in Legoland first – where nearly half of those who answered the door were now Labour – then after lunch to cross the road, cover the old estate with posters in every window, and get McCafferty to meet as many people there as she could.

We walked on to the estate; it was a dismal place. Paint peeled off the doors, cars were few and ancient, and the gardens were threadbare, penned with tatty, unpainted picket fencing and strewn with cheap kids' stuff. In one of these houses, a mate of Tony's had come on a goat tethered to the bannisters; so, said Tony, next time he canvassed here he planned to bring a carrot with him.

A bloke with a belly and a bunch of martial tattoos on his forearms leaned on unsteady, buckled legs in his doorway; he had a poster on a stake in his garden, and Tony knew his story. He'd been a para, his chute had collapsed on him and he'd landed in a ploughed field rather quicker than he'd meant to. He was a party member, said Tony; a disillusioned one.

McCafferty got in a kitchen where a lorry driver sat supping Holsten Super, and he and his wife said they were Labour, definite. She thanked them, and said we had to get rid of those Tories this time. The driver said angrily, 'I dunno 'ow the 'eck we didn't get rid of them last time.'

A few houses along, the garden was overgrown with giant weeds. The woman who came to the door was scrawny, twitching, with long lank hair, shattered teeth, and sideburns. Her hands were claw-shaped, making random gestures; she was totally out of it. McCafferty didn't realise at first and by the time she did it was too late, she was just ploughing on in there. Tony sussed it fast and said, 'Here, I'll tell you what. 'Cause we like your face so much, we'll give you one of these.' He handed this poor bewildered soul a window poster, turned her back with a gentle hand on her tottery way indoors, and pulled McCafferty away. The poster, we decided, was unlikely ever to make it into a window – but it might, I suppose, come in handy if she runs short of roach material.

Tony and his mate went ahead, finding people who wanted to meet McCafferty. Two Asian families were keen to talk; in one of these houses a tall, striking woman in her forties complained with weary resignation of racism and violence. It wasn't everyone, she said, it was a few families; she specified one house by its number, and said how they'd go about the street drinking, swearing, breaking windows. The front garden of the house she'd named was a bare patch of dirt decorated with stolen traffic cones. McCafferty listened sympathetically; she said it would take a long time, but it would get better. The woman replied firmly that her family had lived around Elland since 1979 and it wasn't getting better, it was getting worse.

In another house there was a lad, twenty-two years old and with two kids already, who'd done panel-beating at college but he couldn't find any work, and he wanted seriously to know what Labour would do. If he voted Labour, did he have a better chance of a job? She gave him chapter and verse, and I watched it all float past his head. She was trying her best, but windfall taxes, five pledges, housing revenue accounts – what was all this? Here she was, a politician in his tiny little living room, and she might as well have been a creature from Mars.

She was just finishing when Tony came to the door, wanting to keep her moving; as she stepped out he asked her, 'What was all that about?'

McCafferty said, 'He wanted to know why he should vote for us.'

Tony told her, 'You should have said, 'cause it's worth fifty grand to me. That would have been a lot quicker.'

She hooted with laughter and slapped him about the arms with a sheaf of posters – a much thinned sheaf, because a lot of these houses took one. But not many of them wanted to meet the candidate. It was as if to say, we're Labour, obviously – but let's not bother talking about it, eh? 'Cause there's not much to say, there's football on telly, and it'll not make any difference anyway – not here. We went back to the car, barked on our way by a chained Alsatian.

At Augusta, Tiger Woods stomped on golf as we know it, prompting many jokes about how Blair would love a swing like that one. (My favourite was, Why's Damon Hill jealous of Tiger Woods? 'Cause he'd love to be able to drive three hundred yards.) And the world went on about its business, with FA Cup semi-finals, Eurofish rows, and a continuing scary absence of rain.

Against this backdrop, the election was a news-free zone. With the polls sticking steady, the Tories made wild uncosted promises about grammar schools and launched desperate, increasingly nasty attacks on our Tone. Labour, meanwhile, did their best to say nothing and look nice. The strategy was explained to me by one of their visiting MPs, with the inevitable football metaphor: 'We've won the away leg 2-0. So all we've got to do now is keep the ball.'

The way Labour were playing it, the media were completely institutionalised. At the top level, you gave them one big press conference per day, one photo-op per day, and that was it. In the past – see Kinnock in 1987 – they'd been giving five or six photo-ops a day, but now they'd learnt that wasn't the way to do it, because that way the press got to choose what pictures they used. So instead, you gave them what you wanted to give them and nothing else. You had them at the press conference, you had them on the leader's battle bus (at £7,500 a ticket) and you made sure they didn't get any real news from any of it at all. No ideas, no debate, no nothing. Just the *message* . . . five pledges, and trust me.

McCafferty's next public pitch to the voters was at a hustings organised by the Todmorden churches at St Mary's, an austere old pile in the centre of town. I met Sir Donald outside as he arrived, so we went across the road and he bought me a coke, and we agreed that the government of the Sudan were a rotten bunch. He knew other Tories, he told me, who'd not go in pubs in their constituencies for fear it'd start a row, but plainly he didn't feel he had that problem. Mind you, after eighteen years I reckon he'd know which pubs to pick.

The interior of St Mary's was glossily modernised; the walls were painted bright white, there was a carpet, and comfy padded seats instead of pews. While some fifty people gathered, Stephen Pearson told me (as he would) that it was going well for him; but he said he was sending people out to work their key seats in Rochdale and Sheffield, and that he'd been to Rochdale to support the Liberal incumbent there himself. So he couldn't have had that many hands at his disposal – and everyone else wondered what he was up to. Knowing the man too well, Pam Warhurst had told me that whatever it was, 'He'll have worked out some complex master plan.'

The best guess was that he'd worked his socks off last time and the Liberal vote had still tumbled, so maybe this time he was putting himself in a position where he could say, if it fell further now, that he'd been out working elsewhere for the greater good of his party. That, no doubt, could help him win selection at a later date in another seat he'd be likelier to win. Others of a more conspiratorial bent had a theory that he was counting on Sir Donald winning by a whisker, a Labour government becoming deeply unpopular, Sir Donald kicking the bucket, and then Pearson rides out into the valley to win a mighty by-election triumph. Far-fetched, maybe – but then, anything was possible round this guy. Still, at least he was a man of integrity. Just about every time he got up to speak, he said so.

But it was a Christian evening, so let's move on. The candidates weren't required to speak but only to take questions – about taxes, homelessness, student grants, religious education, abortion and taxes again. Pearson stood up and jack-hammered away, Sir Donald bumbled happily along, McCafferty quietly made her points – on several occasions cannily calling in evidence her experience at the Well Woman Centre, or of the young girl and her baby who'd been living in her house this past year – while Viv Smith wittered aimlessly that, on almost everything, she agreed with everybody.

At one point Sir Donald said, 'If my Dad had had £1,500 I could have gone to King's College, Cambridge, and maybe I'd have finished up a schoolteacher or a vicar instead of an MP. And,' he smiled, 'maybe everybody would have preferred that.'

Pearson was in there like a shot. 'Can I make a contribution, Donald?'

The high point came with a question about tax allowances having gone up by considerably more for single people or childless couples than they had for married people with children. Pearson kicked off the panel's response with an accountant's forensic shimmy through the numbers and then, saying that the current tax system was unfair, proceeded to outline how the Tories had brought taxes down.

Sir Donald said drily, 'Stephen explains my policies very well. I have to take him everywhere with me.'

Pearson leant forward and, with a sudden note of keening urgency, said, 'Please. Please can we debate in Brighouse?'

But Sir Donald only looked magisterially at the ceiling – and all the while, McCafferty was struggling to mask a look of growing satisfaction. When it came to her turn she said sweetly, 'Forgive me if I'm wrong. But am I the only one who thought this question was about family values?'

Yes, said the questioner, and in the quiet church you could hear the point striking home. 'Thanks for that,' she told him, and then she joked, 'I'll pay you later.'

'Oh-ho,' chortled Sir Donald, 'cash for questions, eh?' It got the biggest laugh of the night – but when everything's against you, what else is there to do but make light of it?

A New Labour candidate goes into the barber's shop wearing headphones, and he asks for a haircut. The barber says he'll have to take the headphones off, and the candidate says he can't; the barber'll have to cut his hair around them. He tries his best; then the candidate falls asleep in the chair and so, relieved, the barber carefully takes off the headphones and sets them down to one side. Then he turns back to find the New Labour candidate falling from his chair to the floor, stone dead. Yikes! So the barber picks up the headphones and has a listen, and he hears the voice of Peter Mandelson saying, 'Breathe in. Breathe out. Breathe in. Breathe out . . .'

Two nights after the church hustings in Todmorden, Michael Portillo told this joke to an audience of nearly 200 people at the Elland Cricket Club. They were members of the Halifax and Calder Valley Conservative Associations, and almost without exception they were old. Very, very old. So old that, after I'd arrived and they were gathering about me, I began to fear that I'd stumbled on a meeting of the undead.

It was a glorious evening; the club was set high over the town, with views from the large and well-appointed clubhouse far and wide across the valley. I got a drink and looked edgily out of the windows at this pleasant vista because, behind me at the bar, a fearful crew of wizened creatures was massing amid wafts of cigar smoke and hair lacquer. The men wore blazers and had weird thatches of polished hair (if they had any hair at all) perched stiffly over rheumy eyes and red, pop-veined faces. They said things to each other like, 'Would I like a drink, Tom? What a silly question. You'll be asking me if I'm going to vote Conservative next.' The women were even scarier – ancient and primped and caked in make-up, saggy of jowl and sloped of shoulder, a doddering flock of floral prints and cashmere cardies. What a party of national *vigour* . . . a party of people whose heads bobbled when they talked.

Large and redoubtable, Sir Donald's agent James Davidson moved easily among them, ruddily fresh-faced and charming, obliged in the circumstances to act twenty-five going on forty. And to be fair, there may have been the odd person in their forties or fifties among this throng who'd just unpeeled their tomb wrappings to emerge at nightfall – but among the 200 otherwise there were very few indeed of James Davidson's age. I spotted one or two pimply youths and, bizarrely, a strut-bellied skinhead with a collarless shirt, pressed jeans and a fierce, nervous way of gulping at his drink. Later, I was introduced to a spectacularly gorgeous seventeen-year-old girl, the chair of the Calder Valley Young Tories – and that, on the Tory youth front, was it. I looked at this girl sadly and thought, What are you *doing* here? You're seventeen, for God's sake. Go clubbing, hang out, get a life. Haven't you noticed that virtually everyone else in the room is *dead*?

Davidson said he wanted the Halifax candidate Robert Light going first, then Sir Donald, then Portillo. He didn't want any questions afterwards because he didn't want it getting critical or nit-picking; he wanted Portillo to get up, gee them up and get out – because, he said, 'They're not keen to go out and work, these. They're old, they're scared they'll get mugged – which is nonsense, but it's how they feel. Or they're scared if they put up a poster they'll get a brick through the window.'

A confident lot, this Tory party. I said to Davidson that his prediction of a 3,000 majority when the campaign had begun was now looking, frankly, unrealistic – and he agreed. He said they'd win by 1,500, then he put his hand out, palm down, fingers out, and gave it the wobbly gesture. 'Fifteen hundred,' he said, 'maybe three figures. We've got our backs against the wall here. But I rely on Sir Donald.'

A table was set with three chairs on a small platform before the audience. As we settled down, someone went up to the table and asked the owner of an H-reg car if they could kindly go and move it. The man from the *Courier* chortled, 'H-reg? That's not a Tory car, is it?'

With a ringmaster's flourish Sir Donald said abruptly, 'My friend Robert Light. A big round of applause.' The Halifax candidate was young, balding, and wore very naff shoes. With a lurking paranoia he offered, 'A special welcome to the press. Now this is a proper meeting of proper people, so I hope you'll report what you hear. We don't need the spin doctors of the Labour party here.' So I will, indeed, report what I heard.

Enter Portillo, an odd-looking man of medium height with a head and neck seemingly several sizes too large for his body and a strange, stiff way of walking with his feet splayed and his little shoulders held back, as if someone just shoved a broomstick up his backside. He went to stand at the table and, without notes or any need of the microphone, he spoke with impressive fluency for forty minutes.

He began with three jokes. When he became Minister of Defence, he'd been told that he'd need all his political courage. So he looked back and wondered when he'd needed political courage before – and he remembered, as a young man starting out, a day when he'd been canvassing. Keen to impress his companions with his vigour, he'd vaulted someone's front gate, strode purposefully to the front door and then, as he knocked, he felt a stickiness under-foot. He looked back . . . and the occupant now opening the door, a very large fellow, had evidently just concreted his front path, along which Portillo had now left a trail of footprints.

The man asked, 'Who are you?' Or, said Portillo, words to that effect.

So, Portillo smiled, he summoned all his political courage and said, 'Well, sir – I'm your parliamentary candidate for the Labour Party.'

Fair enough. He got a light batch of laughter. But it does strike me, looking back, that when you're giving a speech whose essence is that you can't trust Tony Blair, it's pretty odd to kick it off by announcing that you're readily prepared to tell a lie yourself.

There was a military joke in case anyone present didn't know what job he was in; there was the New Labour joke, and then a comfortable segue into praising Sir Donald, this excellent Yorkshireman with his many years of experience. As for Robert Light, said Portillo, he was 'The Donald of tomorrow.' So Light looked at his stick-thin stomach and Portillo told him, 'Well, a few meals in the House of Commons'll sort that out.'

Then he got to it. Did we remember 1979? Trade unionists in

Downing Street, rubbish in the streets, 98 per cent tax? And would we care to reflect on the wonders of the eighteen years since? People buying their own homes, buying shares, having choices in education, the trade unionists harried from the field, the government cutting taxes, Britain standing up to the Soviet Union – a time of miracles, nothing less. The paradise years. 'And law and order,' he said. 'In the last four years, rates of crime have been falling.'

Er, 'scuse me. What about the fourteen years before that?

'And now,' said Portillo, 'Michael Howard has had this very brilliant idea that if someone's convicted of burglary three times, they'll get a mandatory sentence and that's it, no ifs or buts.'

This is, of course – as Portillo must know very well – the most brazen nonsense. 'Three strikes and you're out' is an American idea, not Howard's at all. It is also profoundly illiberal, and has as its principal consequence not any great reduction in crime but merely the hideously expensive stacking of the prison system to its rafters with mostly petty criminals serving sentences out of all proportion to their offences. But this audience wouldn't know that, would they? As we'll see, some of the undead here gathered barely knew the time of day. You could tell these people *anything*.

I won't say I felt for Portillo; that would be pushing it altogether too far. But as he extolled his party's achievements (calling in evidence the customary fantastically fanciful economic statistics) and as he sang Britain's praises, I did wonder what he thought as he looked at these people before him. Was he thinking, if we're so great and if we've done so much, how come the only people who want to turn up and hear me tell them about it are so very, very old?

'We are a country whose name means something in the world,' he boomed.

'Tony Blair said Trust me,' he sneered, 'twenty times in half an hour. Trust me, trust me, trust me, and you're counting the spoons. Time for a change, they say. And roughly every day, at about two o'clock' (here he checked his watch) 'they *do* change.'

Ah me, the terrible danger to the holy perfections of our constitution. Ah me, the fearful threat of New Labour in abject surrender to a federal Europe. When, Good Lord, under the Conservatives the UK had become, 'A wonderful brand name in the world.'

That says it all, doesn't it? For all their high words about freedom and the defence of it, we weren't a country to these people, we were a product. Soap powder, missiles, insurance policies, fish'n'chips. Makes you shiver with pride, doesn't it? Indeed he said, 'When I travel on behalf of this country, I hold my head up high.'

And when I think of this preposterous marionette travelling on my behalf, I lower my head in shame.

Against all the evidence, to a roomful of ancient believers in a faith long, long past its sell-by date, Portillo declared, 'Britain prospering and proud. Don't let Labour throw it away.'

James Davidson had said he didn't want any questions. Now Sir Donald stood up and said, 'Any questions?'

Well, to be precise, he said, 'We've got the world's press and the *Halifax Courier* here. If you want to get it off your chest, get it off your chest.'

A lean and cadaverous figure of rumpled military mien, with truly terrible teeth and the skin of his face folded over and over like rhino hide, got up and said, 'Could I ask what the Defence Secretary's thoughts are about sending troops to Bosnia? We've seen a lot of troops going there today . . .'

Someone beside him had to say, Er, actually that was Albania, and they weren't our troops.

The second questioner got up with a rant about the BBC. The first item on Radio Leeds that day had been Angela Rumbold bucking the Euro line, the second item had been some local thing, and the third had been Renault investing £100,000,000 in this country, so why hadn't the good news come first?

And someone beside him had to say, Er, actually, it was Peugeot. 'Well,' howled the questioner, 'they're all French, aren't they?'

Later, someone asked Portillo about Ian Hamilton. I thought, Dear God. He's been in the news for a month and you don't even know what he's *called*?

Portillo answered the questions with well-mannered ease (I'll pass over some deeply nasty remarks about Calderdale Council) and at one point he was asked something about young people and their not remembering a Labour government. Well, said Portillo –

understandably speaking of young people to this audience as if they were an unfathomable alien species – 'There is a tendency for young people to be very idealistic, and perhaps a little credulous.'

I thought, you patronising smarmball. They'd be credulous if they believed in *you*.

Along the way, Sir Donald spoke of how policies evolve and change – like the poll tax. They'd studied it, and they'd got rid of it. So the old bat next to me snarled fiercely under her breath, '*Pity*.' I turned fearfully, wondering if zombie dentures might at any moment be sunk into my socialist flesh . . .

They were so sad, these people, so very sad. Between clinging to their little bits of money and their tightly closed minds, they knew so pathetically little of what went on in the world. But in their fear and ignorance and insecurity, their principal political feature was a clench-buttocked meanness, a truly, madly, deeply repulsive intolerance.

Now, after eighteen years of electing a government to reflect that, their time was past. When Portillo claimed that the tide was running in their favour, I looked about this room of withered flesh and shuttered spirits and I realised that never in my life had I heard a man sound more like Canute. I left and, once I was sure my flesh and spirit were intact, I felt more encouraged than I'd been at any time. Dawn was coming, and for the undead the political grave yawned wide.

21

MELTDOWN

B efore Portillo arrived James Davidson asked me, 'Have you seen this?' He pulled from his pocket a leaflet which had been torn into shreds, and which he'd sellotaped together again. It was printed in Tory blue and it said, 'Conservatives for Stephen Pearson'. The words 'Liberal Democrat' were printed below Pearson's name in small typeface, and the word 'for' was written vertically along the end of the word 'Conservatives'. If you saw it in a car or house window, all you'd register was – as I say, in Tory blue – 'Conservatives Stephen Pearson'.

The text was an endorsement of Pearson by two Liberal councillors who'd defected from the Tories – about one of whom local Labour people, never mind the Tories, had nothing to say that I could possibly print – and the Tories were spitting blood over it. I suspect it had been Sir Donald himself who'd torn up the leaflet; he told me, 'It's designed to deceive. It's not gentlemanly. But Stephen Pearson . . . well, I'm not going into that.'

Davidson said, 'It goes against the grain of the whole campaign. We were under the assumption that we'd play by clean rules here. But if this is how they work, they deserve all the contempt they get.'

I called Pearson, and said he'd put the cat among the pigeons with this one. 'What,' he crowed, 'nice meek mild me? Our party thinks it's *wonderful*. And you only complain if you're losing, don't you?'

He thought McCafferty was sailing home. But whether that was happening or not, the reaction to his leaflet in the Labour camp was one of weary distaste. 'If Donald's astute,' said one visiting MP, 'he'll ignore it. But it can only do us good. Let 'em fight like ferrets in a sack, eh?'

Labour had received a copy of the leaflet by fax from an irate member of the public – a woman who worked in public relations, and who expressed the opinion to Ann Martin (forcefully) that she thought Mr Integrity's leaflet was misleading. Wouldn't you?

While Portillo was speaking, Labour ran their broadcast with the bulldog. The next morning, Alex Powell went to the office in Hebden Bridge and found this message on the ansaphone: 'Hi. Simon Stewart here. I really love the bulldog. Really beautiful racist imagery. Y'know, how far can you take the jingoistic thing, and the racism thing? Y'know, are you gonna associate yourselves with the BNP now? Just lost my fucking vote. See ya, comrades.'

Alex sighed. She said, 'You come in, you think, ooh, messages. Maybe it's a volunteer. And then that. What a sad man, eh? But what a nasty thing to do. There could have been some granny come in and heard that, couldn't there?'

A hundred yards down the road, James Davidson was unpacking boxes of election addresses in a dusty, unlit room on the ground floor of their old house. He said, 'Tempers are getting shorter. Things are getting livelier. Unity, that's the thing.'

Unity – when, even as he said it, at least 150 Tory candidates had already defied the party line by saying 'No' to the single currency in their election literature, and two junior ministers were now doing so too. If the Labour leadership took their workers for granted as they headed towards the sunny uplands of the enterprise economy, how much more were people like James Davidson betrayed, working like slaves while all these rats so precipitously scuttled off the sinking Tory ship?

Ann Martin arrived in Hebden Bridge, and called back to the office in Brighouse. 'No crises? Good.' She was working twelve-hour days. It was a time now when if people didn't have their diaries with them, they couldn't tell you what they'd done yesterday, never mind what they were doing tomorrow. Martin slumped in a chair and admitted, 'I'm very tired. But one goes on. It's the nature of the game. Look at Alex, she's got people on the phone 'til 11.30 last night. And I'm up late keeping the finances up to date – or you get regional office on three phones at once, they all want to know about next Monday when it's only Wednesday, and Monday feels an era away. Oh,' she sighed, 'to be in a majority seat.'

It was five to one; she was looking at her watch. Apart from carrying the can and protecting the candidate, it was also her job to ensure that McCafferty got to places on time – and right now, she smiled sternly, 'She's pushing her luck. Ah well. Times like these, you can get a bit snappy.'

McCafferty arrived, and Martin drove her to the railway station. A man in a bowler hat and a fine belted tweed suit was waiting beside an absolutely gorgeous 1922 Morris Oxford. It was black and maroon, it had 11.9 horsepower, and when this stout fellow had driven it to the French Alps and back last winter, he'd got 28 miles to the gallon. The touch I liked best was the wicker brolly-holder strapped to the spare wheel. McCafferty admired the car; Martin, more practical, took her handbag from her, then got the driver to show the candidate how to open and close the car doors so that she didn't make a bungle of it when the photographers were about. Then, just after half-past one, Mark Covell arrived with Sir Richard Attenborough. He tumbled into the sunshine in a grey suit and a blue Barbour waistcoat, approached the Oxford's driver and told him heartily, 'How magnificent you look, sir!'

He and McCafferty were loaded into the vintage car and driven round the corner to the Hebden Bridge cinema. Waiting on the steps outside were BBC and ITV camera crews, half a dozen photographers, *The Times*, the *Yorkshire Post*, and Val Watts from the *Courier*. No, he told them all happily, he'd never called anyone luvvie in his life. 'But I have called a lot of people darling – because I'm an actor, and because I'm very, very old. So I can't remember anybody's name, darling.'

The cinema was owned by the council, and local campaigners who'd fought to keep it open had rustled up copies of a book about Attenborough for him to sign, so that they could auction them. He talked to anyone and everyone in a flurry of notebooks and flash-bulbs in the foyer, and an old boy passing ambled in to have a gander. Seeing who it was he came up for a handshake and said, 'I remember *The Man Within*.'

It was made just after the War. 'Oh,' Attenborough told him, 'you can't remember that. You were at your mother's breast when that came out.' The old boy wandered off chuffed as punch – but Attenborough had charm by the lorryload. Walking from the cinema to the Little Theatre round the corner, snappers backing down the pavement before him as he went, he put his right arm round McCafferty's shoulders, his left round Val Watts, and when Watts had finished writing enough notes to fill the *Courier* from front page to back, she danced away giggling and grinning as if she'd just lost twenty years, positively rocking on her feet with delight. 'Oh,' she sighed to the local photographer, 'I want prints of that.'

By the post office they came on a mother with her baby in a pushchair. 'Now,' Attenborough stoutly declared, 'anyone who's a decent politician must kiss this baby.'

McCafferty laughed uncertainly. 'I don't think I dare now.'

'I wouldn't,' grinned the mother, 'she'll pull your hair.'

We had lunch at the Robin Hood Inn at Pecket Well, a hamlet up the hill towards Keighley with a corduroy mill, fine views, and farms perched on the rising slopes all about. Attenborough had got back from the States at the weekend, he'd done East Anglia yesterday, it was West Yorkshire today, then Edinburgh tomorrow, the East Midlands on Friday, Glasgow on Saturday, Sterling and Aberdeen on Sunday, Bristol on Monday. He said, 'It's a taxing agenda, OK. But when there's a chance of getting these buggers out, it's a joy to wake up every morning.'

John Major scrapped the planned Tory broadcast about the wondrous condition of the economy, and instead recorded a speech to camera about Europe, and why his wait-and-see position was the only possible policy. It was, in effect, a plea to his own people not to vote Referendum.

He'd said just a couple of weeks earlier that ministers who bucked the line on Europe would be sacked; now two of them did, and they weren't. I was beginning to wonder at what point Kenneth Clarke would finally stub out his cigar, and walk away from this

sorry fevered rabble to join Alan Howarth in the Labour Party –
and on Thursday April 17th, as it happens, Howarth was in
Brighouse to support McCafferty. I asked him about the present
condition of the Tories and he said, 'It's absolutely miserable. It was
very painful to cross the floor – but a not inconsiderable number of
Tories have had a quiet talk with me, and they well understand why
I did what I did. Because, for traditional Tories, this just isn't their
party any more.'

They went out canvassing, and an old lady in a purple suit said to
Howarth, 'I'll tell you what I'm not happy about. It's this single currency.' So I offer to her – and to all those like her – and to all those
xenophobes in a crumbling Tory party whose only logical end-
game is secession from the European Union – one simple fact.
Two-thirds of manufacturing industry in West Yorkshire exports
into Western Europe. And you want to leave?

The following day McCafferty, Alice Mahon, and Barry
Sheerman – the incumbent Labour MP for Huddersfield – had a
working lunch at the Kirklees and Calderdale TEC. On the other
side of a large and gleaming table sat five suits: four men, one
woman. One of them said, 'We're in Europe in a big way here.
We've got £5,000,000 coming from Europe for a number of very
exciting projects – so we really need to be in there with a lot better
grace. We have so much to learn from them, on so many fronts.'

These were, remember, senior people responsible for the management of a Conservative-created quango – and they were linked
into Europe in all kinds of ways both via the TEC and, in one case,
as a private sector exporter in his own right. The idea of withdrawal
from Europe was, said this man, 'A total nightmare.' So I held up
the Tory ad showing a weeny Blair sitting on the knee of a giant
Chancellor Kohl. 'What do you think of this?' Across the table, a
contemptuous curl of the lip: 'It stinks.'

One of them said, 'I deal with Europeans all the time. They ask,
Why is the UK so anti? Or they ask, Why is the UK *media* so anti?
And the more informed among them say – in impeccable English –
"You've got some very strange people wrapping themselves in the
Union Jack, haven't you?"'

Yes, they conceded, some of the European bureaucracy needed
sorting out – but then, so did a good deal of ours. Comparing our
civil servants with theirs, one of them said, 'The quality of some of

the people running these European programmes – we just don't sit at the same table as them.'

It became a strand of the conversation: how both the structure and the mind-set of the civil service in this country could be a significant hindrance to progress – but then, it was instructive to see the tone of this meeting altogether. In essence, members of the governing party in waiting were being briefed in some detail on the current state of skills training and education on their patch, and taking note of how it might be better done. The windfall tax was welcomed, more devolved regional policies and a saner approach to Europe were devoutly hoped for – until eventually Sheerman said, 'When we're in after May 1st, you feed us this information, and we'll feed it on up.'

Also interesting was the reaction when, carefully, one of the suits raised his concern about how willing Labour really was to embrace Blair's drive to the free market. Amongst the Labour people facing him, it was the supposed firebrand Alice Mahon who said firmly, 'We want to govern. After eighteen years, you'll not find many people who want to rock the boat.' She repeated, 'We want to *govern*.'

The Tory party couldn't even govern themselves. With the count of Tory candidates expressly opposed to a single currency rising all the time, I called James Davidson and put it to him that this was now an absolute shambles. The Prime Minister wanted to leave his options open, yet half his own party had closed the option tight shut. 'What can I say,' he replied, 'without getting myself into trouble? What can I say?'

He said, 'I think these people that are saying they don't want to be in Europe are in line with the majority of Tory voters.'

But they're not in line with Mr Major.

'Mr Major's looking after the best interests of Britain. Whereas if Mr Blair goes to Amsterdam . . .'

I'm not talking about Blair, I'm talking about Major. How can he look after Britain's interests, if he can't even look after his own party? I repeat, it's a shambles.

'No, no, no, I disagree. It's not seen that way.' He paused, he gasped, he struggled for a formula. He said, 'There is no uproar in the party ranks over this, because it's what the party wants to hear.'

In that case, the party doesn't agree with their own Prime Minister. Either your options are open, or they aren't. If they aren't, you defy him.

A long, long pause. 'Oh dear.'

If they aren't, I repeat, you defy him.

'Hmm. OK. Correct.'

So it's a shambles. This is meltdown.

'No, no, no, it's not. Among supporters, it's not seen that way.'

Well, if it's not a shambles . . .

He said helplessly, 'It's a broad church.'

It was stretched so broad the bleedin' roof was falling in. Look, I said, either the Conservative Party backs its leader, or it doesn't.

He said, 'You're asking me the wrong question. You're giving me a question I can't answer. What you've said is right to an extent, but I can't agree with you, and I'm not going to say what you want me to say. 'Cause I won't do that. I just won't.'

I felt for him, I really did. He was a nice bloke – but a tad too large, I fear, to be forced to dance on the head of a pin.

As you'd expect, Gillian Shephard, the Secretary of State for Education and Employment, coped with this line of questioning rather better. Basically, she coped by refusing point-blank to accept that there was any difficulty here. She said, 'It's absolutely not a shambles at all. The Prime Minister's made it absolutely clear that the government's position is negotiate-and-decide. On that, back-benchers will have a free vote, which I have found up and down the country to be extremely welcome.'

But, setting aside the fact that Major had produced the free vote out of thin air only forty-eight hours earlier, it remained the case that around two hundred Tory candidates weren't going to negoti-ate and decide because they'd decided already.

'When those candidates are elected, as they will be, they'll have a free vote. So there's no problem.'

It *looks* like a problem . . .

'Well, it may do. But I assure you that up and down the country people much prefer a party that allows free speech, to one that's putting elastoplast over the mouths of all its candidates. *Big* gagging.'

I tried another tack. The English, I said, like united parties and a strong leader — and the Tories didn't seem able to offer either of those things.

'That's nonsense. If you look at John Major in this election campaign, nobody, but *nobody*, can be in any doubt about the leadership he is showing. But there are, I'm afraid, still very big doubts about the courage of Mr Blair, who doesn't seem able to pluck up enough of it . . .'

I'm not talking about Mr Blair . . .

'To pluck up *enough* of it to face John Major in a debate.'

Red herring alert. I said, look, two weeks ago, Major said if a minister stepped out of line, he'd be sacked. Two just did . . .

'And they've retracted. They've retracted, and they've signed up to the government view. The government view is negotiate-and-decide.'

But all these candidates have decided *already*. In logic, I can't see any way round it.

'I think you're being blinded by your own logic, if I may say so. The government . . .'

An option is either open, or it's not . . .

'Do you wish me to answer these questions, or would you prefer to answer them yourself? The position is this. The government will negotiate and decide . . .'

Round and round we went and Jeremy Paxman, I guess, can rest safe in his bed. Mrs Shephard was flawlessly impenetrable — but claiming her party didn't have a problem was a porkie as big as a palace.

She was visiting Brighouse to support Sir Donald; the visit finished over coffee in the Black Bull, and one of those present was the chair of the Yorkshire Area Conservatives, Mrs Jean Searle OBE. Searle was a tall and strikingly handsome woman, I'd guess in her fifties, immaculately and expensively turned out — and she was also an angry woman. She said, 'A lot of these candidates have behaved appallingly. It makes it enormously difficult. I pleaded twelve months, eighteen months ago that everybody should be united and loyal on *all* issues. But these candidates do their own thing, and I think it could do irreparable damage. It looks like disloyalty, disunity — so I ask myself, have they got another agenda? And if that other agenda is a different leader in opposition, they want their heads seeing to.'

It looked, I said, as if the Tories faced electoral meltdown.

'I think all I can say to that is yes. I think you're quite right.'

And you're being betrayed.

'Yes. I quite agree with you. The Prime Minster's *pleaded* with his candidates that we should wait and see – and they're destroying the party if they don't do that.'

A different line, I think, from the state of denial inhabited by Mrs Shephard; and Jean Searle said that, after the election, she was going to get all these candidates who'd bucked the line together for a meeting, with their constituency chairmen too, because they'd been just as bad. She said, 'If we win, I shall ask them if they're going to behave. And if we lose, I shall tell them why.'

Mrs Searle struck me as a formidable woman. I was, therefore, very glad indeed not to be one of those candidates. They would, I suspected, be finding themselves elegantly but most comprehensively horsewhipped.

While she was there, Mrs Searle checked that Sir Donald wasn't taking money from the Yorkshire businessman Paul Sykes, who'd offered campaign funds to any candidate who'd say 'No' to the single currency. (They're so easily bought, these people, aren't they?) But Sir Donald, of course, was doing no such thing – that wouldn't be his style at all. On the other hand, his own formulation in his election address still sailed pretty close to the wind. He'd written, 'I shall oppose further politicisation of Europe and cannot see Britain joining a single currency.'

I asked him what he felt about the outright rejectionists and he said, 'I feel let down by these guys. What I've said is broad enough to be read between the lines – and you shouldn't be a politician if you can't make a political statement. But these guys, they're either naïve or selfish. About half and half, I should think. Still,' he shrugged, 'if we lose, they lose.'

I said it looked like they'd be losing in a big, big way.

He sighed and said, 'Well. We'll see.'

22

BLIND STUPIDITY

A man in Halifax changed his name by deed poll to Alice Mahon, and came within an ace of getting on the ballot as the official Labour candidate. Labour's lawyers got it thrown out in court – with five minutes to spare before the deadline for nominations closed. An election pulls crazies out of the woodwork all over the shop – though to be fair, the bloke in Huddersfield who once changed his name to Mr Singh didn't do it because he wanted votes; he just wanted to ride a motor-bike without a helmet. Presumably it didn't work, because after that he changed his name to The Occupier.

Back among the sensible people, Davidson said Shephard would be turning up at Kwikfit – appropriate, seeing the Tory wheels were coming off.

Around the corner, Labour had a white Mercedes van covered in posters, with loudspeakers on the roof-rack. In the office, Mick Clapham and two other Barnsley boys set off with great bundles of balloons. 'Oh, I love it,' chuckled Ann Martin. 'I love it when we get going like this.'

Just yards away, Shephard arrived in Jean Searle's Toyota jeep; she set off round the streets trailed by the *Courier*, *The Times Educational Supplement* and the BBC. She could charm for Great Britain, this woman – while Sir Donald knew everyone, and if he didn't, in the haze of bonhomie he made it look like he did. We met people he'd been at school with; so I can reveal that he was slimmer back then, a handy rugby player, and he came bottom in Latin.

We went to a Girl Guides' bookstall; Mrs Shephard bought a Fay

Weldon novel, and an ancient tome called *Modern Practical Cookery*. Well, she'd have more time on her hands soon, wouldn't she? In the background, Clapham's voice boomed about the town asking people to vote Labour.

Later, when we had coffee in the Bull, Labour's van was parked right outside. Sir Donald pointed it out and said, 'It's a measure of how sensible Chris McCafferty is that they can be as close as that and there's no bloody silliness. It's a bit old-fashioned – but it's how it should be.'

His body language suggested he'd conceded already – and I never noticed him actually ask anyone how they were going to vote. But you wouldn't want the knockbacks, would you?

McCafferty asked people straight, 'Can I ask whether you'll be voting for us?' In a session outside Tesco two hours later, the answer she got from young and old, men and women, poor and well-heeled alike, was Yes, yes, yes, yes, yes. Then she got a woman who said she wasn't quite sure. She was teetering Labour's way – and from something this woman said, McCafferty got the impression that she'd previously voted Liberal, so she asked if that were the case. The woman snorted and said, 'I work in the education depart-ment. I *know* Councillor Pearson. And I wouldn't vote for a man like that in a thousand years.'

The following morning, Sunday April 20th, the Liberal candi-date met five members of his party in Todmorden. A short distance from where they parked, there was a road called Major Street; fit-tingly, it was a dead end. But then, the Liberals were meeting at the end of Every Street, which was equally appropriate. This was, after all, the party that offered us everything. For just a penny!

As Warhurst had predicted, Pearson had a master plan. He wasn't going to stand again as a Liberal candidate for parliament – he'd promised his wife this – and instead, he was now working at the grass-roots. The bulk of his effort in this election went on promot-ing the Liberal candidate for a council by-election in Todmorden; come May 1st, he expected people in Tod to vote Labour nation-ally, and Liberal for the council.

In the 1980s, the Liberals had fifteen seats on Calderdale Council. By 1992, this had collapsed to a rump of five, for a variety of reasons. They won a couple back – then they fell at each other's throats when Tim Swift made a bid to oust Pearson. If you believe Swift, he left; if you believe Pearson, they kicked him out. But either way, it was nine months of bloodshed, their vote flaked off – and on top of that, Pearson made what he described as, 'The biggest political mistake of my life'.

He became Mayor of Calderdale for a year. During that time, he was a busy bee with a chain round his neck and he couldn't be politically active – but, he said, every local party depends on one or two individuals. 'So for a year, I've left it to others – and to put it bluntly, fuck all happened. We didn't put leaflets out, we weren't organised on council; it was a personal triumph in terms of the Mayorality but underneath that, politically, nothing happened.'

A personal triumph. Don't you love it? The man's middle name was modesty. But now his year of triumph was past, and he was riding back to resurrect their local fortunes. Labour would win the election, they'd be as unpopular in government as they were unpopular on Calderdale, so starting now – with the Tod council by-election – the Liberals were going to build their local vote back up, and thus rise to recapture the balance of power on the council. Labour, he said, would lose control by 1999 – with Pearson, no doubt, at the helm of the Liberals in their glory regained.

The Liberal candidate in Tod was 23, a supermarket manager in Oldham, and he seemed pleasant enough. But from the way Pearson delivered his instructions for the leaflet drop that morning, I suspect if Pearson said jump, this young man would ask, How high?

Pearson had the election all worked out; McCafferty would win by 2,000. He gave Viv Smith 500, Tony Mellor 1,000, himself 7,500; so if 55,000 voted, that left Labour and Conservative 46,000 to play for, and McCafferty would get more of them.

For himself, his worst case scenario was that his vote might be squeezed as low as 6,000, a fall of over a third. If that happened, he said, 'I'd be very, very upset. And it's no good people saying, Don't take it personally – 'cause when it's you on your own on the Friday after polling day, it *is* personal, isn't it? 'Cause I've worked like *fuck*. And if it happens, I'll probably say something I'll regret.

That I was the best candidate, and that I've been shat on from a great height.'

He was not the nicest man I've ever met, and he had an ego the size of a house (detached, with many bedrooms) but it was still possible to have sympathy for him. A wee bit, anyway – because he was bright, capable, hard-working and well-informed, and in my opinion he was right on a good number of things. He was a unilateral disarmer, he wanted PR, on race he was sound as a pound – and his analysis of the present situation was both realistic and principled. He said, 'After eighteen years, I can understand what Labour are doing – but the political system breeds dishonesty, doesn't it? It forces them to do it, and at what cost? What happens afterwards? Maybe there'll be two hundred Blairites in Westminster soon. But if they've abandoned socialism, let's hope they don't abandon social justice too.'

I couldn't have put it better myself. So why did he have to spoil it by saying such unpleasant things about people? Like, 'McCafferty is so wound up in her own self-importance.' Pots and kettles, boy, pots and kettles.

He went to work with a sidekick producing leaflets to hand out at a rugby league game that afternoon: Halifax away to Castleford. He thought this was clever, as he did the blue leaflet that had so exercised the Tories. But personally, if I was a rugby league fan and some bleedin' politician came up and hassled me when I was out to watch the game on a Sunday, I'd have decked him.

After the echoing, empty-office longueurs of the early weeks, Labour now had so many people working for them that their desktop printers couldn't keep up; that Sunday afternoon, they ran out of letters to put into envelopes. MPs and other workers were coming from Doncaster, Barnsley, Bradford, Rotherham, Sheffield, Shipley, Newcastle, even from London – this last in the form (among others) of Nick Brown's assistant Tom Greatrex. Greatrex, as far as I could tell, was making a very good job of organising his boss's campaign schedule around the Fulham fixture list – he'd managed to watch them lately in both Carlisle and Doncaster – and very happy he was about it. Fulham promoted, Labour winning – what more could a boy want?

In the background, Tim Swift was working quietly with

McCafferty. He applied careful spit and polish to her press releases; he boiled Labour HQ's target letters down from two pages to one (so they could print them in half the time, spend half the money on paper, and not make people have to read so much), and he was cautiously confident. His attitude to the polls was that the size of the lead didn't matter, what mattered was the trend – and since there was no downward shift of any significance in Labour's lead, he had to believe it looked good. Besides, he said, 'The Tory campaign's been so bad, hasn't it? That golden touch they had, it's just gone. Their ads have been awful – and the Chancellor's Joe Bloggs now? You just don't say that sort of thing, do you?'

So he was confident; but then, with a nervous laugh, he put in the careful caveat. He said, 'I'm as confident as a person who thought Labour'd shade it in '92 can be.'

Another day, another bunch of MPs. Helen Jackson brought a crew from Sheffield, Derek Fatchett came from Leeds, Hugh Bayley came from York; McCafferty was beaming. She'd got a lovely letter from a couple of Tories who lived in one of the poshest houses in Mytholmroyd, wishing her all the best, and telling her that when the Tories canvassed they'd told the caller, No, not this time. Categorically not.

She'd also been sent a packet of Clorets – a minor but brilliant piece of marketing. If you're out kissing babies, they told her, you'll be needing fresh breath.

She did some GOTV work with Fatchett in Hebden Bridge – this acronym being an American import, short for Get Out The Vote. You hit the places where your people are; you remind them how you need every one of them in the polling booth come the day. They visited a clutch of back-to-back terraces tucked away between the river and the canal, behind a mill with a giant blackened chimney. Washing lines hung across the alleys between the houses; a man getting his washing in said, 'They're all socialist in this street, mate.'

Posters went up in every window. It was the same in a bleak stack of flats across the river; up dark, bare stairwells, people smiled and took posters. Even the people behind the door with the sign saying 'Go Away' were friendly. One shambly old cove came out in his slippers, clutching his cat, and said, 'I'll not be voting any other way, will I?'

McCafferty told him, 'Well, get your posters up then. Or you're getting no more kisses from me.'

'When yer get in,' he asked her, 'will yer let me come down an' 'ave a look at them 'ouses of Parlyment?'

'I will. But not if you don't put those posters up. And,' she wagged a finger at him, 'you know I mean what I say, don't you?'

They moved on to Tod to help their council candidate Steve Martin work an estate up there; Labour manifesto summaries went through every door, and Martin had a leaflet for the by-election folded round each one. Pearson, he said, had put out four leaflets already; he'd been working the place to death, and now people were telling Martin they were sick of it. How much stuff were they supposed to read? A woman came to her door and said she'd always voted Liberal, but she was Labour this time – and when, she cried, was it all going to end? 'It's driving me *mad*.'

Fatchett laughed and told her, 'It's driving us all mad too.'

He predicted a Labour majority of fifty, maybe more.

Talk was starting about the post-election Tory leadership campaign. Pearson thought it was Portillo or Redwood; he thought they'd swing messily, nastily, xenophobically to the right. I thought Shephard looked good, on the grounds that the other two are weird and slimy and bonkers – but maybe, given the state of the Tories now, those were the qualifications you needed. As for the prospect of Michael Howard, that was too ghastly to bear thinking about. Several Labour MPs, meanwhile, sagely advised me to keep an eye on William Hague. 'He's human,' said one. 'It does help.'

Assuming Labour won, they'd be facing a different order of problem altogether. Hugh Bayley's visit was organised round a surgery in Todmorden; amid the increasingly chaotic schedule there'd been talk of Labour's health boss Chris Smith coming to do this one, but in the manic compression of the campaign his visit got pulled (you could always blame the IRA) so the GPs got the more junior health man instead. Bayley was on Smith's team – he'd been a health economist before he won York, he'd been on the health select committee – and the doctors didn't mind. As far as I could tell, they figured they were better getting someone who had the ear of the top folk for forty minutes than someone more senior who zoomed in and out, shook a lot of hands and was gone before they'd opened their mouths.

We sat in a meeting room in the surgery: Bayley, McCafferty, two doctors, the practice's business manager, two Labour minders from regional office and the local press. These last got their quotes, and were swiftly despatched. Then we got down to it. One of the doctors had prepared a résumé of their problems. It said, 'The NHS will need more resources to deliver what the population needs . . . 'Reduction in Bureaucracy' will not yield enough, nor quickly enough. We worry that Mr Brown's stringency will hamstring us . . . we are *not* self-interested people who must be defeated. The NHS runs on altruism. The enthusiasm to go the extra mile (for free) is being knocked out of us . . . we cannot cope without more resources. HELP!'

Bayley told them, 'Overall, the Labour party's committed to match the year-on-year growth promised by Stephen Dorrell. There is no commitment to increase NHS funding beyond that; that's the floor set by Brown. There is the ability to rise above it if circumstances allow, but I don't think it will rise in the first two years. Given the state of the public finances, it's not credible to borrow more, or to tax more. There are options to shift our priorities about, but to say we can solve our problems with one penny, or whatever, we don't think is politically or economically viable. The intention is to shift incrementally from welfare spending to public services – not as far as we'd like, maybe. But towards the end of a Labour government, I think we'll be able to increase public spending and obviously the NHS will be in the queue for that.'

There followed much detailed talk about how Labour could help these people to do a better job – the essence of which, when you got away from the money, was that doctors were not stupid people. One said, 'We've been treated unfairly; we're not seen as professionals but as unreconstructed trade unionists. I want to be a partner with government, not an adversary to be beaten down with well-honed phrases . . .'

McCafferty said, 'I've heard head teachers say exactly the same.'

So they wanted respect for their views – but, at the end of the day, it still came back to money. They were increasingly overworked as more and more health care shifted out of hospitals into primary care in the community, and resources failed to follow that shift. In their own words, HELP!

But Labour, basically, weren't offering much help. We all knew that health care (like education, transport, everything) needed more money. Not fine words, but money. And we all knew that scrapping the assisted places scheme, or 'cutting bureaucacy', didn't begin to provide the sort of money required. The money wasn't there, because Labour couldn't say they'd raise taxes to bring it in – so, basically, we were shafted.

About this time, one of the phalanx of Labour MPs now marching through this key marginal said to me, 'Politics begins again on May 1st. New Labour have been absolutely brilliant at organising to win an election – but once you've won it, that agenda's over, isn't it? They may have the PR sorted out for Blair's move into Downing Street on May 2nd, but what next? On May 2nd, you're in the real world then – and it's going to be very interesting. Because even the five pledges aren't easy, never mind anything else.'

It felt as if we were living through a game-show. New Labour, come on down . . . the electorate were being invited to play a political version of 'Blind Date', and the whole tone of the thing was blind stupidity. While the hard work went on day by day on the doorstep, at the leadership level the debate had all the intellectual gravitas of the primary school playground. Trust me, cried Blair. A federal Europe, threatened Major. They might as well have stuck out their tongues at each other and shouted, Pooh.

All the while, I'd tried to remain cautious. Don't believe the polls, keep an open mind, be afraid – be very afraid – that the Tory machine could still, somehow, finally get into gear. Then, with two weeks to go, I'd begun to feel certain that the Tories had lost it; that they were all ninety-five and gaga in blazers; that Europe was destroying them.

Liberal and Labour people said Europe wasn't an issue on the doorstep. But then Jaques Santer weighed in, berating the sceptics, and I began to wonder again. One Labour MP said, 'Europe's still dangerous for us. If the Tories come out the other side of this as a totally anti-European party, that could still hurt us.'

The ironic thing about these sovereignty junkies, of course, is that they all love NATO. For goodness' sake, we'd pooled – indeed, submerged – our sovereignty on defence matters under the American banner for the best part of fifty years; but logic didn't enter into it any more, did it? We were ten days away now, and it was coming down to who could shout Pooh the loudest.

23

POLLYWOBBLES

———————

Have you seen a Tory MP about here?

The bloke was bald and grey-bearded; he wore blue overalls, and was lugging what looked like boiler components out of a workshop at the bottom of an old mill. He looked up at me and said, 'No. But if I did I'd direct him that way.' He waved behind him and said, 'Right in canal.'

I found Sir Donald at the other end of the mill; he was visiting a firm run by a friend of his, one Elizabeth Greenwood. A striking, rather theatrical woman in a green felt hat adorned with a pheasant feather, she'd been born in Czechoslovakia, schooled in Austria and at the Sorbonne, and she now employed twenty-eight people – twenty on site, eight outworkers – making textile goods for horses. They made leg protectors, winter rugs, saddle pads; they turned over nearly £1 million, and 90 per cent of it was export. Boxes were stacked up ready for despatch to the States, Bahrain, Denmark, France, Japan, and to trade fairs at the world championships in Gothenburg. The *Courier* came – and Greenwood told them business was as bad as she'd known it in ten years.

Whoops. Business was bad because the pound was strong – France and Germany were difficult, she'd lost her Spanish market altogether – and she was mortified that she'd not explained that. She cried, 'It's not Donald's fault!' But she hadn't said so to the *Courier*, and it was a bit of a bungle. Sir Donald shrugged, as if to say, there's a bit of comedy for you.

We walked through the workshop, past women cutting and

sewing at wide tables. Sir Donald said contentedly, 'I've known some of these ladies longer than I'd like to remember.'

'I'm only thirty-nine, Donald,' one of them told him, 'don't you be giving any secrets away.'

He chuckled, 'Thirty-nine *again*?'

During an election, he said, you couldn't just drop in on people who'd never seen you before. You wanted a friendly reception.

A man in his forties asked him, 'Are you canvassing for Labour?'

Sir Donald looked moon-faced. He asked, 'Why?'

''Cause everyone else is. And I hope you get in. I doubt you will, mind.' He then launched – amiably, but firmly – into a complaint about the distribution of the lottery money. London got it all – bleedin' Wembley, bleedin' opera, all that. Vainly Thompson told him Calder Valley had had £2 million – to which the bloke asked, how much was £2 million then?

Before he left Thompson said, 'It's as hard a fight as I've ever had. We'll see on the day whether eighteen years makes any difference. A chap can't expect a personal vote of more than five or six hundred – but,' he sighed, 'it might be enough.'

Greenwood told him she was sorry to say it, but a lot of people would vote for the Referendum man. 'This single currency,' she declaimed, 'nobody wants it. The French, the Germans, nobody.'

Sir Donald took the knocks with good grace and gave her a parting kiss. He said a lot might depend on Pearson's vote – and then he asked me, Had I seen the BNP leaflet? It was, he said, 'A nasty, grubby little thing.'

I say, put this man in the House of Lords. Until we abolish it, anyway.

This assumes, of course, that McCafferty would beat him – which continued to be a rather reckless assumption. She went canvassing in Stainland, and met a woman who said she'd voted Labour before but this time she wasn't right sure. She said, 'I'm in a difficult situation, 'cause my husband's an avid Tory.'

I'm still trying to fathom the implications of this statement today. I did at least manage to restrain myself from telling her that obviously she should leave him.

Back in the office, Ann Martin announced that Blair was coming and that she had to find a brass band. She was not best pleased. It had been marked in the diary for weeks that on the campaign's final Saturday, Calder Valley would be blessed with a mystery celebrity – so why did they never tell them in good time who it was? Why did they keep it secret all that time and then, with just four days' notice, finally spring on them this requirement for the instant provision of a brass band?

They called the best local outfit, the Brighouse and Rastrick, but they couldn't do it; they'd be off in Rochdale recording a CD. They called the Friendly band – there really is a place called Friendly – and they called the Walkley's Clogs band, but it was pretty short notice. The Friendly man said cautiously that they had a slow melody contest coming up the next day, and it depended besides whether the solo euphonium was available.

Martin said, 'They expect you to work bloody miracles. Maybe I'll just pull me tenor horn out the wardrobe and do him a solo.'

Jack Straw's visit the following morning had also had its timetable shunted about at the last minute. McCafferty looked at the new schedule and sighed, 'Tell me. How am I going to survive the next nine days?'

I went to fill the kettle. When I came back Martin asked, 'Did you hear that? ICM's got the Labour lead down to nine points.' There was a long, long pause while that bad news sank in. Then Martin said fiercely, 'It's *crap*. The Tory vote's stuck solid on thirty points. As long as that stays, the size of the lead doesn't matter.'

I said that nine points was good enough.

McCafferty said, 'I don't know if it's good enough for me.'

Away in a corner, Tom Greatrex played solitaire on one of the computers. He was waiting for someone in London to page him with the latest Gallup Poll, to see if it was any better than the ICM. On the screen, the cards weren't coming out right.

Martin asked what day it was. We discussed that for a while, because I wasn't too sure either. Eventually we decided it was Tuesday. I went home, and left them wondering where they'd find a brass band.

The poll was worse than we'd heard. Labour's lead hadn't fallen to 9 points, it had fallen *by* 9 points; ICM had them merely 5 points ahead. Gallup, on the other hand, had the lead climbing to 21 – but it's the one that looks bad that makes you nervy. At 9.30 the next morning Steve Martin, Labour's council candidate in Todmorden, found me waiting for Jack Straw outside the cop shop. He asked if I'd seen the poll, then he said, 'It's a blip. It's got to be a blip.'

I could hear the silent scream of taut nerves, nails breaking as they shrieked down the blackboard. He said, 'Since Major spoke on Europe last week, it's been the only issue on the doorstep. Pearson's putting all these leaflets out saying Labour won't build Todmorden a swimming pool, but I'll tell you, they're not talking about swimming pools. All of a sudden, it's Europe – which is ironic, 'cause most people in Tod think Halifax is a foreign country, never mind Brussels. But still, I saw that this morning and I thought, *Oh my God.*'

The worst thing about the poll was the truly ludicrous information that the Tories now rated eight points ahead of Labour on Europe. This despite that fact that the policies of both parties on the single currency were identical, barring the one salient difference that in the Tories' case, half their candidates didn't agree with it.

While we mulled it over, the BBC were waiting, and the local paper; Straw was fifteen minutes late. Martin said, 'He probably heard the *Today* programme and decided to go back to bed.' Filling time, the girl from the local paper – right on top of the news agenda here – started interviewing another Tod councillor under the mistaken impression that she was McCafferty. Well, they were both blonde. It turned out that this councillor's son had had a minor car crash, and the reporter brightened up. A story! Lad rolls car, no injuries! Who needs the election?

The real McCafferty arrived. She'd had a brake light out; she'd set off for Tod thinking, My God, Jack Straw's going to be following me to three police stations the length of the valley and my car's illegal. Then Ann Martin rang on the mobile, said Straw would be late, and she thought, There *is* a god. She found a garage, and stood fretting while they fixed it – but she needn't have worried. There was still no sign of Straw.

He finally arrived an hour late, with two cars, four minders and a *Guardian* journalist. He apologised, saying something about 'geographical difficulties'. No brass band, a tumbling poll – what else could go wrong? Maybe, after all this time, Labour were going to lose because their map-reading was lousy and they didn't have a euphonium.

Look North pounced, and asked how Labour were going to sort out the criminal justice system if they stayed inside existing Tory spending limits. Straw headed away from that one at the speed of light, and did his hard man act. You couldn't trust the Tories. Labour would be more efficient, more draconian, more responsible and just generally brilliant. Look out, you crims, here comes Big Jack, armed to the hilt with ferocious pledges. Piffly guffle spew. There wasn't any more *money* . . .

He stepped into the station, shook hands with two coppers, then put his hand out to a woman standing to one side of them. 'It's all right Jack,' she told him, 'I was in the car with you.'

The door was being held open behind us by another of New Labour's crop-haired youths with the shades, the dark suit and floral tie. I think they must have been cloning them.

We scuttled in, scuttled out, went to Hebden Bridge and did the same, then went to Brighouse and did the same there too. Straw shook hands, swapped pleasantries, inspected computer systems and talked to Radio Leeds. In one room there was a board of mugshots and ugly character histories: recent releases, active crims, this month's targets. Straw asked, 'Are they all on drugs?'

They weren't – and I asked him if the standard of debate wasn't just woeful. He said, 'With the public it isn't. What is appalling is the culture of British political journalism; it's all concerned with process, not with issues. It's navel-gazing by bored journalists; the British press are de-skilling the British public, and the Tories are complicit in this. They trade in fear, and they want to bore the electorate . . .'

But Labour aren't saying much either.

'I think we're being *more* explicit this election. We *can't* bump up taxes, and people may not like it but it's the truth. And don't worry, we'll win. Any seat with a Tory majority less than two or three thousand, we'll take it.' And off he went, next stop Dewsbury. But what he'd just said implied, of course, that they might not win seats like Calder Valley – in which case they might end up the largest party, but not have an overall majority.

★

Ann Martin's horoscope said, 'Life is changing for the better.' This was more acceptable than the polls.

The Blair visit was on hold; whether he came or not, material for The Last Five Days had arrived. There was bunting, balloons, flags, paper hats, majorette's pom-pom sticks – all the trappings of a serious debate. It was in the new design livery – purple. One theory had it that this denoted passion. Another was, purple's what you get when you mix up red and blue.

Everywhere you went among Labour people this theme recurred, this ironic and resigned acceptance of their campaign as a necessary exercise in marketing flummery. The following morning, with Gallup and MORI showing Labour's lead holding at 19 or 20 points, the Pollywobbles receded; the Guardian thing had surely been a blip. What worried Labour people more, all the while, was that they weren't really running a Labour campaign at all.

It was so safe, so nervously righteous, so polished and American – and it wasn't coming clean about the money. Certainly, it was difficult. Labour had to say they were different – but at the same time they had to reassure a timorous electorate that they weren't too different. With seven days to go, however, the result of this was the reaction reported to me by one of a crew working Hebden Bridge market. She said, 'People are positive that they want the Tories out. The trouble is, they're not so positive they want us in.'

McCafferty was above any worrying, feeling much refreshed. At 4.30 the previous afternoon, getting home from door-knocking, she'd called Ann Martin and asked what to do next. 'You're tired,' Martin told her, 'you stay there. You sleep.'

No, said McCafferty, I can't do that . . .

You can, said Martin sternly, and you will.

McCafferty lay back on her bed, and the next thing she knew she was waking up to find three whole hours had gone by. She slept all night, too – unheard of – and now she was up for it. On her way to the market, when a woman said that this time Labour had to win, she told her firmly, 'I know. And we will. I shall be disgusted with myself if we don't.'

'Well,' this woman muttered nervously, 'I've still got this sneaky feeling. 'Cause they're right devious, aren't they?'

Someone gave her a balloon for her kid's pram. It was the New
Labour spin doctor's prescription; if afflicted with the pollywobbles,
take one balloon daily.

Kinnock's biographer Eileen Jones arrived, and she was even
angrier than she'd been six months back when Brown first
announced his target of a 10p tax rate. She waved her hands about
and said, 'I *want* to pay more taxes. They just don't *need* to go so far
to the right.' Pointing at McCafferty busy stroking a voter she said,
'It must be invidious for her to have to stand in the street and virtually defend Tory policies. I've found it more and more distressing
as the campaign goes on; to say that an incoming government will
run on the same economic basis as the Tories just beggars belief. I
hear them wriggling, and it just turns my stomach.'

Anyway, she said, she had to rush off, she had to meet a friend
for coffee. And agreeing with her's one thing – but another thing is,
Kinnock lost. And look, here were these people out working for a
Labour win while Eileen Jones scampered off for coffee – with, I
must add, one of the crew saying wearily to her departing back, 'It's
all right her saying she'll pay more taxes. She can afford to, can't
she?'

By a fruit-and-veg stall, I saw a man watching all this with a wry,
dry hint of a smile. He was a college lecturer in sound studio technology (an exotically implausible job description – but this is
Hebden Bridge, remember) and he was, he said, just sick of it all. It
was saturation, it was altogether too much. Mind you, the
Referendum mob had sent him a nice video, he enjoyed that. That
Goldsmith, he said, he talked all that time and he *never blinked*. Was
he real? Or was he computer-generated?

Anyway, now it was only a week off, he supposed he was beginning to think about it – and Donald Thompson had never done
him any personal harm, he said mildly, but he felt it'd be a shame to
add to his tenure. He'd probably vote Labour. With, I have to say,
a gaping lack of enthusiasm.

Back in Brighouse Ann Martin and Alex Powell sat alone, stamping McCafferty's signature on 10,000 letters to weak Labour
supporters. That's a lot of stamping – and while others nattered,
people like these were working their arms out of their sockets.

Martin once said to me of Alex, 'How can you put a value on someone you can't do without?'

What Alex had to say about people who didn't work for the party because of their fancy principles had best go unprinted. She laughed at herself and said, 'I'm turning into a right little fascist.'

I was directed to the Blakeborough Working Men's Club, two minutes' walk away, to find fourteen members of the Brighouse Pensioners' Association sitting on red plush banquettes under paintings of scenes from World War Two and a D-Day commemorative plaque. McCafferty arrived with Tarlo, and told these people that she felt pensioners had been left out of the election. She didn't know if that was the fault of the Tories or the media, but they had been.

'And another thing that's been left out is the privatisation of the pension. It's in their manifesto, and I'm *outraged* that it's not a bigger issue. But we will never, *ever* go down that road. It was your generation who gave us what we have today, and we will *never* forget that. Whereas we feel the Tories have betrayed your trust; they're forcing 40,000 people to sell their homes every year to pay for long-term care, when those people scrimped and saved to have something to pass to their children, and they end up having to give it all to the government . . .'

She spoke fluently and well for twenty minutes, about carers and the NHS, about crime and the climate of fear. It was in small moments like these that the election had its passion, moments that I've no doubt were repeated in seat after seat all round the country; but where was it reported? Where was it in the national campaign? Nationally, instead of passion, we got purple posters.

When the time came for questions, a spry old woman in a bright red coat said immediately, 'I'd like to be the first. I've been a Labour member a long, long time, and we fought on socialist principles – but we haven't heard a single socialist word in this election, and I'm quite sick of it. I feel that fiercely about it, I'm not even sure how to vote. We've lost the spirit of the Labour Party. We're *pink*!'

She made McCafferty struggle; as she tried to answer, her questioner's interjections were intense, articulate and acute. Finally McCafferty drove on over them and won out when she said, 'Look, I've been a member of the Labour Party thirty years, and I know why I'm standing. I'm standing because I believe in justice and equality. That doesn't mean I want to see the rich brought down; it means I want everybody else brought *up* . . .'

Yes, this game old bird was nodding vigorously, yes, yes, yes.

She came up to me later, a peppy little bundle of bright-eyed energy, and she told me, 'I'll tell you what's wrong with the Labour Party. There's too many college boys and not enough workers. And then, *this* man (here she gestured at a picture of Blair), I saw him on Dimbleby saying he's done this for the Labour Party, he's done that, he's changed this, he's changed that. Oh, it made me want to *vomit*. I was in the Labour Party when he was in *nappies*. I tell you, when he gets in, I'll be *watching* him.'

With, no doubt, a most sternly alive and beady eye. I said to her (somewhat tentatively, as you'll imagine, for fear of having my head cheerfully parted from my shoulders) that she'd said all this, it was understandable – but surely she wasn't really going to vote for someone else?

She said, 'Oh, I'll be voting Labour. Of course I will. If I didn't vote Labour, my old man'd come down from heaven and chop my fingers off.' Then she turned to McCafferty, pointed to Tarlo and said, 'He's quite dishy, isn't he?'

She had a laugh like stones falling into water. Still thinking of this gem of a woman, I went back to the office – and as I came on to the main street I saw a wee bout of road rage. A fat guy in a BMW was terrorising a woman over a parking spot, snarling and waving and throwing her the finger. The woman fled; the fat guy backed so ferociously into the spot that he came within an inch of knocking down an old fellow with a stick crossing the road behind him. And fat rich bastards being angrily rude, mowing down people in their way . . . it was an image in miniature of the last eighteen years.

In the hope that the next eighteen years might be better, I'd used my postal vote for Labour that morning. The question now was, would enough other people do the same?

24

THE LAST FIVE DAYS

On Friday April 25th, I called James Davidson; he had his hand stuck in a broken photocopier. Amid small grunts and wrenching noises, he said it had gone on so long now that by rights polling day should have been yesterday; everywhere people were saying, let's get it done with. Still, it was the last big push now. By Thursday every candidate, every agent, would all be absolutely knackered. 'And then,' he said, 'we'll have to stay awake for a possible recount.'

Given his original prediction of a win by 3,000, this was hardly a confident suggestion; and if everyone was twitchy, the unknown trajectory of Tony Blair was adding to it. Davidson had heard he'd be in Halifax and the valley that day; Ann Martin hadn't. If the Tories thought he would be, she said – half-amused, half-irritated that she didn't know where her own party's leader was – 'That'll get them worked up over nothing.'

Meanwhile, after many parched weeks, the cricket season had begun; naturally, it started raining. Most people stayed in stuffing envelopes; the Tories were writing to doubters, which struck me as another nervy sign. In Brighouse, the official Labour Party rain ponchos arrived; more of the jollity package for The Last Five Days. They were thin, they were pink and, said one volunteer, they made you look as if you were modelling condoms.

Tony the Denim Geezer wouldn't have been seen dead in such a thing, but he wasn't going to let a spot of rain stop him either; he was a man on a mission. While Tarlo saw to the top of the valley, Tony the Geezer wanted to cover the bottom end with enough

posters to make your eyes ache. He set off with a bloke from
Bradford in a beat-up old Nissan hatchback stuffed with stakes,
placards, bags of nails, plastic tie-bands and a sledgehammer. They
had a list of people who'd said they'd take stakes in their gardens;
anyone else who'd got a window poster up, they doorknocked
them too, trying to make them go one better. In a T-shirt and a
jacket hanging open to the grey and watery day, Tony picked a fer-
tile street and they went to work bedecking it with McCafferty's
name.

He was thirty-nine, a big, strong, quiet-spoken man; he was on
the dole at the minute, working sporadically on a notion he had for
a television drama, but he'd not written much lately. He'd always
voted Labour – then in 1987, the Labour rooms were opposite
where he lived, so he'd gone in and started helping. He said, 'You
don't intend to get this involved, do you? But there are never
enough people. So,' he shrugged, 'you just admit to yourself after a
while that you're doing seven days a week.'

He had a job once selling loft insulation door-to-door, making
good money; now he went door-to-door for nothing. But the
thing was, 'You get obsessed. You want to see just how many
posters you can do. We did an estate round the corner the other day,
it was brilliant. When we got there, there was nothing. It started
out a virgin – and half an hour later it was a whore.'

The street was narrow, lined with long terraces in pale Yorkshire
stone behind pocket-handkerchief front yards. A woman taking a
poster on the outside of her house advised them of the political
affiliations of everyone she knew who lived there. 'Her over there'll
have one, and her over there. My friend up there's poorly in her bed
so don't knock, just stick one up for her.' While she pointed to this
house and that, a scrap collector took two posters for the back
windows of his van; an old boy walking past said, 'I'll have one in
my garden and all.'

One door where Tony knocked, the woman said she'd be voting
Labour but she'd not have a poster, not even in her window. 'I'm
not a fanatic.'

He smiled and told her, 'The Labour Party guarantees a
Caribbean holiday to anyone who gets their windows broken . . .
no? All right then. Thanks anyway, see you now.'

Other people told me they'd tried to persuade him to stand for council; between his work-rate and his local knowledge, he might well have been an asset. But he always turned it down; he said, 'I've got no nerves about doing this. But the idea of running round saying vote for me, vote for me – I wouldn't want to do that. Besides, if you get in, sooner or later you've got to lie, haven't you?'

He came on the poster man's wet dream – a prominent gable end looking down across the town. They had big boards, four foot by five, and the owner said sure, you can stick one up there. As he stood looking at this site, crooning with glee, I asked why he was doing all this. He said, 'I'm doing it 'cause I don't want it to get any worse. Her there, she'll be paying for her privatised lampstand if that lot get another five years. But this is my watershed. I've done this ten years and if Blair gets in now, good. Then I'll give him twelve months. If he turns out to be a Tory, that's it. I'm off.'

Saturday 26th April

The balloons, the flags, the leaflets and lapel stickers all said the same. 'Now Vote. Because We Deserve Better.' It was ten in the morning, and the office was humming with people. A gang from Barnsley set off into the rain with all their purple paraphernalia; across the road, Donald Thompson stood in his pinstripe outside the Black Bull with a long face on. He was, he said, just putting in fleeting appearances, showing himself about the place – and as the Labour wave emerged, he scooted off to Elland.

He left behind him Councillor John Foran, one shy middle-aged man, and two old women. They had drab leaflets, plain blue stickers, and nothing else. As Labour's team took up positions across the way, so the flow of people going past clutching red balloons steadily increased. The Tories were sadly outnumbered, and they looked as if they knew it. Foran was saying, You never know, you never know – but he did know. They were gone. He consoled himself by saying, 'They'll be a one-term wonder, that's all.'

David Tarlo turned up, daftly vivid in a pink poncho and a purple paper hat. 'You,' Foran told him, grinning, 'look a *right* fairy.'

Tarlo happily retorted, 'I see you've got the A-team out.'

One of the old women was leaving. Her friend pleaded with her,

'You'll be coming back, won't you?' But she didn't look as if she would be.

'Ah well,' Tarlo smiled, 'you'll have time to reflect, won't you? In the next eighteen years.'

'Oh, *don't*,' Foran laughed, a throaty chuckle. 'It'll be hot baths and opening veins time.'

I put to him the prospect of Portillo, Redwood and Howard scrapping for the Tory leadership, and he visibly shuddered at the thought. Tarlo said of that idea later, it'd be like *Invasion of the Body Snatchers*.

He and Foran joked about the fact that Blair wasn't coming after all. Foran said he'd given up on Labour in Calder Valley, Tarlo said Labour in Calder Valley didn't need him – and these two talking together was a heartening, very English scene. While their party leaders traded increasingly foul and hysterical insults, here you had the business type in his smart, heavy overcoat with the blue rosette, and beside him the Labour man in his baggy jeans and tatty trainers, dolled up in the daft livery of the final days, nattering away like the best of friends. But as Tarlo said later, 'You want to get along, don't you? There's no point being bitter. If they're losing, let's be magnanimous.'

As he went back to nail up some bunting round the front of the office, it was raining harder and harder. Labour people spilt in and out; their van rolled past, loudspeakers booming. Alex came in and said, 'Those three Tories, they're still out there.' She might have been talking of a disappearing species, the last remnants of an obscure sect.

Ann Martin said, 'It's a miserable time for them, isn't it?'

'Yeah,' grinned Alex. ''Cause they've got no ponchos, have they?'

By lunchtime it was chucking it down. Tarlo clambered into a battered old post office van full of stakes, posters and boxes of material for Tod; the dashboard was littered with computer debris, a jumbled slew of empty ink cartridges. We set off to the top of the valley, and Yorkshire in the rain somehow seemed more like Yorkshire again; dry-stone walls darkly climbed hillsides drenched in mist, and the green colours seemed all revived.

Tarlo was buzzing. He said, 'It's a bit audacious for a man nearly fifty to go round feeling like he's in the vivacious party. But I *do* feel young. When you look at the Tories, they're so old, so bereft – and we're going to win the country. It does put a spring in your stride.'

Still, he found the idea of his wife becoming an MP pretty daunting. People told him of the changes it'd make to their lives, but you could never really know. For a start, he could see himself spending more time in London than he'd have liked. He gestured about him and said simply, 'I love being here. I love the people. I love running in the countryside.'

Whether she won or lost, he was touchingly proud of her. He said, 'I don't know how she keeps track of everything. Often, what appears to me to be new, she's already dealing with it. And it does take courage to put yourself forward as a politician – because we're not well thought of, are we? It can be ever so disheartening when people have that perception that we all piss in the same pot, that we're all just lining our pockets, when you know it's not true, when you know public service is an honour and a privilege. But public service,' he sighed, 'those are two old-fashioned words these days.'

'Funnily enough,' said McCafferty, 'I'm probably the least fraught of anybody. I might be a bit frayed at the edges, but that's all.'

She'd been working off a stall in the middle of Hebden Bridge, meeting and greeting in the rain. Now it was early afternoon, she was driving down to Brighouse, and she was mulling carefully over the matters that could yet derail them – which, in essence, was the council. 'Frankly,' she said, 'some of the Labour group are not as bright as they think they are' – and only yesterday, one of them had passed information to a *Courier* journalist (with the appropriately hackish name of Nick Drainey) concerning proposals for a new power station on a business park in Elland. Given that only six months earlier they'd blown up the old one, cleared the site and were now hoping to get companies to move in and make jobs, this wasn't a welcome idea.

McCafferty went ballistic; she didn't know what material had been passed out when for over two years now, nothing connected to her had been released without her knowledge and approval. Nor could she believe that this councillor had expected a journalist to observe an embargo on the subject.

Drainey worked the phones; faxes and mobiles fizzed in all directions hunting statements, comments, confirmations. Then, in the office, one of the computer boys found the material that had been given out. McCafferty was in her car, halfway to Hebden Bridge; Martin called to say it was OK, it was their own prepared statement – literally seconds before Drainey was on the mobile wanting her position. So the *Courier* went with 'Storm Over "Secret" Power Plant Talks', and McCafferty was quoted in vigorous opposition, which was where she wanted to be. Thompson, on the other hand, said any new plant would look better than the old one – 'probably like a modern factory' – which, given that the power plant would only have nine jobs in it, rather missed the point.

The story was knocked off the lead anyway by the bizarre news that Mr Alice Mahon (who'd tried to stand against the real Alice Mahon) was a porn dealer. But while McCafferty didn't get caught in a bad light on the power plant, all the time you never knew where the next wobbly was coming from – and hanging over everything was a full meeting of Calderdale Council on (of all times) the Wednesday night before the general election. To put it mildly, this was bad planning; but the only way to defer it now was to call a council meeting anyway, and the press would have been all over any call for a deferral like rats in a grain store.

Labour parachuted their local government guru Howard Knight into Brighouse; he was now writing the Labour group's script for the council meeting, hoping to massage the event so when the *Courier* came out before noon on election day, the front page wouldn't be some loony left horror-show that'd blow Mahon and McCafferty's chances right there at the death.

Knight was a quiet, faintly nerdy bloke with a beard, a laptop, a heavy cigar habit and a spookily ruthless clarity of mind. He said, obviously, you couldn't mend Calderdale's dodgy image in one week – so the job was to manage the press releases, put out good news items and paint the best picture possible in the time that remained. He prepared a dozen 'friendly' standing order questions for Labour people to take to council; he prepared the answers too. Say the Tories attacked the level of Calderdale's debt. Your response: Compare debt to assets, then equate that to a graspable reality. It equates to a fourteen-grand mortage on a fifty-grand house — sounds pretty prudent, yes? And that way, you win the media game. A paper like the *Courier* had not, historically, been friendly to Labour — but Labour had been hostile to them too, because they didn't understand how newspapers worked. Labour didn't understand *stories*.

Knight gave an example from an authority that modernised a council estate. Two leaflets went out. Labour's leaflet said, In line with our policy of good housing for all, your council has upgraded 150 houses despite government cutbacks in our funding. By contrast, the Liberal Democrats' leaflet had a picture of Mrs Jones in 32 Acacia Grove saying, My neighbours and I are delighted with the improvements. The double glazing is especially welcome. We're very grateful to our Liberal Democrat councillor who's done this for us. And, said Knight, which one would you read?

Whether telling the right stories in this way could keep Calderdale from looking bad in the *Courier* on May 1st remained to be seen; there might be no problem in the first place. But at least Labour was ready for it — and there was, said Knight, another basic aspect to this. He said, 'People forget that journalists are lazy. If you give them 200 words of well-written information, they'll use it. If you give them 500 words of meaningless crap, they won't.'

If Knight's presence helped to manage the news, good — but while she never admitted it, if Ann Martin didn't feel this was also a pair of eyes from on high watching her run this key campaign, she'd not have been human. And as the pressure mounted, if she was ever annoyed with McCafferty — for being late to this or that, for fretting over the other — she never went at the candidate over it, because the candidate was the candidate and the agent protected her.

So other people got it in the neck. If David Tarlo stood there being indecisive about something — was he going to take this box of stuff to Tod now or not? — she'd tell him sternly just exactly what to do and she'd be smiling while she told him, but she'd not be smiling in her eyes. And Tarlo was by no means a man as relaxed inside as his demeanour would suggest; he was sensitive, easily stung, the woman he loved was on the line, he was trying to help, and he could be snappy right back. So it didn't matter any more if people liked each other; things remained mannerly, just, but the tension was bubbling ever fiercer underneath.

McCafferty worried that Martin felt blamed for every little thing – and she said it would be grossly unfair if she was, because people higher up should have cottoned on weeks ago to how tight it was in Calder Valley. But there's an old adage in politics that shows how this unfairness works. They say, if you win, it's because you've got a good candidate. And if you lose, it's because you've got a bad agent.

Overall, said McCafferty, 'The situation is very, very nerve-racking. We're all very, very tired. And in a way, if you start feeling confident that we'll win this nationally, that makes the idea of losing here even worse. Because for all that Donald's delightful, *he's a Tory.*'

A bunch of flowers lay wrapped on a desk; two lifelong members in Rastrick were celebrating their golden anniversary and, in the middle of everything, Ann Martin had still clocked that. 'All tribute to her,' said McCafferty quietly; then she sat to write the card, paused, looked up and smiled. 'What should I say? Friends and comrades? Are we allowed to say comrades any more?'

The party was organised by the son of these two; he was a probation officer who lived with his family on a pleasant suburban estate. The living room was packed with friends and relations; the woman for whom Martin had got the flowers was sadly stricken with Parkinson's, so McCafferty knelt by her, took her hand and told her her husband must be all right if they'd gone fifty years. And it was a big day for her, wasn't it?

'Oh,' said this brave old soul, rocking and twisting in the trap of her breaking body in her chair, 'it's a big day next Thursday as well.'

She'd been a councillor for many years; she said it felt good that the party had thought of her today, and there was a little moment where a few came close to tears. McCafferty said later, 'It's women like that who did the spadework that have made it possible for me to be a candidate now.'

I stood out of the way at the back; I talked to this woman's grand-daughter, and she said she was deeply disillusioned with the

Labour Party. She supposed, grudgingly, that she'd vote for them – but she'd been heavily tempted by the Liberals.

'You do that,' her father told her, 'your bags'll be on patio.'

Ann Martin had a glass of sangria, said that being out of the office was like escape from a cage, gave it forty minutes, then decreed that it was time to return. On the way back she smiled and said, 'Now the slavedriver's been out for an hour, they'll all have gone home.'

But they hadn't; still the printer chattered and whined, still the volunteers toiled, while from the corner came the chink of mugs being washed and another brew on the go. Barry Sheerman was over from Huddersfield, taking stakes out to a poster-blazoned Galaxy, one of those flash roomy minivans. He said that at traffic lights, people were winding down their windows to tell him, This time you'll do it. He said, 'It's spontaneous. Last time we told them it was time for a change; this time they believe it.'

There came more good news. One of the people McCafferty had helped over their objection to the building development at Greave House Fields in her ward – a group she now fondly spoke of as 'the Greave House Tories' – had called to ask for six stakes. Six! She said there'd never been a Labour stake in that road since it was built.

Sunday 27th April

SPICE GIRLS CRACK UP!
8–BABY MANDY IS PREGNANT AGAIN
ULRIKA GOES TOPLESS
MY LOVE FOR DI'S MOTHER
By Britain's Top Burglar

As ever, the tabloids paid close and intelligent interest to the vital issues of the day. Both tabloids and broadsheets, however, agreed that the election was over; it was going to be a landslide bigger than Clement Attlee's after the war. Edwina Currie said Labour's majority would be one hundred, minimum; she said John Major was incompetent. Maybe so – but in Brighouse, Howard Knight said he still didn't believe the polls; he figured a majority of fifty, maybe eighty. He had all the papers, and he was scouring them for bad news. But there wasn't any.

All this and, for the first time in 109 years, Barnsley won promotion to the top flight of English football. The Barnsley crew turned up in a minivan with a Tykes scarf flying from the driver's mirror; one of them came in with his arms raised and said, massively grinning, 'Barnsley up. Blair in. Double whammy.'

In the old bakery in Hebden Bridge, McCafferty sifted through fifty letters; what did she think about this, that, the other? Fifteen were from field sports people. She left Megan Swift to get replies out, then headed for Brighouse. Teams from Sheffield and Rotherham were delivering letters there already; the Barnsley crew waited to go out with the candidate. They'd been brilliant; they were solid, gritty and mightily sociable. One of them said simply, 'We're happy to do it. We'd love to see her win.'

Like Barnsley, my own Wakefield seat was Labour – not wholly solid, but with a notional majority after boundary changes of about 4,000 – and in my village, a friend told me this was the lowest-key election he'd ever seen. At my house we'd had one small drab Tory leaflet, one large bright Labour one, the mad Referendum video, a nervous Tory woman who was politely sent on her way – and that was it.

But the truth was, there wasn't one election but seven. There were the elections in Scotland, Wales and Northern Ireland; these are different countries (even if John Major hadn't noticed) and they had their own national business. The fourth election was the freak-show in Tatton. The fifth was the election in seats like mine, where nothing too much seemed to be happening at all. The sixth was the mad whirl of the marginals where everything was happening, and where local Labour parties had supplies of material that their solid seats could only dream of. Then the seventh was the media construct, a vapid slop of spin-doctored nonsense that had less to do with reality than any of the other six. It's democracy, Jim, but not as we know it . . .

Still, if the polls were to be believed that Sunday morning – holding steady on Labour leads in the high teens or early twenties – the result was a foregone conclusion. The broadsheets said:

STARTING THIS WEEK: A NEW ARENA

LABOUR LANDSLIDE

IT'S ALL OVER, ADMIT TOP TORIES

McCafferty arrived in Brighouse, and found she'd lost her car keys down a hole in her overcoat pocket. Candidate loses keys, I told her, marbles to follow. She grinned and said, 'I've lost those already.'

We hit a patch of Elland to Get Out The Vote; a zone of narrow terraced streets with bigger semis beyond. On a small estate of tidy council flats, a thin old lady with a daffodil in her raincoat lapel asked, 'Who are you canvassing for?'

McCafferty laughed, 'Myself.'

'Well, there's something good in all of them.'

'I should hope so. Otherwise they shouldn't be standing, should they?'

The old lady was fierce and frightened and teetering. She pointed across the way and said, 'How have we let it get so bad? That lady over there had her four tyres slashed last night.' McCafferty suspected she was a Liberal – but she admitted her memory wasn't so good these days, so she might wake up something different come Thursday.

Up the road, Tony the Geezer had a couple complaining that they'd not seen anyone. 'You've seen no one,' he told them, 'now here's the next MP. Can't say fairer than that, can I?'

The woman at the door was a qualified nurse who said she couldn't find work because she was fifty-one. She gestured about her and said, 'From here downwards, there's maybe five people in employment.' From there downwards, there were a lot more than five houses. I went across the road to inspect an intriguing institution called Leon's Biosthetic Cottage ('Your Skin Is For Life!') and when I got back, the nurse was saying she did a charity stall by Elland Town Hall on Saturday mornings. Every six or eight weeks, Thompson did his clinic there – but, she claimed angrily, 'He's *not* there. He's in the fish'n'chip shop across the street, he's left a note, I've *seen* him. Then he comes and chucks a fiver on my stall and I feel like saying, I don't *want* your patronage.'

McCafferty kept her smile to herself and said, 'I don't talk about my opponent. I only talk about my policies.'

I enjoyed the face-to-face stuff. You met your fair share of idiots and foul-mouths, and the woman we met one time in the Tesco car park had some gall on her. She said she was glad to meet the candidate, but she wasn't voting for anyone who didn't come to her door. Fine, said McCafferty through gritted teeth, and she took the address, thinking, Would you like me to lick your front path clean with my tongue while I'm at it? But in a heartening number of cases, the debates you got into were intelligent and worthwhile. By now, many people had thought hard about their concerns, they were glad of the chance to discuss them, and they were usually understanding as well when the candidate said she had to move on.

Grammar schools came up now and then – Halifax has two of them – and occasionally Europe did. When it did, it was usually debated with a sight more calm reason than was on offer from the Tory party. The Child Support Agency came up as much as anything, and was plainly an institution very widely reviled. People with children worried about education, drugs and unemployment; low wages were often raised, with a lot of interest in how a minimum wage would work, and what the windfall tax on the utilities was meant to do. Amongst all this, a lot of people also said that what they really hated was the slagging off, the endless shouting about sleaze and lies.

McCafferty told people it wasn't like that in Calder Valley; that Donald Thompson was a decent man, and that they didn't attack each other. After some of the muck that had been thrown at Alice Mahon in the past, she was a bit surprised about that – but she assumed if anyone on his side had wanted to go that way, plainly Thompson wouldn't have it.

It was quarter to one; down the warren of narrow streets, the rest of the crew were out of sight. McCafferty called the office on her mobile, the office called Tony on his to tell him the candidate was gone, and we headed off to the White Lion in Mytholmroyd.

An old stalwart in his eighties had left a message on McCafferty's ansaphone. 'When,' he barked, 'are you going to start your campaign in Mytholmroyd?' Crash, down went the phone – and the answer was, now.

In the pub's car park there was a Rover saloon, a Nova and a Corsa, a Citroen ZX and an ancient Commer van with a sticker saying, 'Jugglers Of The World Unite!' – this last driven by a bloke in a very fine Brazil World Cup 1950 T-shirt. Tarlo arrived in the Volvo, with a loudspeaker on the roof playing 'Things Can Only Get Better'. There followed an infectiously jubilant ten minutes of car embellishment; posters were taped to boots and doors, flags and balloons went on aerials and roof racks. Tarlo asked, 'Have we got the manifestos?'

One of the other drivers grinned and said, 'Don't talk about *policy!*'

The cavalcade set off, drawing wide eyes and smiles all down the road. Slowly we paraded up a side road until we came to the Nest Estate, a circular array of red brick semis and bungalows built on the flank of the hill just after the War. The canvassers tumbled from their cars in festive mood and, inside an hour, they'd knocked on every door in the place. Kids flocked on their bikes to get hats and balloons; McCafferty zoomed about among them to see anyone that wanted to meet her.

This was her ward; when one fit old lady asked her to get a new 'No Cycling' sign put up on one of the footpaths, she knew the spot she meant straight away. Then the old lady was telling us her story. She said it was a lovely little estate, she'd lived there forty-seven years; she was seventy-seven now, and she'd moved in with her husband when they left the RAF. She remembered her Dad helping them move in; the rent, rates and water were fourteen shillings and eightpence all in. Then she said she'd lost her husband a month ago, and she'd found their love letters in a box the other week. There was one she'd written all those years back that told him, 'I've got the key!' Well, she said, he'd gone very sudden – and her clear eyes watered just a little as she said, 'You've got to keep on living, haven't you?'

McCafferty touched her hand and said you did, you had to, but she knew it was hard – and she'd make sure and get her that 'No Cycling' sign, so she could walk down the path and not be afraid of the kids on their bikes. And you go through your life, you think everything's fine – but an election throws you into everybody's lives. Behind one door here and another one there you find pain and problems, strife and loss. The worst to hear of was the children who'd died – and the battle buses don't come on all this, not unless it's been pre-prepared by the media management team flying point. But the candidates do. So while there are no doubt some heartless and calculating ratbags among them, don't anyone ever tell me again that MPs don't know how we live – because for sure, they know a lot more about it than I do.

Tarlo stood in a doorway earnestly trying to argue the case with a spotty young man who said he'd be voting for the Referendum Party. How, Tarlo cried, could you trust James Goldsmith more than Tony Blair? But this lad only said, 'I don't want to live in a federal Europe.' It was dismally clear that he had no idea what a federal Europe might be: that it was just some vague and monstrous ogre out there, to be fended off by voting for a billionaire who didn't go in much for blinking. I watched for a while, wondering about this boy. You live tucked away in this tatty patch of brick semis on the edge of a nowhere little town in a valley no one's heard of, and your biggest worry is this phantasmic spectre of Helmut Kohl coming to tell you you've got to eat straight bananas? Is everything else in your life OK then?

Tarlo was wasting his time – but this was a man who'd try to reason with a brick wall if it had Tory graffiti on it. He simply could not accept that sometimes there wasn't a way through, that some people were no more rational than a leaf on a stream – so you had to ease him gently away, because if you didn't do it gently you could hurt his feelings. In these last days he'd be lively, he had his quick dry wit, then something would vex him – and you'd see that inside he was taut as a rubber band pulling near to its limit.

At least sometimes you got a warning. After we'd quit the acned Europhobe, we were walking up the street and another member of the caravan told us, 'Don't go to number twenty. All you'll get is a mouthful.' I asked, A mouthful of what? He said, 'Oh, nothing political. Just, you're all a bunch of shite.' And Tarlo would have tried to reason with that, too.

★

We moved on to the Banksfield Estate on the other side of the valley, where the state of the original housing was a disgrace. Built with wooden frames in the 1950s, they'd been condemned as fire risks, and a good deal of the increase in McCafferty's vote when she was re-elected to council had come from her involvement in the current programme of refurbishment. 'Refurbishment' was something of a misnomer; in reality, they were building new houses by putting up brick skins round the existing structures, then tearing down everything inside except the staircase and starting again. This tortuous process – the daft business of having to leave the old staircase inside the new house – was a sharp ruse by which the council had got round the government's ban on them building new homes. But some way had had to be found, because these people were living in the housing equivalent of a box of matches.

Tiered lanes stepped up the hillside; it was hot work trooping up and down them. Everywhere people said they'd be voting Labour, don't you worry – and then we came on a man whose life had been ruined by the Conservatives. He was a lorry driver, a strong barrel-gutted bloke with fantastical sideburns, and a pretty little daughter holding his hand. Buy your own house, the Tories told this guy – so he did. The trouble was, if you'd bought your place before it was condemned you were OK, you were part of the rebuilding programme – whereas if you'd bought it after they'd been condemned, then in law the council couldn't help you.

The result was that rickety originals still stood here and there amid the new brick skins, as if a dentist had passed over a few rotted teeth in an otherwise well-restored mouth. And you may ask, why would a man buy a condemned house? He'd do it because they were sold at a knockdown price, he'd been told the mortgage would be cheaper than the rent, and he'd swallowed it. It might not be too bright, but not all of us can be – and now he was a home-owner in a home that wasn't worth anything, a fire risk with leaking windows. He said simply, 'I was caught in the Tory trap' – which seemed a modest phrase for a circumstance that would surely drive you to despair.

The only thing McCafferty could tell him was to apply for a council grant to get at least some of it seen to, but she had to be honest with him. Funds were so low, and the waiting list so long, that it would most likely be two years before anybody even came to look at it, and five years before something got done. And that's where Tory housing policy had left him.

It didn't stop there. Further down the estate there were people living in bungalows that had been built just after the War, and which had only been meant to last for fifteen years. A game old boy with a smoker's croak, a walking-stick since he'd had a stroke and painfully arthritic hands said his place still had the original bath, the original sink – and he'd had to pay out £56 to get new taps because the old ones were going through washers like nobody's business, and with his hands bad he'd had trouble with them. McCafferty sighed, looking genuinely pained and angry; she said, 'That's out-rageous. I could have got you some taps.' But again she had to tell him that, with the council's capital receipts locked in the bank by the government, these bungalows could not yet be included in the rebuilding programme.

Two doors along, a woman asked what she had to do so her disabled daughter could vote – while in the sitting room through the kitchen another daughter, a tall, petulant young woman, announced with a deliberately hostile sneer, 'Don't look at me. I'm Con-*serv*-ative.'

Her mother snapped, 'Oh shurrup. You dunno *what* you are.'

'I *am* a Conservative. I live in a big house, me.'

McCafferty had to wrestle a shade here to contain her sharp dis-dain. She snorted, 'So do I.' And I could hear her thinking, Can you not look about you?

The cavalcade drove up to the tops through the village of Midgley, and back down through Luddenden to the Kershaw estate. A sticky heat lay heavy on the hills; the moors along the skyline were fuggy-edged in the haze. We parked in front of the Parish Pop-In shop and Mr Singh's little supermarket, music blaring; one of the lads idling on the low wall along the front of the store wan-dered off with his hands over his mouth to mimic the tinny rasp of the microphone. 'Vote Labour,' he crackled, 'Vote Labour'. Plainly the phrase had no more meaning to him than a slogan in an ad.

The troops gasped off round the houses in the heat; McCafferty went to see a woman she knew, and called out to Tarlo that her friend would take a stake. Tarlo sat in the passenger seat of the Volvo, dog-weary, and muttered, 'People think I'm *made* of stakes.'

He walked over towards the house and I said, I thought you were the vivacious party?

He said, 'I am,' and he gave a small hint of a dry grin. 'It's just, do this, do that . . .'

He started putting the stake up in the garden and the woman in the house told him, 'Better not. Leave my husband to do it. He'll not vote for you if you've done one of his plants in.'

Tarlo looked quietly to the heavens, contained himself, laid the stake on the lawn and went back to the car. McCafferty said, 'I know how he feels. But we'll go into reverse by Thursday. All of a sudden, by then, we'll be wanting another week.'

Another woman came up to her, looking nervously apologetic. She said, 'You're going to be very cross with me, but I've an eighteen year old and he's not on the register. Is it too late?'

McCafferty said nothing. She leant forward and rested her head on this woman's shoulder. The woman said, 'Oh sugar lumps.'

W hen we drove about with the music and the banners, kids would laugh and dance on the street as we passed; adults walking or driving by would smile, wave or give the thumbs-up. But inside the cars, people were fraying. Children needed feeding, the letters and leaflets were mostly done – it was enough. Tarlo stood by the open boot of the Volvo, tizzed up with indecision – should he do the boards in Ryburn? Should he get the letters up to Tod? There was the Dodd Naze estate . . .

McCafferty said gently, 'David. You're losing it.'

'I've lost it already.'

'Well, *get it back*.'

She came back to Brighouse in my car while he headed for the top of the valley, talking all the while through the speakers. 'Vote Labour,' he was saying, 'for a brighter better Britain' – but he'd forgotten something in their car that needed to go in mine. As we approached the junction to the main road I could see him flashing us in my mirror, and I assumed he was just saying goodbye, but then the voice coming out of the speakers said something different. 'Vote Labour,' he said, 'I need to talk to you.'

We pulled up, and he handed over a box of letters that had been one box too many for the workers in Luddendenfoot to deliver. We took them back to the main office, McCafferty wondering how they were going to be got out, knowing Martin would be bothered about spending money on stamps – and when we got back Alex Powell quietly nodded, took them from her and said she'd handle it. McCafferty sighed, 'We'd have been right up the swannee without Alex.'

Meanwhile, events were becoming more bizarre with each fatigue-raddled day. While the cavalcade did Mytholmroyd, Tony the Geezer had the Barnsley crew out leafleting the Field Lane estate in Brighouse, preparing it for a second visit from the Prezza Express – and a mad bloke went and bit him. Now you're not a true leafleter until you've been bitten by a dog, but getting bitten by a man – that was something else.

'We get there,' said Tony, 'and this bloke's bashing his girl's head against the wall. He puts her down, he's got his foot pulled back to kick her head in – so I put him on the ground. He's tiny, early twenties, only about nine stone – but he's out of his shaven head, staring eyes, mental. It took two of us to hold him down. Then we had to let him up 'cause his mates were gathering, one of them had a bottle, and he's running about just hitting anyone that's there. He's stripped to the waist, he really *wants* to fight – so we get him held again, and he sinks his teeth into the inside of my arm like it's a joint of meat. Well, it's mobile telephones everywhere now. The police come, three cars – they took that long, I think they came from Alice Springs. Anyway, he's in the cop shop in a straitjacket. But he's only just out from another GBH, he's perambulating round that estate fucking people's lives up – so I'm pursuing it. 'Cause never mind liberal solutions, he needs putting away, this one. All that,' Tony shook his head, 'and the bloke that took me to hospital got a puncture. Lively days, eh?'

It gets weirder yet. Back on the Banksfield estate in Mytholmroyd, one of the canvassers had called us over to tell us, 'There's a bloke up there says Sir Donald's jumped off a bridge.'

We're thinking, Get on. Donald wouldn't jump off the bottom step of a flight of stairs – but we go to see this bloke, and he's adamant. It was a Tory, he says, definite. Went off that narrow bridge in the middle of Mytholmroyd. His mate's in the fire brigade, he told him they had to fish this big bugger out of the river there and get him in the ambulance. Now what the hell was this?

*M*onday 28th April

Of course it was nonsense; of course Donald Thompson didn't jump off any bridge. His agent did – and now he was in the Halifax Royal Infirmary with a broken leg.

There's a narrow old bridge over the Calder in the middle of Mytholmroyd; looking at it from the main road, a footpath runs immediately beside it to the right. To the left, there's another footpath – but this one isn't connected to the main bridge; instead, there's a fair gap between the two.

Late Saturday afternoon, James Davidson packed up work and went for a beer with a friend. (And if that doesn't speak volumes about the Conservative campaign, when 10 o'clock at night was an early finish for Ann Martin, what does?) Now James is a big young lad, and he likes his beer – as he put it himself, 'The first one doesn't seem to touch the sides' – so a little bit later he's gambolling back from the pub over the footpath on the right, the one that's connected to the road-bridge, and he decides he'll jump over to the other side. He's assuming, of course, that the other footbridge is connected to the main bridge like the one he's started out from. So he hops over the low stone wall from the first footbridge to the main bridge, crosses the road, jumps over the far wall . . . and I prefer not to imagine his surprise as he discovers in short order that where he thought there'd be a second footbridge, there isn't. Down he goes, some twenty feet into the shallow river.

A further detail provided by other Conservatives was that a game of poohsticks was in progress at the time; James himself didn't volunteer that information. But either way, he was a lucky boy; he could have broken his neck or his back, even killed himself outright. Instead he had a double fracture of the left leg above the knee, and that was quite nasty enough. So his mother rang Sir Donald and told him he'd had an accident. Donald's first thought was an aghast imagining of his agent mangled on a motorway somewhere, but then she told him what had happened. Donald asked if he was allowed to laugh.

It was terrible, I know – but how could you not laugh? Were

things not bad enough for the Tories, that their agent had to jump off a bridge as well?

On Monday morning in Brighouse, McCafferty folded and stuffed seventy letters to farmers. A few days back, she'd had a successful meeting with the local branch of the NFU; Labour sent in one of the agriculture front-bench team to back her up when it got technical, and one of the NFU people said subsequently that the session was notably more worthwhile than the meeting they'd had with Donald Thompson. The NFU locally hadn't met any Labour person for ages but now, while the Tory agent was jumping off a bridge, Labour was marching unfazed into the heart of Tory territory.

Outside the office, a hired bus waited on double yellow lines across the road; today's hoopla involved twenty-two MPs descending en masse to Get Out The Vote. At one point in the planning, it had been mooted that this event might involve as many as sixty MPs, even a hundred – a quite giddying prospect. I imagined the good folk of the valley cowering in their attics from such a tsunami of electoral persuasion. Even twenty-two was a fair old bunch – and around the office people racked their brains for the appropriate collective noun. A caucus? A bevy? Derek Fatchett from Leeds, a slim, mildly-spoken and rather acute individual, later smiled ironically and said, 'I know it's not a noun – but how about a wasteful?'

The room began to fill; most of the MPs had brought people with them, friends, spouses, party workers from their seats. The atmosphere was charged with expectation, everyone feeding each other good news, the bright feel on the ground in their constituencies. One local journalist cooed with glee at the acuity of Labour producing an MP for each Tory tax rise; he was informed that this was of course merely coincidence, that this was just the number that had happened to make it, but he went ahead and used it in his story anyway. Lazy, like Howard Knight said – but it did make Labour look sharp.

Another journalist wafted a list of the twenty-two tax rises under McCafferty's nose, then – crafty beggar – turned it face down and asked her what they were. It was common knowledge that most candidates didn't know all twenty-two off by heart; McCafferty's

mind raced out of gear for a second, then she smiled and said that
actually there were now more than twenty-two. There'd been the
landfill tax, she told him, and started explaining away. His eyes
brightened; he didn't know about that one and off he set to scribbling, happy to be given a new line.

The feeling now was plain, that Labour were unbeatable. They
didn't know how much they'd win by, but they knew they'd win.
At the beginning of the campaign they'd been riddled with a terrible anxiety – that they had this mighty lead and all they could do in
six weeks was cling to it, gnawed with a dreadful anticipation of the
moment it started sliding. But it never did slide; they had the
monkey of 1992 perched on their shoulders, but the monkey never
chattered.

Early on, David Dimbleby skewered a sweating Blair on the
BBC; in 1983 he'd stood for parliament on all those old Labour
policies, and why should anyone trust him if he'd changed his mind
so much since then? This line of questioning recurred again and
again, most recently on that morning's *Today* programme – and
everyone was lifted by the increasing confidence with which Blair
handled it as the campaign progressed. On Radio 4 that morning,
he'd just brushed it aside. One MP said, 'The temptation must be
unbearable. They ask him, Come on, did you *really* believe in unilateral disarmament in 1983? And it must be so difficult not to look
straight back and say, You must be fucking joking.'

Two fiercely capable women from regional office sped about
the room discussing details of the day's itinerary; Ann Martin distributed campaign packs stuffed with posters and leaflets and pledge
cards. The tall, sardonic figure of Donald Dewar called the room to
order. He raised a laugh by telling them he was a most unlikely candidate for giving anyone a pep talk, then he gave them a pep talk.
'You're going to be catapulted out there to meet the public, so let's
dispel any apathy, let's dispel any eccentric notions that they can
vote for fringe candidates; let's get them voting for us. The Calder
Valley's like the Somme; we've fought over it again and again, and
we've lost. But not this time. There is a real feeling of bounce and
optimism in the marginals, so let's go out and add to it. I know it's
been a long, long trip – but let's keep going, and let's give Chris a
real boost here.'

Earlier he'd told me that he was a feel politician, and the feeling was good; that it was difficult for the Tories to get out of jail now. 'Sometimes I actually have to moderate optimism; I'll be with a candidate that needs a twelve per cent swing, and he thinks he's got it – well, maybe he has. But there's the old, old problem of people's ancient myths and remembered fears, and there's also the feeling that the third party's a safe option. But,' he smiled, 'even we can't throw it away now.'

He said of course there'd be unexpected triumphs in individual seats, and there'd be bitter disappointments as well, that was always the way – and I could only stand there praying that one of the disappointments wouldn't land on me here.

Getting the MPs on the bus was like airline boarding; it involved much bunching together for photographs, and much scuttling back and forth for posters and slogan boards. As people ran to and fro the boards flapped and buckled in a gusting wind; specks of rain began falling from the thickening clouds that hurried across a darkening sky.

I stood over the road watching the bustle with a delightful traffic warden, a woman in her thirties with a great beam of a smile. She said she'd not booked the bus for being there all that while, of course not; they had their business to be about, and good luck to them. 'But the thing is, I don't recognise any of them. Who's who, eh? There's one I ought to know . . .'

Donald Dewar?

'That's it. But I don't know him. Still, I'll not tell. Wouldn't want to disappoint them.'

Then an overweight and seriously obnoxious man – naff lemon polo shirt, baggy pink shorts, pricy trainers, your genuine country club clot – came and got in her face. He was full of bluster and arrogance, full of a ghastly itch, a horrid, powerless, wriggly resentment that Labour were all over the centre of Brighouse like this. That bus had been there all this time, he told her, when was she going to book it?

Mildly she told him, 'They're just going off now.'

He barked, 'Now means *now*.'

The smile fell away from her face. She looked up at him with her big lovely eyes all stern and unanswerable and she told him, 'Now means when they're ready. I've given them my permission, and it's in my power to do that.'

The fat git stared at her, humourless and seething, and for a moment I thought he was going to get really unpleasant – then he walked away, visibly stunned that the world wasn't doing his bidding, that it was changing right in front of his eyes.

The traffic warden sighed and put her smile back on. She said, 'Some people, eh? They think 'cause I've got this uniform on I'll just stand here and tek it. And I *won't*.'

The bus went to blitz an estate in Sowerby Bridge; McCafferty went with Dewar on to the streets of Brighouse. The first person they met said, 'I'm not changing. I'm happy with what I've got.' What she'd got was a Barbour and too much lipstick.

'So you're a true blue,' said Dewar, 'and you're quite entitled to it. But I think you're going to lose.'

She shrugged and said, 'Everybody's got to lose sometime.' She didn't seem unduly bothered.

Down the road the candidate said, 'I'm Chris McCafferty . . .'

'And I,' said a rather wide-eyed and hectically smiling woman, 'am Mrs Batty of Mrs Batty's Nursing Homes. Oh,' she then cried, catching sight of Dewar, 'I think you're *wonderful*. And so does my mother!'

Dewar responded with genuine charm and a most gigantic smile. The conversation was a tad hard to follow, Mrs Batty being radiantly effusive as she was, but somewhere he said that English politics was tolerant . . .

'Quite right,' she forcefully averred. 'No nasty jackboots here.'

Dewar wound up by saying, 'Give my regards to your mother. I've never met her, but I'm sure she's a splendid woman.'

We trooped down the road – Dewar, Barry Sheerman, McCafferty, one of Dewar's aides, Val Watts, and the *Yorkshire Post*. Outside a chemist's shop a ferocious old man with a body the shape of a tea chest, wearing a trilby, a tweed jacket with a para's badge and carrying a walking-stick, turned out to be entirely mad. 'I fought for this country,' he shouted at Dewar, 'did you? Knickers. You buggers are all the bloody same.'

Dewar accelerated away, the old guy racketing after him. When he'd escaped Dewar said, 'You get one of those every day. But there's a bit of opposition here, isn't there? It's a tough nut to crack.' Then, referring to this book, he asked, 'What if Labour win and we lose the Calder Valley?'

I said we only made the semi-final in 1990, and I did all right with that – but inside, by now, I was jangled all over. The only difference between me and the candidate was that I wasn't asking people to vote for me. Otherwise, every night she went home and worked the phone, and every night I went home and worked the word processor. It had been seven days a week for six weeks now – and what if we were doing all this for nothing?

Dewar had to go to Batley and Spen. One of his people asked if he wanted any lunch and he said, 'No. No lunch. Lunch is of no importance.' So he had a quick brew and zoomed off; before he left he told McCafferty, 'I'll see you on the 7th. But you'll get your first letter before that. They're ready to go out on Friday.'

When he was gone McCafferty grinned and said, 'Did you hear that? The first letter already?'

'That,' said one of the volunteers, 'is in case you have a thought out of line.'

It was raining heavily. We found the bus in Sowerby Bridge; they were finishing up, so we went ahead to the Trades Club in Hebden. Eileen Jones was there, Kinnock's biographer, collecting a bag of leaflets to distribute to parents at school turning-out time. She said since she'd been on the market the other day, and seen all the cheer and bonhomie, she'd felt guiltier and guiltier. She'd been reading everything, watching everything, she thought Blair had had a brilliant weekend, so now she'd come round to join in. When one of the volunteers stuffed a letter in her bag for a Liberal squeeze, she laughed and said, 'That's me!'

Tarlo had got me a present; it was a copy of Jones's Kinnock book, and the price he'd agreed to pay her was a penny for every seat in Labour's majority. So, he smiled, he'd be out sixty-four pence. I told him it looked as if he'd be paying more than that – but still none of us knew what was looming.

Outside in the rain there was now the bus, three carloads and a Galaxy. After lunch we set off, the cavalcade rapidly fell apart in the usual dreadful traffic on the A646, and none of us knew where we were going. Tarlo was ahead of me in the Volvo; from my passenger seat, McCafferty rang him on her mobile. This had a small but delicious absurdity about it, the husband and wife yammering away from one car to the other, lost in the rain in West Yorkshire. Tarlo gave her Howard Knight's number – he was on the bus with the wasteful, he'd know where we were meant to be going – so she called Knight and got his answering service. She called Tarlo back, said what had happened and burst out laughing. 'He says,' she told me, 'I thought he was supposed to be a director of communications?'

We knew the general goal was Hipperholme and Lightcliffe; we got there, drove round and round, and ended up parked outside Sir Donald's house. Tarlo came over, wrinkled his brow and said, 'Why doesn't he have a poster up?' Looking puckish, he went back towards the Volvo, meaning to turn on the D-ream tape and give the Thompson manse a blasting. 'No,' McCafferty screamed. 'No! David, NO!' She sighed, 'Let's have some etiquette, shall we?'

Tarlo obeyed; we drove off round a big estate, and he waited until we were away from Thompson's house before he turned the tape on. Meanwhile I was thinking, How can you lose twenty-two MPs? Mind you, it was chucking it down now; if I was out knocking doors in this, the first friendly voter I found, I'd be in for a brew with them in no time.

Eventually we found some MPs sheltering at a bus stop; one of them told McCafferty it looked good. Some Tories were sticking, but others that were down as Tories on the sheets from the phone work were coming over. 'Keep going,' he told her, 'only three more bloody days.'

We went back to my car, but on the way she saw a man in his drive. She went to shake his hand, then told me she could feel OK about getting back in the car now she'd met a voter. As she got in the passenger seat and slumped backwards with her eyes shut, I thought for a second she was going to pass out. I let her be for a minute; she pulled herself together, then asked what day it was. When I told her Monday she said, 'I wonder when I should start freaking out about Thursday?'

★

Back in the office, we got the news that the Tories had cancelled their press conference that morning. One of the union men told me, 'It'd take a major disaster to shift things now.'

He was preparing the Dixon boards for polling day. From the computer, you print off every voter who's told you they're definite for Labour on thin strips, ordered street by street. Each strip's taped to the board, side by side; each board covers a polling district, or part of one. Between now and Wednesday night, over a hundred of these would be made up in committee rooms all round the valley; come the day, as the number-takers bring in their lists of who's voted from the polling stations, you can mark off your people who've voted and chase up the ones who haven't. That way, you turn out every promise. In theory . . .

At another desk, Howard Knight was working up a story. One of the MPs had turned up a man sixty-five years old who'd not voted in forty years – and now he was coming out for Labour. Knight liked that a lot; his fingers flickered across his laptop.

At the centre of things, Ann Martin watched the rain. Prezza was due back tomorrow, but they'd had to change the location for the visit; he'd been set to go to Field Lane but, after Tony the Geezer got bitten there, they were going to take him somewhere else. They didn't want the risk of the mad biter's mates deciding to give the Labour Party a bricking – but this meant the new destination had to be canvassed, to find friendly households that'd want to meet Prescott, and still it was raining. Two young men up from London, union boys from the CPSA, were game to do it; but the trouble was, they said, the rain turns all your material into *papier maché*.

Martin lit a cigarette. 'So this will happen,' she said, looking at her watch, 'ah . . . at some time in the near future.'

A volunteer took her overflowing ashtray to empty it for her; a key campaign task, since she was now living almost entirely on Raffles cigarettes and mega-size Mars bars. She talked for a while with McCafferty about the count, about who their allotted fifteen spectators would be, about how tight a limit that was and all the people who'd be disappointed – and she told the candidate firmly that she didn't want her turning up there any time before midnight. McCafferty embraced her. She said, 'You can protect me from everything else. But you can't protect me from the count.'

I went to see James Davidson in the Royal Infirmary. McCafferty told me to pass on her sympathy (non-politically) and to say that if the press got hold of it, it wouldn't be from her.

'Put in your book,' said James, 'that I'm a bloody idiot, and I've no excuses.'

They'd opened him up that morning to pin the bone together; they'd given him an epidural but he'd asked for a general as he didn't want to hear them wrenching about at it. He'd gone out like a light, and that had been nice. He liked the morphine too, but it wasn't strong enough; he was in a lot of pain. He had some happy gas to breathe at, and a saline drip in his right arm. A bar hung over the bed for him to tug at, to try and shift himself with his left arm if he could; his left leg lay bandaged on two pillows, yellowed from the operation. 'It's raw,' he breathed, 'it's that bloody raw.' Still, he said bravely, 'At least I'm seeing how good the NHS is in Calderdale.'

He'd said a few weeks back that he'd have a nice rest after the election; he tried for a grim flicker of a smile, and said he surely would now. But he'd booked a holiday in New York; that was down the pan. And the party . . . he supposed he'd go on sick pay, unless they sacked him. I looked at him lying there and I thought, the Tory Party's not an outfit renowned for its sympathy. You had to figure, sadly, that he'd jumped off more than a bridge; unless he was fiercely determined and very fortunate with it, he'd jumped off a career in politics as well.

An auxiliary came to give him a drink of water. A game lad, if somewhat behind in the gender wars, he told her, 'What I need's a good rub-down from a raunchy woman.'

She was a tiny, twinkle-eyed brown raisin of a woman; she told him smiling that she'd be no good to him, she was just a little stick of a thing. Well, he asked her, 'How much do you charge then?'

'You couldn't afford me, love.'

She moved his leg for him; it was plainly agony. Then, when she left, he asked how it was going out there. I didn't say anything, I just looked at him. After a while he said quietly, 'It's not good, is it?'

★

*T*uesday *29th April*
I rang Thompson's office, and they didn't know where he was.
Dear God, the state of them. McCafferty, meanwhile – with her
agent's permission – was having her hair done.

In Brighouse, the phones were humming. John Prescott was
due on Whinney Hill at one-thirty. Ann Martin said, 'We're crowd
building.' Another call came in, a man seventy-three years old
who'd voted Tory since 1945 and now he wanted to vote Labour,
but he was worried about his private health care. And while you're
there, he's got the Burma Star, blah blah blah . . . Martin cradled the
phone on her shoulder, let him ramble on and had another go at
her Mars bar. She kind of nibbled them round the edges, like a
chipmunk.

A parcel firm delivered a box of purple Labour lollipops; that
Peter Mandelson, he'd stop at nothing. An old boy wandered round
with a hoover; New Labour, said Martin, got to be tidy. Other volunteers worked on Dixon boards, while a computer whiz sorted
out a programme for extrapolating from the tally sheets during the
count and transferred it to a laptop. The tally sheets gave you the
total votes from each box; with this programme, as the counters
worked through the eighty-six boxes, you'd start getting a picture –
a virtual result – well before it was finally announced. The whiz ran
a model to check the programme worked; the model gave
McCafferty a majority of 13,000. He smiled and said, 'OK, I'm
biased.'

The candidate arrived with Megan Swift, and another volunteer
was sent to buy a needle and thread; one of her buttons had fallen
off. Megan asked if I'd seen the angel-in-a-taxi broadcast last night;
she laughed and said, 'I'm just relieved the angel didn't turn into
Tony Blair.'

McCafferty sat at a desk with her mail. She'd sent a letter to all
the market traders in Hebden Bridge about what might be done to
improve the flow of traffic (and hence their business) on the A646.
One of these had been sent back with something added to her
slogan along the bottom, 'Caring For Calder Valley'. The addition
said, 'Joke. Caring For Yourselves.' On the back, handwritten in
scrawly capitals, was the following reply, which I reproduce
exactly:

What you have written sounds nice + well rehersed, but I don't think this is a major issue in Hebden Bridge, how about:

1. Scraping Parking Meters (Labour Council)
2. Policing The Streets, more visable police on foot not in cars
3. Security cameras on streets

After the couple of year as we have seen a Labour Council in Halifax, God help us if you ever get to govern this country I have never known a party to cheat + lie as much yes the goverment are not perfect but they will get my vote come Thursday. God willing we will have a Tory victory come Thursday.

And I'd take this person more seriously:

1. If they'd had the bottle to give their name and address, and
2. If they could spell.

Jokes about 'scraping' undesirable items were *de rigeur* from here on.

On our way to the car, the Tesco manageress came out and told McCafferty, 'I'm that stressed about this election.' I thought, try standing in it. Or, worse, try doing what John Prescott had done. The big Geordie advance guard said they passed the 10,000-mile mark in Chorley that morning ('about ten past ten, something like that'). They'd done Colne Valley, they were here, then Halifax, and they'd spend the night in Leeds. I asked what they'd done yesterday; he said, 'Was it Monday yesterday?'

On Monday they'd done Stafford, The Wrekin, Rhyl, Bangor, Chester, Wirral South, Blackpool, and got to their hotel at 10.30. He said, 'I'm that tired, I ache.'

We were with a crowd of about fifty, maybe more, in a small car park amid a spread of plain brick bungalows. Tony the Geezer rattled round planting posters to brighten the place up. A gusty wind plucked a bundle of balloons from someone's hand, and sent it rolling and tumbling over the rooftops into the bright sunny sky.

I talked to McCafferty's brother-in-law from her first marriage; he'd flown in with his wife to see how she went. Eileen worked for the UN's Drug Control Programme in Vienna; Roy ran computers for the UN in the Gaza Strip. His next-door neighbour was Yasser Arafat, so the security was good; not much chance of getting burgled. On the other hand, when things got iffy, you had Israeli jets breaking the sound barrier five feet outside your bedroom window; that could be unsettling. Anyway, he said, he was here now; they'd do some doorsteps this afternoon. 'Hello. I've just popped over from the Gaza Strip to support your local Labour candidate . . .'

We heard music growing louder in the distance, and a cheerleader's voice calling out loud and crackly, 'It's the Prescott Express! It's the Prescott Express on its 10,000-mile tour! Welcome to the people of the Calder Valley!' The bus pulled in and out popped a minder and a roadie. The roadie had a speaker and a mike, and he set them up in front of the bus. One old boy behind me in a row of four cloth caps said, 'Let's give him a reet cheer when he comes out, eh?' Out he came, and they did.

Prescott took the mike and launched straight into speaking – a burly, dark-suited music-hall turn with bags under the eyes and a voice so hoarse it must have been painful. But it didn't stop him. His free arm wheeling as he spoke, he said, 'This is the cul-de-sac the Tories are stuck up, eh? There's no way out for 'em. He's on the run, isn't he? Into that helicopter, it's the flight of the bumble bee. But look, this is the ninety-fourth seat I've been in. And we don't hope for a Labour government, we *vote* for a Labour government.

'Oh, but have you seen all those police he's surrounded with? Set 'em off him, we could halve the crime rate. Look into my eyes, he says. Gor blimey, look into my eyes. The eyes of a man in charge of the most incompetent, sleazy government ever. I mean, he's got three or four parties, hasn't he? And Paul Daniels is going if Labour win? Jim Davidson, he's going. Cilla Black, that Lloyd Webber – well I'll tell you what. Friday, I'll be down at the airport waving 'em off.

'Sleaze. £25,000 in the back pocket. He's gone, hasn't he? And I hope that other bugger in Tatton goes too. 'Cause while they're taking that money they're deregulating wages, people are on starvation wages – that's the *stench* of hypocrisy. Well, I'll tell you, we'll bring back brown envelopes all right. We'll bring back decent wage packets for ordinary people.

'We know we'll inherit a mess. But look at the record. Fifty years ago we created a welfare state, we dealt with poverty and squalor and ignorance – and we did something else. The greatest gift we ever gave to the people of this country: the National Health Service. Now, after eighteen years, what have we got? Tuberculosis and rickets are back. A health service where if you've got private insurance you go to the front, and if you haven't you wait. You wait, wait, wait. A two-tier system – 'cause it was always the Tory way. But look . . .'

He held up a pledge card and started in on what Labour would do – and all the time he'd been speaking, the four old boys in cloth caps had been muttering along, Yer reet, yer reet. Now I looked back at them and one of them was crying. His face was red, his head was shaking, he had his glasses off and his hankie to his eyes, and even as he smiled and listened and said Yer reet, the tears were streaming down his face.

I felt like joining him. I was now incredibly tired, and we were getting so close.

If McCafferty lost, her husband had strict instructions to get her out of the country inside twenty-four hours.

In the afternoon she went leafleting in Hipperholme with Roy and Eileen, Megan Swift, another woman and a councillor from Dewsbury. Or from somewhere, I don't know. They were too many to count now; they were Labour, and that was all I knew.

She told them not to knock, just put in the leaflets; she said people had had enough now, it was getting too much. An old woman with a sour face confirmed it when she came to her door and said, 'I had someone yesterday.'

'You've had a lot, have you?'

'Too many.' Then she slammed the door shut.

As we walked down the pavements in hot, sticky sunshine, McCafferty tripped on a step and nearly fell. Megan said softly, 'I think she's had enough.' When the candidate came away from the house her friend told her, 'Early night, love. And make sure you sit upstairs, away from that phone.'

We came on houses divided into flats, one up, one down, with outside steps to the top door. I watched her stop at the bottom, take a deep breath and start climbing. I thought, this is getting ridiculous and terrible, and I told her to stop, really, stop. You give me those, I'll do the rest, and to hell with just watching and writing, or striving to maintain any last vestige of impartiality.

I took the leaflets and a weird thing happened. I'd been feeling that the exercise was pointless, that these people were just doing something now for the sake of doing it, that they were walking about in a sun-cooked daze putting leaflets through doors for the simple reason that they had some left, when everybody in the place was sick to the back teeth with bloody leaflets, and when really it was over now – when it was come to the point where whatever happened, happened.

But once you've got those leaflets in your hand, it feels different. You become suddenly obsessed. You think, I must get shot of every one; any one of these might mean another vote, and it's that damn tight that just a couple more votes might make the difference. Then you turn a corner and the road in front of you looks so long, it must run half-way to bloody Cornwall – and you think, all right, I'll have you. You go at it in the broiling sun, up and down the paths, one door to the next, closing every gate carefully so you don't have someone vote against you because you didn't close their gate, and your elastic band round the leaflets breaks and you think, OK, no problem, I've big hands, keep going, keep going.

Two women were minding their kids in their front yards; one took her leaflet and said, 'I'll be shocked if you don't win this time.'

I thought, You'll be shocked. I'll be torn to bits, me.

In the car on the way back Megan told McCafferty, 'I'm the most pessimistic person there is. But I think you've won here now.' She paused for a moment and then she added, 'If Labour can't win Calder Valley now, we'll never win Calder Valley. We might as well not put up a candidate.'

In the office, Ann Martin filled and signed forms about spectators and counting agents, then faxed them to the registration officer. People came and went, taking Dixon boards and boxes of number takers' sheets to the different wards. The word was that they had enough manpower lined up now for every ward except maybe Greetland and Stainland – and they were all Liberals there anyway.

McCafferty sat with a cup of tea, talking to Megan – then a man came in and sat beside her, listening. He was balding, in a yellow sweatshirt. Martin looked up, eyebrows raised, and asked him, 'Have you come to help?'

He said, 'No. I've come to ask about policy.'

The candidate gave a quiet little laugh and put a tired hand on his arm. He said, 'Public transport . . .'

'Come and sit over here.' She left her friends to go and talk at another table about why Labour couldn't renationalise the railways, about regulating the buses, about why he'd heard so much about education.

Finally Megan drove her home at 5.15, while her agent settled in for the night shift – and you remember the people I bought my house from? The couple who moved to Brighouse, and they were Tories? Three weeks back Paul had been undecided, and his wife Leslie said she wasn't voting Tory, so she'd probably not vote because she couldn't vote Labour.

Now I met them again – and Leslie said she was voting Labour. One of the reasons was that on Sunday night at 11 o'clock they'd gone past the Labour office, the lights were still on, someone was working there – and she thought, if they're working that hard they deserve it.

I asked Paul what he was going to do, and he put up a number of reasons for voting Conservative again. He put them up without conviction, as if expecting me, almost wanting me to knock them down – so I did, but still he wasn't sure. Eventually I told him, Look. If you help put McCafferty in, I'll sell more books. He laughed like a drain – and he voted Liberal.

*W*ednesday *30th April*

Alex Powell came in bubbling. On the bus from Hebden Bridge a bunch of old ladies were talking about how they'd all vote Labour – then they saw the rosette on her knapsack and they started singing. She had these pensioners gleefully chanting at her, 'Come On You Reds'. 'But oh,' she said, 'it's like being pregnant today. You feel great, you think something great's going to happen – and all the while you fear something terrible.'

Outside, the guy from the MSF put posters on his car; thirty yards away, Sir Donald stood outside Tesco with a few of his people. I asked how it was going and he said, 'How can you tell? You only hear what you want to hear, don't you?' I told him I'd seen Davidson in hospital and he said, 'It hasn't helped. I expect his mind's in turmoil, isn't it?'

An attractive woman of a certain age came and told him, 'Oh, I *do* hope you win. This European thing is absolutely *terrifying* – to people of my generation, anyway.'

Gallantly Thompson told her, 'You're just a young 'un.'

He was standing in a gap about eight feet wide between two parked cars; a woman coming through said, 'Excuse me.'

He budged and chuckled, 'I take up so much room, don't I?'

I asked what he'd do if he lost. He said, 'I don't know. Something'll turn up. But I've had a good time of it, haven't I? I've had a good eighteen years.'

He left for Todmorden as, once again, the Labour wave came spilling from the office with all their glossy purple clobber. The MSF man was playing clips of Blair and Prescott speeches cut into the D-ream theme from his car; Sir Donald's car, by contrast, had tatty boards tied to the roof-rack, with his message handwritten on them in blue felt pen. In true idiosyncratic style the message read: 'Sir Donald Thompson for Calder Valley. Very Sound – Industry, Education, Police, Social Services, Finance, etc. Well Done John Major. Vote Conservative.' It was sweetly, woefully amateur – and I thought Central Office were supposed to be good at that kind of thing. But it seemed the Tories couldn't even decorate a car any more.

Ten Russians turned up at Labour's office, members of a tour group from the New Perspectives Foundation spending a week observing the election. Their principal project back home was to get people, especially young people, to participate in the democratic process; watching that process in Britain now involved them hitting the streets and the marketplace in Brighouse with two lads from the CPSA and a lot of balloons. Theoretically, of course, they were neutral – but Labour's spirit was too infectious for them, and in no time these big smiling Slavs were taking pictures and video-tape of each other decked with flags and waving pledge cards.

As we roamed through the market stalls one of the union boys said with a smile, 'How bizarre does it get? You watch an election in Yorkshire, you end up with two blokes from London and a bunch of Russians. Mind you,' he went on, 'it's felt bizarre from the day we got here.'

I don't know if the translation was iffy, but the Russian group's slogan was apparently, Get Plucked Up. (As in, Gee yourself up to go and vote.) Their leader was a tall, substantially built man called Andrei, from Volgograd; their translator was a truly handsome woman, tanned and hawklike with jet-black hair. They were full of life, fascinated with all they saw; they were also fabulously courte-ous. Andrei declined to make a prediction, on the grounds that it would have been impertinent; but he said everywhere they went Labour were more active, more alive, more flamboyant. As the translator put it, 'His impression is that the Tories in their heart think they'll lose. They have no enthusiasm, no belief, no fighting spirit. They are not very happy. It's a kind of stagnation with them.'

Were they aware that what they were watching was historic? She translated the question and everywhere heads vigorously nodded, *Da, da, da.* 'It's my first election,' said the translator, 'and it's won-derful.'

She went to thank Ann Martin, saying she understood how hectic a time it was for her; Martin said, 'No problem. It's lovely to see you. I hope it's given you a flavour of what we do.'

One of the union boys laughed and said, 'We wander about with a bunch of balloons.'

And now I'm the proud owner of a T-shirt that says, Get Plucked Up.

I took McCafferty and Megan Swift to Hipperholme, then to Hebden Bridge. In the car McCafferty said nervously, 'The Tories are invisible. Just because you don't see them doesn't mean they're not out there.'

'Come polling day,' Megan fretted, 'they all come off the tops in their four-wheel drives.'

In 1992, McCafferty knew Labour had lost by 7.30 in the morning. She was taking numbers at a polling station in Mytholmroyd; a senior Tory man was there too. In the first half-hour, she said, there must have been fifty people turn up on their way to work, all driving Mercs, Jags, Rovers, BMWs. This had been her ward for a year by then, and she didn't know any of these people, but the Tory guy knew every one of them by name. She watched and she thought, we've lost this.

Pearson had known they'd lose it too; she said she'd met him on the steps of the Town Hall the night before and he told her then that Labour couldn't win, that his vote had collapsed – and she went off thinking, How does he know that? He knew because in 1992, when Labour still didn't know the difference between a computer and a compost heap, the Liberals had a system called EARS: the Electoral Agents' Registration System. It was still reckoned now to be a fair bit better than Labour's Elpack – though on the other hand, given the nature of the Liberal candidate in Calder Valley, they might have been better off calling it MOUTH.

On the day, several hundred people would be working for Labour in Calder Valley; taking numbers, running committee rooms, giving lifts to the elderly and infirm. In the office, Ann Martin tried to organise all the manpower. Howard Knight said, 'We're going to win.'

McCafferty discussed with Megan Swift the letter they'd have to get out to thank all these people who'd helped; they'd have to change the letterhead, ditch the slogan off the bottom. They'd need a new letterhead, they mused, saying MP on it.

I thought, Don't say that. Please, please, don't say it 'til we know . . . and I cannot overstress to you how frightening this now was. My stomach felt permanently hollow with anxiety; I was waking up in the small hours every night. When you follow a football tournament, at least you have regular bouts of action; there's a discernible narrative progress marked by the simple matter of scoring goals. As it goes along you either win or lose and, ultimately, if you lose it doesn't matter. But when you follow an election, there's only one game; it's a tournament where the only match is the final and in the weeks before that all the polls, all the software packages, all the canvassing in the world can't tell you for sure that you'll win it.

Moreover, unlike football, it matters like hell that you should win it – which makes the last days an echoing abyss of uncertainty, a hideous void of mood swings from jubilant anticipation to the most gut-wrenching dread. You can know in your bones that this time, surely, the Tories are finished – I'd known it from the time I saw Portillo speak to that wrinkled crew at the Elland Cricket Club – but all the while you're aware in your belly that you don't actually *know*.

On the eve of the election, it felt like coming to the end of a tightrope walk. Safety on the platform at the end was just there, just another few feet away . . . but all the while you're looking behind you, terribly afraid that some part of the rope is unravelling, and just when you're nearly home it's going to break and you're going to fall. In my personal opinion, it would have been a fall from which the country could never have recovered.

McCafferty went to a photocall at the Trusthouse Forte; the candidates' last supper. The hotel had prepared appropriate meals for each party; an odd idea, maybe, though not as daft as the lifestyle feature she'd had to do for one of the local papers. What's your favourite dress, how do you keep fit, what do you like to eat? This had involved Tarlo cooking her dinner, and her then pretending to eat it for the photographer, at 9.15 on a Sunday morning.

She got to the Trusthouse and found Sir Donald waiting. Oh Donald, she told him, we're alone; that felt a bit nervous, so they both went to the loo. Eventually the photographer turned up and told Thompson he was looking well, he looked as if he'd had a tonic.

What man, this wonderful character replied, gesturing to McCafferty, wouldn't find it a tonic to be in the company of this lovely young woman?

Well, she said, her hand over her mouth, what on earth could you say to that?

Thompson shot off; McCafferty and Megan Swift found themselves alone, so they ate the Green Party's meal – bean curd – and then discovered they'd been locked out on the terrace. They wandered about a bit, and the only way back in was through a function room packed with business types in expensive suits. They're thinking, Oh cripes – so they try and edge through unobtrusively, but one of these big men turns to her and says, 'Are you the Labour candidate?' So she's thinking, Here we go. I'm in for an earful now.

But the earful consisted of an older man saying the Tories were finished, it really was time for a change, and a younger man telling her he knew a lot of people in his company who voted Tory last time, and who would not be doing so again.

At four in the afternoon, three Tory men and John Foran's daughter waited on the corner of Sunny Bank Lane, just outside the centre of Brighouse; Peter Lilley was coming to visit a big photographic concern tucked away just up the road. Foran's daughter was twenty-three, and had ambitions to become a candidate herself one day; at the moment, she worked for Thompson in London. While we waited, I asked her if it wasn't just really demoralising for them.

She said, 'Nothing's ever certain. Last time . . .'

This isn't last time.

'No. But if I start off my political career believing these polls and getting despondent I'll not get very far, will I?'

I told her her father had accepted defeat. Not very kind, I know – but if she wants to be an MP, she'll come up against folk much nastier than me.

She said, 'I'm surprised he'd say that. And I just cannot accept that the British people would elect the party of Ken Livingstone and Bernie Grant.'

I think they're electing the party of Tony Blair and Gordon Brown . . .

'I cannot believe the electorate would be so naïve as to vote for a marketing campaign. I'd be stunned.'

Bit harsh on the electorate there? Naïve?

'No. But look, nothing has been made of the fact that a substantial part of the Labour Party, including its principal backers, have been gagged for now, and will very soon return to influence a Labour government.'

I suggested that this was a world view seriously detached from current realities; that as a consequence, she and her people were about to lose and lose big. But she simply could not accept that. She laughed and said, 'Ask me on Friday.'

The first car had two minders; Jean Searle came behind in her jeep, with Peter Lilley and two other suits. Lilley was on the phone. Searle stepped out, radiantly good-looking, and announced herself to be extremely optimistic, really buoyant. She was either extraordinarily brave or utterly deluded. She was still furious with all the candidates who'd taken money from Paul Sykes – who were *still* taking money from him – but it didn't change her apparently secure belief that the Tories could yet win this. She asked me, 'Who have the polls interviewed? I've yet to meet anybody they've interviewed, or anybody who *knows* anybody they've interviewed. *Our* returns are on a par with '92, except with far more don't-knows – so this is anybody's election.' Which raises the question, never mind the pollsters – who in God's name were the Tories talking to?

Thompson arrived hotfoot from the Trusthouse; he told the Secretary of State for Social Security, 'We're in Calder Valley. This is Brighouse.' That was that sorted out then. Lilley looked tired, but said he wasn't.

The photography firm was called A. H. Leach & Co.; the boss showed us round, through several floors of white, polished rooms producing fine glossy enlargements, through big dark-rooms, past large and featureless machinery. Quite what the Social Security Minister was doing going round a photo shop I don't know; maybe it was one of the few places left where they knew they wouldn't get a barracking. Members of staff explained to Lilley how they produced their pictures; he stood stiffly upright, his left hand holding his right forearm behind his back. The fingers of his right hand twitched and scraped repeatedly across his palm. One of the staff took him across the room to stand by a giant print of a lunar sci-fi landscape; I was keening inside at the *Courier* photographer, for God's sake, can't you see it? Surely you *have* to get this shot? Minister on the moon . . . but he didn't.

One of his minders told me, 'Don't grab him now.'

I wasn't going to.

'You grabbed Gillian Shephard.'

I did. But what was he going to say now? That it was all to play for, there were lots of don't-knows, blah blah – and before he left I told him I didn't have any questions, 'cause I knew he'd only say that. He smiled wearily and with a nice touch of irony he said, 'Not at all. We'd have an intelligent discussion of the issues.' Then he was gone.

Thompson told me he'd known the boss of this firm all his life, he was the fourth generation in the business, and his son played for the rugby club of which he himself had been chairman. 'So,' he concluded contentedly, 'we're all interbred.' He had a way with words, didn't he? When I checked a detail, I slipped; I said, Tell me again, you were chair of the rugby club . . .

Thompson laughed. He said, 'Chair*man*. None of your bloody furniture.'

The boss of the firm, meanwhile, was a big local booster, much involved in the Build A Brighter Brighouse campaign. He said, 'That should be worth a chapter of your book on its own.' I groaned inwardly at the very idea. Brighouse, frankly, was not the most exciting place in the world; most of the shopkeepers I talked to said it was dying on its feet. All the Labour Council's fault, of course, them and their car-parking charges; nothing at all to do with the fact that a lot of the shops were rubbish.

The booster asked me when the book would be out. I told him and he said complacently, 'Send me a copy.' I thought, you cocky bleeder. You can get your wallet out.

The result of the postal vote came in. The total votes cast were 1,545. Of these, McCafferty had 711 and Thompson 536 – 46 per cent for Labour, against 35 per cent Conservative. Historically, the Tories had been better at turning out postal votes; now people looked at each other and told themselves, That's it. Surely we've got it now.

I drove Alex Powell back to Hebden Bridge. She'd turned twenty-eight since conference; she was a short, attractive woman with black hair, a pale face, a quick, winning smile – and the election, she said, was costing her a fortune. Her boyfriend was looking after the kids but they'd fallen out, so now she was having to pay him to do it – and all her friends thought she was obsessed.

She, in her turn, thought it was sad that none of them was really interested. She said they'd all vote Labour, they knew how horrid she'd be to them if they didn't – but she said they were right, because she was obsessed. 'It's Labour this, Labour that; it's going to be really weird next week, having nothing to do. You're with these people all the time, Ann, Tony, Chris – I've just loved it so much. You feel like you're doing something proper, like you're a proper person. When I go out and people ask me how it's going, I feel like it's my election, like I own it. Ah well, I suppose it'll be back to boring old CLP meetings. We've got this Labour Into Power document I'm supposed to read, but I haven't, not yet. 'Cause what if we don't win?'

She wasn't going to the count. It was in Elland, too far from Hebden Bridge; they were putting up a big screen in the Trades Club, and she'd watch it there instead. They had a late licence 'til four. But apart from the distance, the other reason she wasn't going was plain dread. She said, 'If I've got to go home crying, I don't want it to be a long way home.'

I dropped her off and parked outside the old bakery. Tim Swift was arriving at the same time. 'So,' he asked, smiling, 'are you expecting a tense, close count?'

I said I wasn't – with fingers crossed so tight you'd have needed pliers to part them.

McCafferty said Viv Smith had got three postal votes, and she asked Tim what that said about how the Greens were doing. He grinned and said, 'It says they're doing very badly.'

Megan produced a bottle of whisky. She said she'd been conned into buying an expensive brand because the bloke told her he'd vote Labour if she did. While we talked, volunteers were putting out 3,000 eve-of-poll leaflets – 3,000, in Hebden Bridge alone.

Pages and pages of instructions lay spilling from McCafferty's fax: instructions on what she should say in her acceptance speech. 'It's going to look pretty stupid on TV,' said Tim, 'if everybody says the same thing.'

McCafferty smiled and said, 'We're only making five promises anyway.'

'So,' laughed Megan, 'you just say, one a year, and I'll see you.'

It was a quarter to eight. McCafferty said she didn't know how she felt; she was in a state of disbelief. 'It's been two years and eight months since the start of the selection process, it's been six weeks of campaign – it's been since October, really. It doesn't seem real.'

'And,' Tim told her, 'the next campaign starts on Saturday.'

Liam, the little boy that Tarlo and McCafferty had taken in with his teenage mother, poddled around our feet on a toy car. The day we voted would be his second birthday; he was a beautiful child, tranquil and confident. 'Car,' he said, 'car. Key gone.' His mother came to take him for his bath.

I asked the others for a spot of help; I had to go on Radio 4 on Friday afternoon to talk about the election and they wanted six bullet points, six things I'd be saying. Megan said, 'Just give 'em the five pledges. It's all we gave anybody else. Why should they have six?'

Tarlo got back from the council meeting with a huge load of Chinese take-out. The meeting had passed quickly and smoothly. 'So apart from the fact that Calderdale's falling to bits,' he grinned, 'everything's fine.'

Megan said she'd bought a lottery ticket. She'd decided she was going to win the jackpot on Wednesday, and McCafferty was going to win the election on Thursday. 'Well,' said Tim, 'as one of those things is a lot more likely than the other . . .'

'Oh, come on,' Megan told him, 'don't be getting Chris down here.'

We watched the 9 o'clock news. 'After one of the longest election campaigns of modern times, the last speeches have been made, the last interviews given . . .'

Chris McCafferty said quietly, 'Amen to that.'

25

POLLING DAY

The alarm in my hotel room went off at 6 a.m. An hour later, I watched the election begin at Colden Junior and Infants' School, way up on the tops over Hebden Bridge. McCafferty's son had gone to this school; the house she'd lived in back then was three fields away, and she'd watch him walk down the winding little road every morning from her kitchen window.

A year ago to the day – a year ago to the minute – she'd been back up here, taking numbers in the local elections. Twelve months on, as she sought election herself, it seemed a good place to start. It was the smallest polling station in the constituency, a place of decision for just 190 people; it was a century of education built in solid gritstone on the grand expanse of the uplands.

The morning was bright and crisp; the moon was still up in a wide blue sky faintly traced with veils of high white cloud. The fields, neatly squared off with their dry-stone walls, glistened silver-green with dew. Sheep bleated, the air trilled with bird-song, a cock crowed and inside the school the presiding officer, herself a retired head-teacher, made ready for the day. On the door, Labour's number-taker made ready too – a man called Graham who'd never done this job before but was doing it now because, he said, it was just so important to get the Tories out. Mind you, he'd been told to bring a good book; he'd been told this wasn't a frenetic place to be. He was alone; neither the Tories nor the Liberals had a number-taker here.

At two minutes past seven, the first voter arrived. A small man about forty years old, or maybe less, he was balding, and smart-casual in creased trousers and a fleece top. When he came out, he wouldn't say how he'd voted – but everything about him said he'd voted Conservative, and that he was ashamed of it. He was a shy Tory; he was a wanker.

'So at the moment,' said Graham, 'they're ahead.'

The second voter came in at 7.13, an attractive woman aged thirty-one with short blonde hair, wearing leggings and a T-shirt. She voted Labour; she was a residential social worker and, she said, 'I shouldn't imagine anyone I work with'd vote Tory.'

I asked how she felt about casting her vote and she said, 'It feels important. It feels a necessary thing to do. In everyday life, you don't count for much outside your own little circle. But today, you do.'

And that, I thought, was the English electorate for you. One decent soul and one shifty onanist.

At twenty to eight in the church hall in Heptonstall – a village so beautiful that it's now populated almost entirely by people from the television industry – business was brisk. Of 928 voters, thirty-two had been through already and more were coming all the while. Again, there was no Tory taking numbers. The Labour man said he knew most of these people by sight, a lot of them by name, but it was no guarantee of what they'd do in the booth. You took their numbers, and you prayed.

A large and alarming biker came out, wrapped in leather from head to toe; he had a Kawasaki 1300. Before he put his helmet on I asked him – somewhat nervously – how he'd voted. He looked me up and down for a moment; maybe he was going to tear my head off here, and piss down the hole for good measure. He said, 'Conservative.'

Ah. Er, ho hum. What do you do then? I'm thinking, a spot of casual rape and pillage here, a bout of indiscriminate chemical abuse there, beat up the sex slave for relaxation at the weekends.

He said, 'I'm a policeman.'

I got to the old bakery at eight. The Swifts had come by at quarter to seven to take Tarlo and McCafferty out leafleting, but the

candidate hadn't slept all night so they left her to herself. She was
getting out of the shower when the others returned, and Tarlo was
chuffed, he looked happier than he'd been for days; he'd voted. 'It
was,' he said, 'like having a really good dump after weeks of constipation.'

Shelves and mantelpieces were filled with cards from well-
wishers. See you on *Question Time*, said their friends, save a peerage
for me. The candidate came down dressed and ready, and Liam
edged his way down the stairs behind her. She ruffled his hair and
said, 'This is a historic day. You're two, aren't you?'

We went into town; I'd booked breakfast at my hotel. Before we
got there, McCafferty popped down the street to the beauty salon;
she had an hour's worth of pampering lined up, something Tarlo
wasn't supposed to know about. 'So that,' he said, 'is where she
spends my money.' Then he grinned fiercely and said, 'Never mind.
I'll be spending hers next week.'

As she went down the street, a well-dressed woman climbed
out of a big estate car and jabbed a finger at her. Oh God, thought
the candidate, I'm going to get it in the ear now – and the woman
said sternly, 'I'm voting for you, you know. For the first time in my
life.'

The Old Civic Hall Hotel did the business: two rashers, two
sausages, two eggs, beans, a plump tinned tomato, two fried slices,
a mountain of toast and marmalade. Now that's what I call this
England – but while we ate, conversation was tense, a blurred mix
of nerves and laughter. Tim Swift said anxiously that if you looked
at the good Tory areas and the good Labour areas in 1992, the turn-
out was 10 per cent higher in the Tory patches.

McCafferty said if they didn't turn out in the Labour zones after
all the stuff they'd had this time, they never would.

Megan said, 'We should have a leaflet saying, If you don't vote
you'll get four more leaflets.'

Someone came up with the ultimate nightmare scenario – a
recount to see if the Referendum crew had lost their deposit or
not – and of course we wondered what Donald Thompson had
been doing. Why, in a key marginal, had his campaign seemed so
penny-short? We speculated that maybe, behind the apparent strategy, they knew they were losing all along, so they were only
defending really hard in those seats with the bigger majorities. Or

maybe some right-wing clique in Central Office had decided Sir Donald was expendable. Maybe this, maybe that . . .

A woman came in to work, and McCafferty knew her. They exchanged friendly greetings, then the candidate demanded, 'But have you *voted* yet?'

She said, 'Not yet. I'll do it tonight, then I'll go and have a beer.'

McCafferty voted at five to ten in the Hebden Bridge Methodist Church. 'Right,' said the presiding officer, 'I'll not ask who you're voting for.'

'And,' she smiled, 'I'll not say.'

Again, Labour had a number-taker and the Tories didn't. Where were they?

I drove to Elland; the sun was shining, Simon Mayo was on the radio, Labour were winning and all was right with the world. Even the latest batch of Yorkshire Water roadworks couldn't get me down.

Labour's base in Elland was the upstairs room of a pub called the Old Bailey. Tony the Geezer and a local councillor called Shaun Topham were crossing off Labour voters on the Dixon boards; around five different polling stations, they said, they hadn't seen a single Tory number-taker. This was unusual for a local election; for a general, it was unheard of.

Topham said it looked good. 'We're coming out in numbers, and the opposition aren't. I'd rather be us than them, put it that way.'

'We turn up,' said Tony, 'and there *is* no opposition.'

In Brighouse at 11.15, Howard Knight said it was either incompetent management, or surrender, or both.

Ann Martin said, 'The turn-out is very brisk, and that's good for us. I'm very heartened right now. If we can get them out on the council estates, there's no problem. I'm not saying we'll have a landslide in Calder Valley – but we'll have a comfortable majority. I feel good.'

She hadn't felt good the night before; she'd felt terrible. Her mother had gone in for a hip replacement on the eve of the election and, obviously, she couldn't be there. Then her father – who, she said, was a little lost lamb without his wife – had left the phone off the hook all night. He'd probably just not put it down properly, but it left Martin ravaged with worry. Finally she called a neighbour who went round to put the phone down, and at last she heard her Mam was all right, she was sitting up, they'd taken the drip off – it was a mighty relief.

But it didn't stop her thinking about the candidate. She wanted McCafferty resting in the morning, she wanted her resting in the afternoon, 'Because this is the first day of the rest of her life. I don't want her trooping round any streets any more – she's done her job. Mind, when did she ever listen to me?'

This was comic stuff. McCafferty right now was flat out in the beauty parlour having a facial – but, thinking that Martin would want her out working, had strictly forbidden me to say so. Still, the way things were looking, the pair of them could have gone hang-gliding in clown suits for all the difference it'd make. There wasn't any science in this, and there was a long way to go until the end of the day – but it felt as if Labour were walking it.

I went back up the valley to the Tory office; since Davidson had gone off the bridge, it was being run by a woman called Brenda Lowe. She was an experienced agent who'd worked for the party for many years; now she'd come out of retirement to see Thompson through – and she said you couldn't say they were losing because nobody knew. Well, I said, there were Tories who said they'd lost . . .

She said, 'There are natural pessimists. It felt at one time in '92 as if I was the only person who thought we'd win, and people laughed at me – but we did win. Now I admit, this one's more mixed up, the Referendum Party's clouded it – but that's just the English for you. We don't like foreigners, do we? We don't like Lancastrians, never mind Europeans.'

Setting aside this peculiarly relaxed acceptance of xenophobia as a tolerable national trait, we seemed to be sliding somewhat off the point here – and the point was, there appeared to be an election going on out there at which the Tories simply hadn't turned up.

Lowe said, 'We're as organised as we can be.'

Which was, not very – and, as in Wirral South, the contrast between the two party headquarters was striking. While Ann

Martin in Brighouse ran a big modern office full of life and colour in the centre of town, with people of all ages coming and going, the Tory base in Hebden Bridge was two unvisited biddies in a dusty old corner.

The other woman there, Thompson's PA, was originally from the Seychelles. (Another of Thompson's staff was an Asian–American called Samidha – and I thought the English didn't like foreigners?) Anyway, this pleasant woman explained that she'd arrived in Hebden Bridge from a tropical island because, 'I don't like Labour. My mother used to say, Born under the British flag, die under the British flag. I'd say, Yes Mum. Then Labour let us go and look what 'appen. Communist dictatorship. So I came here. And if Labour win now, I'm off. My husband's in the bush in Tanzania, and I'll go join him.'

Similarly, just about everybody on the Labour side said that if the Tories won, they'd emigrate too. So I stood there thinking that one way or the other, by the time you're reading this the country'll be half empty.

At the Labour office in the Trades Club, the word was good; 35 per cent of the electorate had voted already. 'They've been waiting for this,' said McCafferty, 'it's retribution.'

Megan said, 'I wonder how it feels to be a Tory. It can't be very nice.'

'Well,' said the candidate fiercely, 'it's about time.' And both women were grinning – but still that small itchy worry nagged in the back of your mind. We still didn't know anything for certain – and the Tories might be invisible but they knew their people, they'd be ringing them up . . .

Megan said, 'I'm 99 per cent sure. But,' *sotto voce*, 'when you want something really badly, there's always that fear until you've got it.'

It was one o'clock; the candidate's job now was to tour the committee rooms, to put in an appearance everywhere to thank all the people who were working for her. Tarlo told me, 'Come into the battle bus' – the Volvo – 'and it is a battle bus, too. It's wrecked.' The lining of the roof inside had been punctured all over by the stakes; posters and tattered hats and bits of popped balloon lay all about, a morass of electoral debris.

We left the Italianate jumble of over-and-unders clambering up the Hebden Bridge hillsides, and headed west for Todmorden; Tarlo played D-ream through the speakers, driving with one hand and holding the mike in the other. Each terrace we passed, he told them, 'Today is polling day. Use your vote wisely. Vote Labour. For a brighter better Britain.' But he was tired, and it kept coming out wrong. A biter breton brotten. A bratter bitter bitten. A batter blatter bratten. Burgly bargle bog.

Well, he said, you know what I mean — and as we curled up the valley under the silver-blue sky, the trees in blossom along the river and the green land shining in clear bright heat, past signs for places with names like Mankinholes and Lumbutts, people were dancing and waving as we passed. Those long eighteen years were coming to an end at last — and when we got to the Labour rooms in Tod, Pam Warhurst looked up from the voter lists, grinned enormously and said, 'Landslide.'

She and McCafferty embraced. Warhurst's T-shirt said, 'We must have faith, courage and chocolate fudge cake.'

Soon afterwards, we met a Labour man who'd bumped into Donald Thompson in Ripponden and, he said, he'd not looked a happy man. He'd said this good weather wouldn't do him any favours — so, said this Labour fellow, 'I asked him what job he'd be doing tomorrow.'

Then he said, 'I were sat on top of a mountain in Wales yesterday, just sat there in sunshine, and I were thinking what a great day this is going to be. And it is.'

Megan Swift said of the candidate, 'She's done brilliantly. I'd have gone to pieces by now. I'd certainly be in pieces today. I can't imagine what it's like. If you've wanted and worked for something as long as she's worked for this . . . it's got to be frightening, hasn't it?'

It started feeling wrong about ten past two in Mytholmroyd. The Labour rooms were in the borrowed and aptly named offices of Major Financial Services; we met Tim Swift there, and he was worried. He didn't say anything to McCafferty, but he whispered to me, 'There don't seem to be as many Labour voters on the canvass returns as there should be.'

In several rooms round the bottom of the valley, it started looking as if the voter print-outs weren't complete. If it was close, and
Labour didn't have all their promises on the lists so they could go
and turn them out, McCafferty could still lose here. Then, at 3.30
at the Old Bailey in Elland, we found they had a body shortage.
Topham said he only had one driver for the car calls and he needed
someone to go leafleting, to go knocking people up. He was worried about one of the council estates, worried that the polling
station was right there on the end of their road and they weren't
walking down to it.

It was the ratty patch of brick terraces we'd been to a couple of
weeks back, with the battered doors and the drugged-out woman
and the thugs who put the frighteners on the Asians. McCafferty,
Tarlo and Megan Swift grabbed up leaflets, balloons, whatever was
left, and shot off in a fret to try and rouse the place.

Where we parked, bits and bobs of litter lay strewn about the
tarmac and the uneven grass. Twenty kids gathered about us in
tired, grubby clothes to scream for flags and hats; some of them
were as young as four and no one was minding them, they were just
out loose in a pack. When we were driving, little boys on battered
BMXs would scoot alongside, perilously, recklessly close. Who did
they belong to? Did nobody care where they were?

There followed forty manic minutes pelting round in the heat
shoving leaflets though letterboxes, sweating, grimly silent. Megan
looked at her watch and said, 'There's only five and a half hours 'til
the polls close.'

As we headed off to Hipperholme and Lightcliffe to see if it felt
any better there, Tarlo's voice boomed and crackled through the
speakers. I was in Megan's car behind him; the afternoon felt airless
now, and I was sticky with sweat. I'd also been bitten by a dog, and
was worried if it had pierced the skin. As Megan drove she muttered, 'It's no good asking them to vote going past the
crematorium, David.' But her smile was taut with worry; her face,
her whole body language was now rigid with anxiety. Out of the
blue she suddenly said, 'I don't like counts.'

It was getting to me too; I said I'd like to be back in Brighouse,
I'd like to see some hard numbers. Labour were supposed to have
parachuted in some other key-seat bigwig to help pull Calder
Valley through the day; but now Megan said, 'Unless he's a lot

better than any other Labour person that's ever been, he won't have a rotten clue what the numbers are. Or if he does, it'll be wrong.'

We got to the Bailiff Bridge Working Men's Club; Labour were working from a grand, cool, high-ceilinged bar. A stout, cheery woman right out of 'Coronation Street' gave us cold drinks; we collapsed on the padded benches, slumping to a halt. Then I asked another woman how it looked and she said, 'I don't know who's in charge here. I'm not sure what's going on.'

The woman in charge was a slim, calm, capable blonde called Veronica. She said not to worry, there were a lot more known voters out there than there were on these sheets. Megan sat fulminating inside; she felt, understandably, that if her husband hadn't been kept in the background just because he'd been a Liberal once, this computer work might have come off a lot better.

A man came in and said, 'I heard all this noise. I thought, it's some lot of bloody teenagers with a mobile disco. I've come out all ready to give it a bit of abuse – and it's the future Labour MP.'

Someone asked him how it was going and he said he didn't know, he'd only just got back from work. 'So I can tell you,' he said, 'it's going very well in Lancashire.'

I could have screamed inside. Bugger Lancashire, how's it going *here*?

Megan said quietly, 'You know I've been right cheerful? Can I have five minutes off now?' I thought her face was going to crumple. Nnnnggghhh . . .

Outside, McCafferty admitted she didn't feel so positive any more. Megan told her, 'It's 'cause we're at the wrong end of the valley . . .'

'But we've got to *win* this end . . .'

'No. We've got to do *better* at this end. And Veronica says we are doing better.'

Megan got back in her car, trembling. She said, 'It's the area we're in, that's all. It doesn't feel good. But oh God, we *must* win. We'll look such bloody prats if we don't.'

It was all feeling, feeling, feeling. You spent too much time in a place where the Tories had numbers, you could feel it in the air, and then every little glitch, every dud print-out, every doubt expressed by anyone around you ballooned into terror. We were driving about now in a jangled mix of frayed hopes and mounting horror. If this was scientific, then Darwin was a creationist.

Five-thirty, and Ann Martin in Brighouse said it was OK. One of the men running the computers said it was looking good, it was steady. He had a bar chart up, and the red bar was tallest. Someone else said, 'It's bound to get better for the Tories in the afternoon. Wait 'til the workers get home.'

We crawled out into the rush hour in a fug of frazzled speculation. With the shops shut, Brighouse was empty. Rubbish blew down the streets. We crept up the hill towards Huddersfield, turned off into squeaky-clean suburban side streets and found the Rastrick base – a family man's living room on a featureless street of modest, modern detached houses. A sign said, No Smoking, Ken Livingstone for PM.

Tarlo asked, 'Have you got plenty of people to do car lifts and the knocking up?'

'Er . . . good question.'

'But have you got a good answer?'

His wife poured glasses of lemon squash. A glossy cabriolet went past outside, the driver a tanned woman with shiny hair and fancy shades. The Rastrick man peeked through the curtains and said, 'That's our bright neighbour. Who thinks Tony Blair's the leader of the Liberal Democrats.'

On the main road into the south side of Halifax, there's a roundabout at the Calder and Hebble junction. At six-thirty in the evening we crossed this spot towards Sowerby Bridge, and suddenly everything felt better again. We were out of the suburban Tory bottom into the increasingly rural Labour top, and everyone was so sensitised now that you could literally feel it flow through your blood and your lungs, that you were getting back among your people.

The base for Ryburn ward was the front room of a back-street semi on the Sowerby estate, and it was heaving with people. 'Oh,' sighed Megan, 'people smile up here, don't they?'

McCafferty asked the guy running the show if they were turning out and he did indeed smile; he smiled massively. He said they'd been turning out since seven in the morning, and there'd been that many turning out all day they couldn't keep up with them – it had been crazy, non-stop.

These people were a different breed: poorer, noisier, happier. The room bubbled with voices, the atmosphere thrilled and electric. A man came in and said he'd been up on Rishworth tops, he'd just gone round Triangle (there really is a place called Triangle, and there's a place called Slack Bottom too) and everywhere he went the reception was brilliant.

We headed on west, over the back road through Boulder Clough. The valley lay deep amongst the weighty bulk of the hills before us, mill chimneys dotted along the bottom and up the narrow vales beyond. The heat haze was cooling off now; the feeling of relief and release up here was palpable.

We dropped into Hebden Bridge; Tarlo was smiling broadly, playing the music, pointing all his friends out. That man there, he said, was the best children's librarian in Britain. That one there was a good guitarist. There went Chippy the switcher, interviewed in the *Sun* just the other day, out knocking up now, and there was Dave out leafleting. Megan said, 'It's amazing. I feel I'm going to be friends with an MP again now.'

It was past seven, over twelve hours since polling began, and there were still more visits to be made. The Heptonstall committee rooms were in a gorgeous, grand old house with stone-framed windows, a big open kitchen with an Aga, all art and plummy voices and country living. When someone said we still didn't really know how we were doing, Megan laughed and said, 'Why don't we ring Pearson? He'll know.'

Way up on the tops, with the moors lining the horizons all about us, we stopped at Wadsworth Community Centre in Old Town and found three MORI exit pollsters sitting with the Labour number-taker. In the evening sun, a sprinkler played on the bowling green. McCafferty said the MORI team wouldn't get anything too representative up here; with over two hours still to go, 350 voters had already come in out of 500 available, and not many would be Tory.

The Old Town committee rooms were in a wonderful little terrace called Club Houses. Tarlo remembered the house at the far end being bought as a trashed wreck twenty years back for £1,000; now they were warm, welcoming, well-kept homes. The first one belonged to a striking man with longish black hair, a dark complexion, and hawkish good looks like an Apache in a Western; he was a teacher who worked with bilingual kids in Halifax.

The Dixon board on the table was shunted aside; someone produced a steaming, seriously toothsome vegetable curry and a bottle of Sicilian wine. We realised we'd not eaten properly since breakfast and fell on the food, ladling yoghurt and chutneys all over.

When I'd eaten, I stepped outside with Tarlo and the teacher. The view was astonishing; the valley beneath us ran like a jagged scar towards Todmorden, and Stoodley Pike monument – erected after the defeat of Napoleon – stood out sharp and clear on the far tops. Nearer to us, the hulk of Acre Mill loomed on the village skyline; high on the next spur, Heptonstall was a fetching huddle of warm stone. To the west, the sun was a golden disc falling toward the moortops; the sky flared red and lilac. We sat on the wall and gaped at the grandeur of it, the raw beauty of this England.

Tarlo smiled and said, 'This is what I call a committee room. Three people sat on a wall.'

Lambs bleated in the field by the house. The teacher told me that Club Houses had been built in the 1830s, as one of the very first cooperative housing ventures. On the original title there were 147 signatures, a lot of them just crosses; they'd been in a funeral club, and they'd all paid a penny a week from the funeral money to build these. Labour sprang from seeds like that; now Labour was springing back to government.

The teacher came to see us off. With an ironic smile he told McCafferty, 'I shall be writing to you in your new capacity . . .'

The candidate laughed. 'So will every other bugger in Hebden Bridge, I've absolutely no doubt.'

In the Trades Club at eight-thirty, with ninety minutes of voting time still left, they said it was all over; everyone had voted already. A slight man named Fred Bascombe, with a beard and glasses and a mild manner about him, told McCafferty, 'You've won. I'm a bit worried about the size of the majority – but you've won.'

Bascombe worked in community care for the social services; he was a school governor as well, and in 1991 he'd been Tarlo's agent when he and McCafferty got on the council. He was, said Tarlo, an extremely soothing presence, and he had a very good nose – so I asked him to describe how it had been.

He said, 'They've been coming out in droves all day. From ten o'clock when I've gone round collecting the number sheets, the turn-out's been high; we had over fifty per cent of the electorate before teatime. And it's always unnerving that you never see much activity from the Tories – but today they've just been invisible. Us, since teatime we've been scraping round for people to get out. We've not got all of them logged, obviously, and we should have done – but it's a win. You never know, not definitely, until you start seeing the bundles on the racks – but I'm confident.'

McCafferty was on the mobile to Ann Martin. Bascombe looked at her and her husband and he said, 'I think they're tired. I should think Donald's tired too. But just another few hours, and this could be a very emotional night. You look back, '83, '87, '92 – '92 was supposed to be the year, but it never looked like that here. This time, it clearly does.

'As for them – well, I think they're standing up to this far better than when they first stood for their wards. That was their initiation to this caper and it was a tremendous double act, to stand together for adjoining wards – my job then was just to keep them sane. But this time they're more experienced, more confident – and I think she'll be brilliant.'

She got off the phone; the numbers from Martin indicated that, of the 36 per cent of the electorate that they knew about, 47 per cent were McCafferty's. Megan told her, 'You've got to have won then.'

The candidate said quietly, 'Don't say that.'

'All right then, Chris. You've lost.'

On the windowsill, the executive committee of the National Society of Dyers and Finishers, 1922 – ten stiffly upright and stalwart old boys in suits and neckties – looked down on us in sepia.

We went back to the old bakery. Walking to the car, Megan told McCafferty, 'I'm glad I'm not the candidate.'

She replied pensively, 'They say your life becomes a maelstrom.'

'I was thinking of the next four hours, actually.'

26

POWER JUICE

McCafferty needed a new battery on her mobile, but her hands started shaking so badly she couldn't do it. The battery wouldn't wedge in; she muttered under her breath, her fingers fluttered, and then the battery clattered to the table top. She looked at it lying there and gave a small, inarticulate moan. It was the first outward sign she'd given all day of what must have been going on inside.

The ansaphone was chockablock with messages, from friends and relatives at home and abroad, from people wanting to go to the count. Suddenly everybody wanted to go. She tried to juggle in her head who deserved it, who'd be really hurt if they didn't get in, who might relinquish their place. One woman on the phone started crying. How she dealt with it all calmly I don't know.

It was nine-thirty. Tim Swift arrived, and asked mildly if anyone had an answer to the really important question: were Bradford beating Charlton?

Tarlo put on a dark suit and red tie. Megan had bought red roses, one for his lapel and one for the candidate. She'd left them in water downstairs; he went to get one and Megan lay back in her chair, eyes closed. She said, 'Can I bang my head against the wall?'

Conversation was a staccato gabble. This person's errors, that person's plans, what might happen in the next hours, what had happened already. There'd been a number-taker in deepest Ryburn who started work at seven in the morning, and somehow he'd been forgotten. At four in the afternoon he'd rung in, plaintively wondering if someone might come and relieve him. We were too edgy to laugh about it; we talked in little bursts, then sat silent. Behind everything lay the impossibility of knowing how close it was.

At ten o'clock we turned on the television; Jonathan Dimbleby on ITV announced that their MORI exit poll predicted a massive Labour majority of 159. Megan's lips trembled, her face was crumbling; she said, 'I want to cry.'

Tim said, 'It was when Paul Daniels said he'd leave the country. Everyone's been champing at the bit ever since.'

We switched to the BBC. David Dimbleby talked about a seismic shift in the electorate; McCafferty smashed a fist in her palm with exultation – but still we didn't really believe it. A psephologist famously observed that what we were looking at was not so much a landslide as an asteroid striking the planet – and from McCafferty, now changing into a fresh suit upstairs, came hoots of laughter. She cried out, 'Am I dreaming?'

The first result came in from Sunderland South; the swing was eleven per cent. Paxman asked Portillo, 'Are you ready to drink hemlock yet?'

Hamilton South swung eight per cent. Edwina Currie blamed the Eurosceptics. Wrexham swung seven per cent. We lay motionless before the screen, dazed with fatigue and disbelief.

We left at 11.45; it took half an hour to drive to Brooksbank School in Elland, through spookily deserted streets. On the radio, slowly the scale of what was happening took shape. When we arrived, I got a badge and walked on to the floor of the school hall. The counters, about fifty of them, worked at desks round three sides of the hall; the black metal ballot-boxes lined the fourth side, and the returning officer's desk was in the centre of the square. On the other side of the desks, counting agents watched the counters' hands flickering through the ballot sheets.

I found John Foran, smartly turned out in a blue suit and rosette; he told me wearily that what was happening wasn't really a surprise. I said half his party still seemed to think so; he sighed and said, 'Well. You've got to have a *little* bit of realism.'

Other Tories had a muffled bewilderment about them, a baffled immobility in the face of something wholly unimaginable. They

simply couldn't get their heads round it. In the hushed and murmuring room, the quiet hubbub pierced now and then by another
buzz and ripple of Labour excitement as news came in of another
seat falling, they stared at the piles of ballot papers and wished the
message to be different. As the night drew on, you could see the life
draining out of them.

Thompson said the news was a 10-per-cent swing, and – defy-
ing mathematics – he said he'd cope with that. Then he said a
young lady had come up to him, told him the Tories hadn't had any
number-takers at the polling stations. Well, he told her sagely, it was
a new system, wasn't it? She looked impressed, he said, and asked
him what the new system was. So he told her, the new system was
that the Tories didn't have any number-takers.

His sense of humour was bearing up; his vote, plainly, was not.

I looked about the room, humming with the tension of the long,
long wait. Viv Smith sat smiling at one of the counters' desks, a great
goofy smile as if it were all a game. The Liberals bunched together in
fierce huddles, concentrating on the simultaneous count for the
council election in Todmorden. The Referendum crew occupied
one corner, and looked utterly barmy. These people Mellor had
brought with him, they made the Addams Family look like *Baywatch*.

I found Med Hughes; he said the BNP had turned up, and they
were a couple of babies. The Referendum lot had more people
than them; they'd had one look and cleared off. But then, who
wouldn't? There was a stubbly dwarf, a tub-shaped woman with
hair like you get on those plastic Disney models from MacDonald's,
and a kind of lounge lizard figure in a bilious tweed jacket. Among
them, Tony Mellor said they'd won the election before it started. I
stared at him. OK, I asked, but how many *votes* have you got?

He blathered; I fled. I found Labour's laptop merchant, and he
said McCafferty was 10 per cent ahead. He was currently predicting a majority over 9,000, but he said that was coming off boxes that
were good for them, so realistically we should expect something
between 5,000 and 7,000. This was, as it turned out, absolutely
spot on, well over two hours before the result came in.

At the back of the room, Stephen Pearson listened to a pocket
radio on an earpiece and said he thought they might have pulled it
off in Todmorden. As for the general, McCafferty had won it, no
doubt. He said, 'I always thought so. But her campaign was a

shambles. They haven't delivered a leaflet. I haven't seen a leaflet hand-delivered locally. They don't know how to work.'

This was one strange man. Why did he say stuff like this? Starting in June 1996, the Hebden Bridge branch of the Labour Party – just that one single branch – had hand-delivered 31,490 leaflets and newsletters. During April alone, in the last weeks of the campaign, they'd done seventeen leaflet drops – and now Pearson said they didn't know how to work. Go figure it.

Nicholas Budgen fell in Wolverhampton. Basildon came back to Labour with a whopping majority. Med Hughes listened in on his earpiece, not to the election but to the news of a man found face-down in the road nearby with a nasty set of facial injuries. So someone in this England, evidently, had been out and about with other matters on their mind than the election.

People came in and out of the hall; they hunched in conspiratorial groups or loitered at the entrance smoking. The steps were littered with butts. David Tarlo, wildly grinning, asked Thompson's assistant Samidha if she wanted a job. She roared with laughter.

Sir Donald continued brave. He said, 'You might be surprised. It's holding up remarkably well, compared to the storms outside.'

Oh come on, I told him – there's a Labour bod with a laptop over there who knows the result already.

He said, 'We don't need a laptop.' Then he paused a minute and said, 'Silly thing to say. We haven't got a laptop.'

It was gone one o'clock. The returning officer announced that the Todmorden council ballot papers had now been separated from those for the general election, and would be counted in a different room upstairs.

Thompson asked me curiously, 'What's he doing with his laptop anyway?'

Foran *fille*, she of the political ambitions, sat on one side of the room. She said, 'If it's 150, stunned would be putting it lightly.' Then she told me that since we'd spoken two days earlier, it had occurred to her that calling the electorate naïve was not, for an aspiring politician, too clever.

I said, if the Conservatives had respected the electorate more, they wouldn't be facing this now.

She said, 'Yes.'

But she was, she said, so stunned at this point that she could not otherwise form any considered opinion.

I wandered off, feeling increasingly wasted; after six seven-day weeks, I'd now been awake for nearly twenty hours. At some point the wild-eyed Referendum lot collared me again, banging on about how Europe was the main issue, the only issue. Mellor flailed his arms, saying, 'We'd certainly hope to retain our deposit.'

Labour's laptop jockey gave them no chance.

John Foran said Mellor was talking claptrap. He said, 'You can quote me on that. And it's a long day as well, isn't it? You can quote me on that, too. Oh, but these Judases are a waste of space, aren't they? Can't carry corn, as my mother would say.'

Nicholas Bonsor fell in Essex to an eleven point swing. Word came in that Labour had Shipley; that young lad who'd gone white with stress in Ann Martin's office had unseated Sir Marcus Fox. Somewhere a Labour voice – not jubilant, but seemingly as stunned as the Tories – said, 'My God. They're *dying*.'

Mildly, John Foran said, 'They're not dying. They're losing an election.' He shrugged. 'It happens.'

Alice Mahon came home down the road by 11,000. David Mellor fell in Putney. I asked Sir Donald how much longer he'd keep on the brave face, and he laughed. He said, 'Until I have to stand up there and hear someone else speak before me.'

But you can't have expected this, this rout . . . again he smiled, but I saw a flash of steel inside. He said, 'Stop talking to me.'

McCafferty said it hadn't begun to sink in yet, it was overwhelming. It'd sink in, she said, 'When I get down there and sign something.' Then Ann Martin came up and they started analysing where they'd done well, where they'd been patchy, and what they could do about it. It was two o'clock in the morning, the result wasn't announced yet, and they were starting work on the next one already.

Across the room, Sir Donald watched one of the counters. He looked sad, and very weary. On the desks in front of him, the piles for McCafferty were very obviously the biggest.

Another Tory, a fierce old woman from Ripponden with a body

the shape of a shoebox, two sticky-thin legs poking out underneath and hair like candy floss, told Med Hughes she was furious with the Referendum lot. She whispered ferociously that they'd been nicking her votes like fuck up there; Hughes mildly raised his eyebrows, and said he thought he'd seen her consorting with them. 'I have,' she said, 'because they've got coffee.'

Anyway, she asked him, 'Why was there a policeman sat on the bench at the cricket ground in Triangle this morning then?'

Hughes held his hands up and told her, 'I've no idea. Was it sunny?'

'Probably watching them caravans, I thought.'

'I must send him on a covert surveillance course then.' He moseyed off, looking deliberately impassive.

The fierce lady told me, 'I'm sick as a chip about Sir Marcus.'

I told her they were now predicting a Labour majority in the Commons of 187 – and she produced the finest bit of spin I heard all night. 'Well,' she growled, 'that's nothing like the three hundred they thought they'd get, is it?'

News came from the Tod count upstairs that Pearson had pulled it off; the Liberals had won the council seat. So now, said McCafferty through clenched teeth, no doubt he'd be presenting her with a train ticket to London and a letter of resignation from her Luddendenfoot ward. She said angrily, 'I'm not mad. If I stand down there he'll go after it with a cast of thousands, and he'll win that too.'

She went off to a dim corner to work on her acceptance speech; outside the hall Jason Jeffrey, the Liberal winner in Tod, came down the stairs with his face flushed bright red, an uncontrollable smile flying all over his face. The power, the power! He was a district councillor!

Another ripple brushed across the room behind me: Martin Bell had won Tatton.

It was two-thirty; a lot of the counters' tables were bare now, and the bundles were stacked up in the racks. The room was quietening; it felt stale, airless, tense with hunger for the numbers. Mellor prowled, looking anxious. Viv Smith sat watching the last papers being counted, still smiling. Maybe she believed in miracles.

Waiting by the stage, Tarlo and McCafferty were wreathed in smiles; she went to speak to Thompson and John Foran and they smiled too, civil and decent as they'd been throughout. To one side, though, Thompson's son looked as if he'd been steamrollered; he looked utterly disbelieving.

Sir Donald slipped away to stand alone, leaning on his hands on one of the empty tables and looking across the waiting room. He'd won four times; he knew this territory, this murmuring hall, these lights and photographers, the TV camera on the balcony, the watching policemen, the rolls of papers stuck in their tin trays on which his fate depended. The returning officer called the candidates into a huddle.

Close by me, one Tory said wearily to another, 'It's like trying to stand up in the middle of a bloody hurricane.'

The candidates went up on the stage; the returning officer announced the result with those brief, resonant, time-worn and hallowed phrases. The people had spoken, and this is what they said:

> Christian Jackson, BNP: 431
> Chris McCafferty, Labour: 26,050
> Anthony Mellor, Referendum: 1,380
> Stephen Pearson, Liberal: 8,322
> Vivienne Smith, Green: 488
> Sir Donald Thompson, Conservative: 19,795

Her smile was wide, her speech was gracious, and so was Donald Thompson's. It was briefly interrupted by the *Courier* man's mobile; Thompson stopped, looked over to the red-faced culprit and told him, 'Tell 'em there's a cheque in the post.'

He said, 'I'd like to thank my helpers over the past eighteen years who've made Calder Valley one of the finest places to live in Europe. May I end by thanking Calder Valley for looking after me so well and generously for so long.'

He drew warm and genuine applause; the others weren't worth listening to. When they were done the stage emptied, and for a brief moment Thompson and McCafferty were alone on it together; they shook hands, he passed her the baton, he climbed down the steps and he left her to the press. And you could see the fatigue falling away from her, you could see the power juice begin to flow – not in any mean or egotistical way, but simply in the sense of a dawning recognition that, my God, I can *do* something now. *It's my turn now . . .*

She embraced her husband in a dazzle of flashbulbs while, all about us, the room quickly emptied. A few men in suits packed up the ballot boxes, a tinny racket of metal thudding on the wooden floor. The *Post* filed, and the new MP talked to Radio Leeds. In the suddenly empty and echoing room, Sir Donald's son stood alone watching a TV lighting man untape his wires off the wall, and then he slowly walked away too. He looked very close to tears.

Outside, Sir Donald told another journalist that it had been his campaign, he'd fought it as honestly as he could, 'And if anybody's to blame it's me. I'll not blame others. So it's thank you, Donald Thompson, and good morning, Chris McCafferty.'

When the journalist was gone, I asked him if he'd seen it coming and he said he had, you could see it building up. Well, I said, he'd had a good innings . . .

He gave a great big laugh. He said, 'Doesn't stop you throwing your bat against the wall when you get back in the dressing-room, does it?' And then he walked away into the night.

Up on the balcony, Yorkshire TV took their turn with the new MP. Someone told me Portillo was gone. At that moment finally I knew, and could start to believe, that after eighteen years this England belonged to Labour.

27

FRESH AIR

It sank in four days later. Doug Henderson was flying to Brussels on the news and I thought, My God. A few days back he'd been knocking doors on the Kershaw estate – and now here he was taking the first steps to the Social Chapter.

As we went into May, it was as if the whole country was blinking, stunned in a great blast of political fresh air; people who'd ordinarily not have the slightest interest were stirred all about the place to an excited wish to talk about it. Of course this will pass – but in the days after the election, I looked back on it and considered myself a lucky man. To spend a year watching this moment arrive was a rich privilege.

I did it in part because I wanted to see what ordinary politicans are like. After eighteen years of Tory rule, a period marked towards the end by an increasingly corrupted arrogance, a creepily decadent mendacity, it's hardly surprising that we'd come to look on politicians with a profound and unhealthy cynicism. It's therefore heartening to be able to report that, on the whole, they're not really such a bad lot at all.

No doubt, among the new Labour intake, there'll be a ruthless witch here, a mean and scheming creep there – but most of those I met seemed to me to be decent, hard-working and intelligent people. They have their egos, for sure, but so do I; and for all that, central to the motivation of many of them is a sincere wish to represent the people of their constituencies, and to seek to improve the condition of their country in accord with their beliefs.

I shall never forget, canvassing on the Kershaw Estate, a woman we met with her severely disabled son. His limbs were twigs, his hands were claws; they waved slowly about him in the unseen winds of his body's dysfunction. He needed care around the clock – and McCafferty had found a special school for this boy that could take him on a residential basis and give him the education that met his needs, and she'd squirrelled out the funding to pay for it. Now, when we went in the room, he knew her, and his smile was radiant. So raise your head from your mistrust, and look around the world; we could, I assure you, be served very much worse.

I also did this because I wanted to see what politicians go through – and, setting aside the fact that a campaign is astonishingly hard work, it's also heartening to be able to report that the democratic process does actually function fairly well. I'd had a mounting fear, as the election progressed, that a lot of the work people did on the ground was rendered pointless by the bawling jabber in the media; but in the final days, when it came down to it, a lot of people made up their minds for themselves, on the basis of their own experience, and a lot of them did it with a deliberate and thoughtful exactitude.

Nonetheless, if the process remains tolerably healthy – if, on the day, a fair proportion of the English still accepted their democratic responsibility with a due degree of seriousness – the system behind that process has fallen into alarming disrepair. The Tories imploded because they became detached from reality – and the system allowed that to happen. To avoid it happening again, it is an absolute imperative that the new government should introduce proportional representation.

It is, I accept, an awesomely tricky task. Having seen it in operation, the traditional link between an MP and his or her constituency has much to be said for it; but it's surely not beyond the wit of our legislators to retain some element of that in a new and fairer system, and we really must have such a system. Otherwise, in time, the impregnable mass of Labour's majority will detach them from the people as surely as the Tories were detached before them.

There is, of course, one drawback to PR: it'll let those Liberals come crawling in all over the shop. Over the year that I've spent watching politics, the Liberals were my biggest disappointment. That large tracts of the Tory party proved to be either ancient, nasty, arguably unsound of mind, or all three, was no surprise. That the fringe groups were bonkers was no surprise either – it is a feature of democracy that anyone can stand, and that no one who does so is obliged to have a good reason for it, and we just have to put up with that. The Liberals, however – I thought they were supposed to be the *nice* party?

I did, of course, meet some nice Liberals. Given their paucity of people and resources, it's also understandable that they tend to require these little Napoleon types to do titanic amounts of work and keep them going. But the fact remains that half the Liberals are really Tories, the other half are really Labour, and the end product is frankly schizoid. First they argue with each other, then they argue with everyone else; hence their propensity to go round slagging off councils that they're actually on.

PR, as I say, will let more of these people through the door; Stephen Pearson, for example, possessed as he is with that unfalteringly high regard for his own abilities, blithely told me that he was positioning himself for a high-profile role in the campaign for this reform in the north of England. So if we do come to it, and you live in the north, expect a short tubby bloke to run around shouting a lot in a newspaper near you.

A fairer share of power to the Liberals, however, would be a just and necessary price to pay for a fairer system . . . and you never know: maybe, if they got it, they'd grow up. In the meantime, it's surely worth getting it if for no other reason than that we would never, ever again have to put up with eighteen years of unfettered and rampant Tories.

It's an irony that, right now, we've needed a landslide majority to start repairing all the damage, when one of the most noble, indeed heroic things that landslide majority could do would be to introduce a system that ensures there'd never be another landslide again. Plainly, Mr Blair has bottle – but does he have the bottle to do this?

We shall see; in the next five years we'll be watching, and in the next five years Blair and his cohorts will be up against a difficulty much more immediately pressing than the voting system: namely, money.

It is a wretched indictment of the past eighteen years that, with the spectre of 1992 at their backs, Labour were obliged to secure victory with promises not to raise income tax, and to adhere to

Kenneth Clarke's spending plans. However seriously middle England may otherwise have considered their vote, in this regard, we stand exposed as a nation all too many of whose people have become greedy, selfish and entirely unrealistic.

There are of course other ways to find the money – and be in no doubt that it will be found, because it must be. Health, education, housing, transport, local government, whole swathes of our national and social infrastructure stand imperilled, nigh derelict. If we fail to address these things because we, as a people, are too mean to put our hands in our pockets when such a goodly proportion of us really could afford to, then all the high hope in these bright first days of May will count for nothing.

At 6 o'clock in the morning of Friday 2nd May, three hours after Chris McCafferty had been elected to serve the people of Calder Valley alongside 418 other Labour MPs, I was in my back garden watching the new day dawn. The sky was clear blue, spun through with thin wisps of cloud coloured tangerine and crimson by the rising sun. A light wind danced through the green shoots of the new crop rising in the field behind my house; beyond the field, the clock-face on the church tower shone dazzling gold in the sunlight. Further off, the last foothills of the Pennines folded down to the flatter plains of east Yorkshire. It's a fine and beautiful country, this England – so can we look after it now?

I'd been awake for twenty-four hours; it felt as if I'd been awake for a year. But that was my season in politics. I went to bed, able at last to turn my mind back to the really big questions. Could Barnsley survive in the Premier League? Why does anybody buy Depeche Mode records? And why, for goodness' sake, did those two lads steal my dustbin?